THE BRITISH
POLITICAL SYSTEM

THE BRITISH
POLITICAL SYSTEM

André Mathiot

Translated by
JENNIFER S. HINES

STANFORD UNIVERSITY PRESS
STANFORD, CALIFORNIA

Translated from *Le Régime Politique Britannique*
by André Mathiot, published by Librairie
Armand Colin, Paris, 1955

Stanford University Press
Stanford, California
Translation © The Hogarth Press Ltd, 1958
Printed in the United States of America
Original edition 1958
Reprinted 1967

CONTENTS

8 CONTENTS

PART III THE LIMITATION OF POWER

FOREWORD

I FIRST read *Le Régime Politique Britannique* by André Mathiot soon after it was published in France, and I at once formed the opinion that this was a book which would help British readers and students of politics to understand and appreciate their own system of government. I therefore gladly agreed to the request of the author and the publishers that I should write an introduction to the English edition.

The author's aim is not to give an exhaustive account of the British system, but rather to describe, explain and interpret its principal features. He concentrates on what he rightly regards as essential, and ignores the rest. He is thus able to provide, within the compass of a book of moderate size, a singularly comprehensive and satisfying view of a complicated political system. The central theme of the book is the source, organisation, exercise and control of political power. Part I deals with the source of power; Part II with the organisation of power; while the third and final part discusses the limitations of power.

Professor Mathiot has a remarkable grasp of English history, and he understands the profound influence which historical events have had on the evolution and working of contemporary British political institutions and practices. Throughout the work he emphasises the extraordinary unity and coherence of the system, and the self-consistency of its several parts. The starting-point of his analysis is the electoral system, the character of which deeply affects the party system, the working of Parliament and the position of the Cabinet. In Great Britain, he points out, the voters do not merely elect members of Parliament: they decide in effect who shall be Prime Minister, which party shall govern and what policy shall prevail. 'This,' he remarks, 'is much more than the people can do in many other democracies which have formally accepted the principle of the popular sovereignty'.

The electoral system has three important consequences. It democratises the parliamentary regime by enabling the electorate to choose the government. It produces stable and strong government. It fosters clear political responsibility by avoiding electoral or parliamentary alliances and bargaining between groups. Such an electoral system, however, demands a high degree of political homogeneity and it necessitates frequent compromise. The members of each party must compromise with their convictions on at least some issues, because the range of choice open to them is so narrow with only two parties. And the party in power must frequently compromise with its principles or policy lest by too rigid adherence to them it should sacrifice the support of the marginal voters on whose uncertain allegiance the result of the next general election will depend. Monsieur Mathiot reminds us that the outcome of a general election really depends on the voting behaviour of a relatively small number of citizens. He also insists that the exaggerated weighting of the party representation in Parliament resulting from the British electoral system would not be acceptable to a people who were concerned with the mathematical niceties of justice. While stressing the importance of the electoral system, the author is none the less fully alive to the other factors which have affected the structure of political parties in England. He does not for a moment assert that the party organisation is the outcome of the electoral system.

The author considers that the grand result of the British polity is that the people are the real source of political power. It is, therefore, an authentic example of 'government by the people'. The Cabinet, despite its vast powers, remains an essentially democratic organ because it derives its authority from the people.

Professor Mathiot's interpretation and evaluation of the British system of government is particularly needed at the present time, when numerous writers who disagree with the policies carried out in recent years by successive governments have sought to show that the balance of the constitution has been upset, or that the constitution is afflicted with some malady of their own devising because the Cabinet can normally get its way with Parliament in its day-to-day activities. This is the theme, for example, of *The Passing of Parliament* by Professor G. W. Keeton; and of Ramsay Muir's *How Britain is Governed*. Professor Mathiot, on the other hand, regards Cabinet government in Britain as a form of government by public opinion because the voters have the last word, whereas in France it is the legislature which both makes and breaks the government, and largely determines its policy. Thus, the preponderant power of the executive in Britain is in his view explicable in terms of the respect given to the primacy of the national will.

The *leit motif* of the present work is that a deep-rooted solicitude for the liberties of the individual is a fundamental characteristic of the British political regime. The growth in the functions of the state and the increased powers of the executive have led some critics to dwell on the dangers of totalitarianism and to invoke the spectre of dictatorship; but Professor Mathiot for his part 'is more struck by the happy success with which the liberties of the subject are still upheld in Great Britain'.

The third part of the book is devoted to an examination of the restraints on the exercise of power exerted by such counter-vailing forces as Parliament, the monarchy, the judiciary, the civil service, local authorities, and above all public opinion.

Individual liberty, he asserts, depends ultimately more on the people themselves than upon any institutions or formal safe-guards. The British people have been ready to face the most severe dangers and to make the utmost sacrifices in defence of their liberties. Throughout the centuries they have zealously guarded their civil rights, and this has led to the growth of a vigorous public opinion which would never tolerate any attempt by the Cabinet or Parliament or the Courts to ride roughshod over the liberties of the individual.

Some readers may feel that the author tends to place too much emphasis on the moderateness of British politics and the common ground shared by the two great parties. It might be contended that the social and economic measures carried out during the post-war years in Britain have produced a more drastic social transformation than has occurred in any other western nation by peaceful means. But this is a point which is only incidental to the book. The main themes of *The British Political System* are based on solid foundations; and the general conclusions of its author are undoubtedly correct. I hope the book will have the success it deserves, and that it will be widely read by students of politics and government. For Professor Mathiot has written a book which is not only interesting but also illuminating.

In conclusion, I should like to congratulate Miss Jennifer S. Hines, M.A., on the excellence of her translation.

WILLIAM A. ROBSON

London School of Economics
and Political Science

PREFACE

MY original intention was to make a comprehensive study of the political institutions of the principal countries of the world, but I was forced to admit that even if I kept to the bare essentials and excluded all detailed footnotes and bibliographical references, such a work would still be likely to assume dimensions that would deter even the best intentioned of publishers. Without definitely abandoning the project, I therefore decided to try to fill another gap by making a series of separate studies of the main forms of government with a view to pointing out their principal distinguishing characteristics. This first volume is devoted to the political system of Great Britain, which obviously deserves pride of place.

I realised from the start that I had set myself an extremely difficult task which might well appear a vain or unduly ambitious undertaking, and I am the more conscious of this now that the result is about to be presented to the public.

It is practically impossible in a mere three hundred pages to do full justice to a subject so profound and important as to be almost forbidding. Those with expert knowledge of British government will no doubt be disappointed to find that I have scarcely ever risen above a strictly 'popular' level.

It is equally obvious that any attempt to find a synthesis in British political life and institutions would run a serious risk of being utterly misleading unless its author were supremely well acquainted with every aspect of the British constitution. He would also have to have mastered an enormous mass of relevant documentary material, to have spent many years making an inductive and comparative study of the regime, and to have cultivated many contacts in all kinds of political circles in the country itself. Moreover, he would need to be completely impartial in his analysis of ideas, mechanisms, changes and events, even when writing of the contemporary scene. Not possessing such experience and qualifications, I have set myself a more limited task. Without wishing to excuse the shortcomings of this volume, I should like to give at least some indication of its scope and purpose.

I have tried to give a straightforward account and exposition of the British political system that might be of interest both to students of law and political science and to a wider public. Though the system has long attracted widespread attention, its singular effectiveness has not always been fully appreciated, and its underlying principles should provide every intelligent citizen with much food for further reflection. It therefore seemed best to omit all footnotes and detailed references such as would be necessary in a more scholarly treatise but might deter the more general reader and would in any case add considerably to the length of the book. Anyone who wishes for further information on any particular point will be able to follow it up through the works listed in the Select Bibliography.

There is hardly room for yet another study of the government of the United Kingdom, but it is perhaps still possible to look at the subject from a new angle and, instead of analysing it within arbitrary subdivisions, to try to see what are the essential characteristics of the regime as a whole. My underlying purpose has been to try to indicate the true nature of British democracy.

If asked to give a single criterion of free democratic government, I should say that it depended on the status of the opposition.

In a democracy, power belongs initially to the people who to some extent actively participate in the conduct of affairs. This necessarily implies government by the majority, where issues are decided by counting heads. Except in the unlikely event of complete unanimity, all are ready to abide by the decision of the majority because in this way no one starts with any undue advantage and there is only a minimum of interference with the liberties of the individual which can never be permanently suppressed.

On any major national issue, public opinion is almost bound to be divided. A very large number of questions have therefore to be decided by the will of the majority. One of the things that distinguishes a liberal democracy from the various forms of 'people's democracy' is perhaps their different concepts of what the rule of the majority really implies.

Without going into the means whereby the majority rose to power in the first place, it may be said that in a 'people's democracy' the people are completely identified with the majority. The majority is never taken for what it really is, that is, the representatives of only a part of the 'national will' or the views of one section of the population. Instead, it is regarded as absolutely comprehensive and infallible. According to this way of thinking, once the will of the people has been made known, the task before the government is to give effect to this 'general will' in its entirety with the least possible delay. Any opposition should be totally disregarded. It cannot contain any element of truth and ought to be suppressed. Anti-government propaganda can be condemned as seditious, and the opposition should be to some extent, if not completely, deprived of any civil liberties that would permit it to criticise the government, to continue to exist as an organised body, or to maintain that there are certain spheres in which the state has no right to intervene.

A liberal regime, on the other hand, admits that the majority is not always right and that others should be at liberty to point out where it is in the wrong, the views of the majority being only an imperfect and transitory reflection of the will of the people. Not only is it considered wrong to suppress or disregard opposition, but it is recognised that the opposition, no less than the government, has its own distinctive part to play. While the majority rules, the opposition must criticise. It has both the power and the duty to keep public opinion on the alert and to try to build up a following so that it may in turn itself become the majority. There are thus two distinct and necessarily unequal elements in the constitution—the government and the opposition—each representing different points of view. National policies are arrived at by means of a compromise between the two.

The great problem is to see that this dualism does not lead to any undue rigidity or multiplication of political divisions, nor yet undermine the efficiency of the government. This will only happen if both sides are ready to maintain an equilibrium based upon mutual toleration and respect. The majority must be a genuine majority that does not get out of touch with public opinion, and it must never forget that it has only been given power for a limited term. The opposition must remain loyal and not try to defy the government or overthrow the established regime. In the British political system, as we shall see, all these conditions are fulfilled in so striking and unique a manner that one could almost study it entirely in terms of the relationship between the majority and the opposition.

Here, however, I have adopted another method of approach in order to emphasise the dominant position of the Cabinet. This is the most striking feature of the whole political system. I have tried to show how the power of the executive is, in effect, based on a form of direct democracy and, in particular, to point out how this elaborate political machine contains an abundance of forces and institutions which combine to ensure the limitation of political power. These other elements are, in one sense, the source of the power of the government. The Cabinet owes its dominant position to the decision of the electorate, the strength of the majority party, the long-established supremacy of Parliament, the extensive powers originally vested in the Crown and the support which it derives from the judiciary. Yet from another point of view all these elements can be regarded as, in varying degrees, important safeguards of individual liberty. Their power, or such influence as they may still be able to exert, combines with other rules and institutions to provide the strongest conceivable safeguard to ensure that the strong executive does not turn itself into a dictatorship.

This study has not been kept strictly within the confines of what is normally regarded as constitutional law. I have allowed myself to be drawn on to try to give an overall picture of the British political system as it really is, and to show how in practice the government is supported or restrained by the other formal authorities in the state—Parliament and the monarchy —and by the administrative system, the power of the judiciary and the firmly established liberties of the subject.

TRADITION AND ADAPTATION

GREAT BRITAIN is the traditional home of liberal institutions. She has been strikingly successful in preserving the balance, flexibility and aversion to violent change that has always been characteristic of her system of government, while at the same time making it singularly effective in discharging all the functions required of a modern state.

The temperament and traditions of the British people have enabled them to resolve their major problems of political organisation in a unique way which well deserves the attention of other countries.

Their political system has a number of features of particular interest. In the first place, it is the political system of a country which still ranks as a Great Power and whose conduct, both in peace and in war, continues to arouse the admiration of other nations. Yet it is not just the system of government of a single country. It has been successfully transplanted, with almost equally happy results, to what used to be the 'white' colonies of the British Empire. These almost invariably looked to British institutions as the pattern to guide them in their evolution towards Dominion status, and although they have now become independent sovereign states within the Commonwealth, this does not mean that they have in any way broken with the basic principles of the British system of government.

Another development of outstanding interest at the present time is the attempts now being made to install parliamentary government on the British model in various parts of tropical Africa. That the British system of government has already been adopted, in varying forms, in the other Commonwealth countries has strengthened the belief that it is capable of being introduced into other colonial territories. The gradual and cautious advance of these countries towards self-government and then towards responsible government provides further evidence of the singularly wide range of circumstances in which it is possible to apply a framework of political ideas that is entirely free from any kind of doctrinaire rigidity.

A number of other monarchies, including Belgium and the
Netherlands, Denmark, Norway and Sweden, have also to a
large extent modelled their institutions on those of Great
Britain. Their present parliamentary regimes have clearly been
inspired by the British, although none has been as successful as
its prototype. At crucial moments in their history, when their
existing forms of government were collapsing, many other
nations, including the French, have turned to Great Britain as
the classic example of the liberal institutions they sought to
emulate. Experience has soon taught them how difficult it is to
reproduce such a unique political system.

The British political system is singularly full of paradoxes.
The fact that it is not based on any logical principles might in
itself be considered a paradox and a sign of weakness, and
would certainly be the despair of anyone who tried to subject
the system to any kind of rational analysis. The difficulty is not
so much that it is impossible to explain its principles, institutions
and conventions, but rather that they mostly contain some
internal contradiction. The more self-contradictory they appear
to be, the more effectively the British seem to be able to make
them work.

It is doubtful whether the British have ever really given much
thought to the underlying principles of their constitution,
although there are some basic ideas that are universally
respected. 'England', wrote Philip Chesterfield, a friend of
Montesquieu, in the eighteenth century, 'is the only monarchy
that can really be said to have a Constitution.' On the other
hand, de Toqueville, whose ideas were moulded by his study
of the American Constitution, considered that there was no
such thing as a constitution in Great Britain. Sir John Simon,
addressing an audience in Paris on 'The British System of
Government' on 28th February 1935, began by saying, 'You
may remember the famous chapter in a treatise on natural
history that was entitled "Snakes in Ireland" and consisted of
a single sentence, "There are no snakes in Ireland." We can
equally well say that in England we have no Constitution.'

Yet the absence of a formal written constitution is really of
very little importance in a country whose whole political
system is founded upon the Rule of Law. Every political community has some rules, and the British is no exception, although
its rules are largely unwritten and sometimes veiled in the haze

of uncertainty that surrounds customary usages whose origins lie far back in history. Nevertheless, these rules are, generally speaking, perfectly well known and more wholeheartedly respected than the constitutional principles of many other countries, even where they have been minutely defined in much-debated legal texts. Legally the British Parliament can do anything that it wishes, but from the political point of view it is very far from being a sovereign body in the same sense as the French National Assembly. The constitutional sense of a nation which reverences its laws and takes a firm stand against any attempt to set them aside is a stronger safeguard against hasty reforms and arbitrary decisions than a constitution that is supposed to be inflexible but in fact merely embodies what was assumed to be the will of the people at some particular moment in history.

Another paradox about British political institutions is the un-usual way in which they were written about and discussed in other countries and became widely known and admired abroad at a period when in Britain itself they were developing empirically and were seldom discussed in theoretical terms, so that the British themselves were not really conscious of the fundamental modifications that were being imposed upon the old system of absolute monarchy. Fortescue in the fourteenth century and Thomas Smith in the sixteenth century both wrote in Latin, and their works never attracted much notice in Britain. It was Montesquieu who first drew the attention of the entire civilised world to the British system of government through his famous chapter in *The Spirit of the Laws*. It was largely through this not altogether accurate description that the British themselves were made aware of the main features of their political system. Blackstone's famous *Commentaries on the Laws of England* appear to have been quite clearly inspired by Montesquieu. It would be true to say that at the end of the eighteenth century there was a far greater understanding of British political institutions on the Continent and even in North America than in the British Isles. There was a considerable body of opinion in France under the Restoration and the July Monarchy which looked upon the British political system as its ideal, and elsewhere other constitutional monarchies were set up in the light of liberal principles borrowed from Great Britain. Yet the British very seldom tried to analyse the system that they had originated and made to work so successfully.

To a foreign observer, the political regime that the British have conceived and elaborated and adapted to changing circumstances either by laws or, much more frequently, by constitutional conventions, looks like an ideal model of a thoroughly harmonious and balanced system of government.

Montesquieu saw in it a living example of the principle of the separation of powers. Even though this may not have been an altogether correct view at the time when he wrote, there can be no doubt that the British political system deserves to be regarded as a masterpiece in the art of governing men. It combines a predominantly elective Parliament and a stable executive, closely linked together by means of a responsible Cabinet. The prerogatives of Parliament are evenly balanced against those of the Cabinet. A set of rules and constitutional conventions ensures strong government and yet at the same time genuinely guarantees a very broad measure of individual liberty. This enviable system of government has been evolved almost entirely without regard to any abstract general principles. It was created and developed empirically, as was only to be expected in a country where logical reasoning is among the most suspect of all the things commonly associated with the Continent.

The course of British constitutional history has been mainly determined by a number of historical accidents, customs which have acquired authority through long usage, and the desire to learn from experience and yet at the same time not to break with venerable tradition. These have been much more influential than any theoretical reasoning or ideas of setting up what was regarded in the abstract as an ideal form of government.

The British system of government is not only a paradox in itself but it contains many other paradoxical features. The term 'parliamentary government', for instance, would appear to imply that Parliament is the chief power in the state. In fact, however, Parliament, which is not at all the same thing as a single-chamber legislature, although in theory supreme, is in practice dominated by the Cabinet, which is formally only the creature of Parliament. The British people strove for several centuries to free themselves from any semblance of absolute monarchy. Yet now that it is no longer the sovereign but the

Cabinet which wields the executive power, they have come to acquiesce in the supremacy of the executive. Thus as the political system has become democratic, the government has found itself in a stronger position than ever before.

Another paradox is the bicameral system. This originated in England, but the form of bicameralism that exists in Great Britain today is quite different from anything to be found in any other country. The upper House has admittedly changed a great deal since the eighteenth century and has been largely deprived of its former powers, but it still survives as a fundamentally aristocratic second chamber.

Despite—or perhaps because of—their anxiety to preserve their historic institutions, the British were ahead of most other countries in curtailing the powers of their second chamber. Since 1911, and even more since 1948, the House of Lords has been reduced to the position of a 'reflecting chamber'.

Yet, as nothing in Britain is really quite what it seems at first glance, the reduction in the powers of the House of Lords does not in the least imply that it has been divested of all political significance. Many highly eminent public figures sit there; public attention may be drawn to important issues by raising them in the Lords; and speeches made there, especially those on foreign affairs, may prove to be extremely influential. The House of Lords might be likened to *The Times* as an important influence in moulding public opinion. It is also a Conservative stronghold that can place considerable obstacles in the way of a Labour government. A number of peers are invariably selected to fill some of the leading positions in the government, and in the Cabinet formed by Mr Churchill in October 1951 the House of Lords was more strongly represented than it had been in any government for many years past.

Peers, together with aliens and the insane, are disqualified from voting or standing for election to the House of Commons. And, for all that it may appear to be an anachronism, the House of Lords remains to this day the supreme court of justice of the realm.

A final paradox in the British constitution is the monarchy. The monarchies which still survive in the west today could almost be counted on the fingers of one hand. The Kings of England often had to face fierce and persistent opposition in the days when monarchy was the normal form of government, but the British monarchy is now, despite all the developments that have taken place in the Commonwealth, as firmly established and highly respected an institution as it would be possible to find.

It is only comparatively recently that the monarchy has become both morally and politically immune from attack. It did not attain this position until the end of the reign of Queen Victoria, that is, just at the time when monarchies were beginning to decline and disappear in other parts of the world.

British sovereigns have been ready to acquiesce in their loss of effective power and have consequently acquired a new kind of prestige. The less they intervene in politics, the more they have been able to inspire the loyalty and compel the respect of the nation as a whole. For anyone not too fastidious about adhering to rigid definitions of his terms, the British system of government might well be described as a republic organised in the form of a monarchy.

Great Britain is still renowned for being the Mother of Parliaments and for having the last surviving monarchy of any real significance. The really important elements in her political system, however, are neither the Queen nor Parliament but the electorate and the Cabinet.

The British political system for the most part defies logical analysis. What we can do, however, is to try to see why a system which appears to be so illogical and out of line with modern political ideas is in fact no less, if not more, effective and successful than many other democratic regimes in dealing with all the infinitely complex problems that arise in the modern state.

Many elaborate and learned answers might be given to that question, but perhaps one explanation lies in the rare if not unique combination of two dominant characteristics, both in the British people themselves and in their political institutions. They have an unshakeable respect for tradition, which they reverence not so much for its own sake as for the good it can produce. Yet this respect for the past is tempered by a complete lack of dogmatic conservatism.

RESPECT FOR TRADITION

'The Constitution which Queen Victoria swore to preserve was the constitution of William the Conqueror.' The historian who said this was not just making a humorous aside, for his remark contains a profound truth. It is a corollary of Sir Maurice Amos's definition of the Englishman, considered as a political animal, as 'law-loving, loyal to his leaders, indifferent to equality, deferential, a lover of liberty, sectarian, individualist, zealous for business, apt for self-government, a lover of compromise, a fertile maker of rules, indifferent to logic, respectful of precedent'.

The British respect for tradition in politics is partly the result of their island situation, which has protected them from the revolutionary movements and new ideologies that have spread across continental Europe.

It has also been strengthened by their relatively happy history, and often by completely accidental historical circumstances. Without going into the political implications of military victories whose effects are often difficult to assess, two outstanding examples may be quoted to show the influence of historical events. First, the loss of their lands in France put an end to English dreams of a continental empire and helped to produce a strong sense of national unity. Then the loss of the American colonies several hundred years later was perhaps the only thing that enabled constitutional monarchy to survive in Great Britain, and there can be no doubt that it considerably simplified the political and economic problems that British governments had to face in the years that followed.

Respect for the past is not merely an integral part of the British national temperament but a tendency that has been reinforced by the respect that the British people have always shown for the laws by which they and their ancestors have agreed to be bound. As Francis Bacon observed, the ancient declaration of the barons in Parliament assembled—that they had no wish to alter the laws of England (*nolumus leges Angliae mutare*)—has been engraved upon the heart of every Englishman. In this connection it is important not to overlook the influence of the legal profession, both judges and barristers, in determining the British approach to politics. From very early times the lawyers have had their own autonomous organisation, the Inns of Court, and have always been extremely active in public affairs and shown themselves forthright champions of individual liberty. Their influence has both helped to ensure respect for juridical traditions and also left its mark on the customs and procedure of Parliament.

Many observers have been astonished at the extent to which British political life is dominated by tradition and contains so many features for which it is difficult to find any rational explanation. The British are not, however, very greatly concerned about having everything cut and dried and giving logical reasons for all that they do. At this stage, therefore, we shall confine ourselves to indicating how their respect for tradition manifests itself in some of the main features of their political institutions.

The British Parliament, unlike the Parliaments of most other countries, did not come into being as the result of a revolution. It is a traditional English institution with an impressively long history. Its origins are to be found in the mediaeval Concilium that the King used to summon when he wanted to confer with the freemen and secure their approval for important decisions. The Concilium had broad advisory powers and also some important juridical functions, as a legacy of which the House of Lords to this day remains the supreme court of the realm. The earliest Parliaments consisted of the bishops and the leading barons. These formed the Magnum Concilium that later developed into the House of Lords. Before this happened, larger assemblies began to be convoked that also included knights from the shires and later burgesses to represent the boroughs and chartered towns. The first Parliament constituted on these lines was summoned by Simon de Montfort in the thirteenth century, and similar assemblies continued to be convoked from time to time. This did not signify any abandonment of power on the part of the King, but was actually intended to strengthen his position. The Great and Model Parliament summoned by Edward I in 1295 was larger than any of its predecessors and the earliest assembly to be in any sense representative of the nation. It included all the members of the King's Council. This, like many other ancient practices, has left its imprint on contemporary British institutions, as all privy councillors, even if not members of Parliament, are still in theory entitled to attend debates in the House of Lords.

The division of Parliament into two Houses is likewise entirely a matter of tradition quite divorced from any kind of rational motivation. The merits and drawbacks of the bicameral system are keenly debated at the present time. It is generally thought to provide a check and balance that constitutes a safe-

guard for individual liberty and improves the quality of parliamentary legislation. Originally the four different categories of
members of Parliament—the barons, the bishops and lower
clergy, the knights of the shire and the representatives of the
boroughs—all sat together, though each group appears to have
met separately as well. But after the lower clergy had withdrawn
from Parliament in the fourteenth century, it gradually became
customary for the bishops and the barons to meet on their own
as they had in the Magnum Concilium, while the knights of the
shire and the borough members, who were both elected representatives and did not come from such distinct social classes
as might be supposed, joined forces to form the other House of
Parliament. Historians maintain that two distinct Houses of
Parliament were in existence by 1341 and the Commons met on
their own in 1351. It is difficult to say exactly when the division
first appeared, but there can be no doubt that the whole
bicameral system as we know it today has evolved out of these
simple beginnings.

It is typical of the British respect for tradition that when they
came to rebuild their House of Commons after it had been
destroyed in an air raid on the night of 10-11th May 1941, it
was decided, on the recommendation of members of Parliament
themselves, to build the new chamber on the same site and on
exactly the same plan as the old. Their decision was the more
remarkable, because the old House of Commons was of no great
antiquity, having been built on the site of part of the old Palace
of Westminster after it was destroyed by fire in 1834. Moreover,
the old chamber had, not originally as the result of any
deliberate policy, been built as a rectangular hall in which the
government and the opposition sat facing each other across a
central gangway, and there had only been seats for about two-
thirds of the total number of members. It might have seemed
more logical to build the new chamber on the semicircular
pattern adopted in most other legislatures and to give every
member a seat and a desk of his own. Yet the British refused to
be guided solely by such theoretical considerations. They
preferred to adhere to their traditional design and were able to
produce many empirical arguments in its defence.

When the House of Commons elected a new Speaker in 1951,
he responded like every other Speaker before him, except
Onslow in 1727, by remaining firmly in his place and putting

up a show of resistance before allowing the two members appointed for the purpose to conduct him to the Chair. This is a survival from the time when the Speaker had only recently ceased to be appointed by the Crown. Anyone then elected Speaker by the House would not proceed to the Chair without first making a profession of his own unworthiness and recalling the dangers to which, as an independent Speaker, he might be exposed.

Every new member of the House of Commons has to be initiated into a special code of parliamentary etiquette. He has to learn that there are certain places where it is forbidden to walk, and certain words and phrases that may not be mentioned in the House. Whenever a member enters or leaves the Chamber, he must bow in the direction of the Speaker, though no one knows whether he is really bowing to Mr Speaker himself or to the mace on the Table in front of him, or simply because of a custom that has survived since the sixteenth century when there used to be a cross behind the Speaker's chair. The reason why they bow does not matter. The rule is that they must do so, and they invariably comply.

When the members of the House of Commons are due to go up to the House of Lords to hear the Queen's Speech from the throne, they wait for Black Rod, an usher who carries a black staff, to come in the name of the sovereign to summon her faithful Commons. The Sergeant-at-Arms will be standing by to shut the door in the face of Black Rod, who is not admitted until he has knocked three times on the door. This is intended to show that the lower House is independent of the sovereign, and dates back to the day in January 1642 when the Commons shut their doors against Charles I when he arrived with an escort of troops to arrest six members of the House.

After the formal opening of Parliament, the Commons return to their Chamber and must immediately proceed to a debate on the address in reply to the Queen's Speech. This debate cannot begin, however, until the Speaker has allowed the House to give a reading to a bill, the text of which is always the same and has not changed for over a hundred years as it is never brought up again later in the session. By giving it an initial reading, however, the Commons reaffirm that they are under no obligation to confine their deliberations to the matters mentioned in the Queen's Speech, which is nowadays actually composed by the Prime Minister.

Many other instances might be quoted to show how tradition has left its imprint upon parliamentary procedure, but it is especially marked in the procedure through which a bill has to go before it becomes law. After a bill has been given a third reading in the House of Commons, it is sent to the House of Lords with the request 'soit baillé aux Seigneurs' which has been used ever since the fourteenth century when the King used to legislate in response to petitions from Parliament. If the Lords give the bill a third reading, nothing can in fact prevent it from becoming law, but before this can happen there has to be a formal ceremony in which it receives the royal assent. On these occasions the Commons are summoned by Black Rod to attend at the bar of the House of Lords. There they find three peers who have received the Queen's commission in respect of the bills in question, sitting on a special seat between the Woolsack and the throne. The Crown Clerk, who wears a wig and is dressed like a mediaeval lawyer, reads the title of each bill in English, whereupon the Clerk of Parliaments, similarly attired, responds in Norman-French with the cry 'Le roy le veult' or, in the case of a bill to grant supply or impose taxation, 'Le Roi remercie ses bons sujets, accepte leur bénévolence et ainsi le veult.' The royal assent has never been refused to a bill since Queen Anne rejected the Scottish Militia Bill in 1707, and it has long been a firmly established constitutional convention that the sovereign should automatically assent to any bill that has been passed by both Houses of Parliament. Nevertheless, bills continue to be formally submitted for the royal assent, and it is still granted with all the traditional ceremony.

The whole history of the English nation is really bound up in these traditional forms and ceremonies. No member of Parliament would dream of trying to do away with them, for by voluntarily continuing to pay homage to the venerable past of the oldest Parliament in the world they are able to invest even their latest reforming legislation with the same sanctity as belongs to their most ancient customs. It seems highly unlikely that this could ever occur in any other country, but it is in fact what actually happens in Great Britain.

The Cabinet is another institution thoroughly steeped in tradition. In the eyes of the law it is nothing more than a committee of the Privy Council of the sovereign, which itself developed out of the Witenagemot that existed right back in Saxon times.

The Cabinet is a corporate body because the King was forced to take into his confidence more than just a single individual or a very small group of privy councillors. For this same reason, the title of Prime Minister was long regarded as a term of abuse and did not come into current usage until the time of Disraeli. The homogeneity and cohesion of the Cabinet arise from the fact that long ago the privy councillors discovered that they had to be agreed among themselves in order to give a satisfactory account to the House of Commons of the advice they had tendered to the King. Not until much later did the Cabinet become politically, as distinct from legally, responsible for its acts when, towards the end of the eighteenth century, a Cabinet set a new precedent by choosing to resign rather than expose its members to the threat of impeachment. There is no law relating to the organisation of the Cabinet. Until 1917 it was entirely without any kind of formal organisation, and even today the rules which govern its activities still for the most part derive their authority from custom alone.

The rôle of the Prime Minister has likewise largely been determined by custom. It gradually became recognised that there had to be someone of this status, and the Prime Minister had become an important figure long before his office was so much as mentioned in any legal text. For some reason that is not altogether clear, the earliest Prime Ministers held the office of First Lord of the Treasury. The Prime Minister still normally occupies this position today, although nowadays he has very little to do with the Treasury, which, for all practical purposes, is under the control of the Chancellor of the Exchequer.

The office which is more full of contradictions than any other, however, is that of Lord Chancellor. His functions display an extraordinary disregard for the principle of the separation of powers that is otherwise as well respected in Great Britain as in any other democracy. The Lord Chancellor is the first subject of Her Majesty, and comes immediately after the Archbishop of Canterbury and before all other members of the government in the order of precedence. He is a judge, and head of the English judiciary. He presides over the House of Lords when it sits as the supreme court of the land, and over the Judicial Committee of the Privy Council. At the same time, he is a member of the government and fulfils many of the functions normally assigned to a Minister of Justice. He also presides over the ordinary legislative sittings of the House of Lords, where he sits on the Woolsack, a special seat upholstered in red plush and symbolically stuffed with wool because this was once the staple of English commerce. When he enters or leaves the Chamber he is ceremonially preceded by the Sergeant-at-Arms bearing the mace, but although he presides over the debates of the House he has no disciplinary powers over its members. His extraordinary combination of functions that are in no way logically connected is really too heavy a burden to impose on any one man and is certainly not dictated by the practical necessities of modern government. It remains as it is, simply because no one wants to undermine the pre-eminent status of the highest office in the state which has been in existence since before the Norman Conquest and the main attributes of which have been unchanged since the reign of Edward the Confessor. It may be an illogical arrangement, but it is one which everyone has come to take for granted.

The monarchy, though but one of many long-established and closely interconnected customs and institutions in which the British political system abounds, is perhaps the most important and highly respected of all these traditional institutions. Itself steeped in tradition, it is also the means whereby traditions are kept alive.

In the eyes of the law, the powers of the sovereign are still almost exactly the same as they were in the days of absolute monarchy. The law regarding the source and exercise of political power has remained practically unchanged since the Middle Ages. Neither the State nor the Nation has ever become a recognised legal entity. All laws are made in the name of the Queen, who is the fountain of all justice and who alone has power to confer any kind of honour. Every ship in the navy is the Queen's ship and every policeman who directs the traffic in the streets is exercising powers that belong to the Crown. An enormous amount of public business has to be referred to the Queen, and there are a vast number of official papers that require her personal signature.

Yet in reality none of the surviving functions of the Crown has more than symbolic value. Almost all the powers of the state remain vested in the sovereign, but the Queen no longer has any genuine political power. Although the sovereign has at times been able to exert some personal influence, this is now generally of quite insignificant proportions. Until comparatively recently, the sovereign remained an important figure as head of the Commonwealth. Even there, however, the idea of common allegiance to the Crown and all that it used to imply has now been supplanted by the concept of a 'Crown without a sceptre' that is merely the symbolic head of an entirely voluntary association of states.

Respect for the past thus pervades every aspect of political life in Great Britain. It is reflected in the spectacular pomps and traditional ceremonies and in the retention of impressive and outmoded costumes and language. These are a valuable asset, as they help to stimulate a sense of national unity. Although some democracies have thought it possible to dispense with this kind of patriotism, it is something which all totalitarian states have tried, by more artificial means, to revive.

Respect for tradition in politics is a more specifically British characteristic, but it too fulfils several important purposes. Every state opening of Parliament serves to remind the country that, as they are proud to recall, their political system rests on firm foundations. In spite of all the new political ideologies put forward since its first youth, their Parliament, although re-newed at regular intervals, still survives in much the same form as it assumed seven centuries ago. The historic rites are also evidence of the political sagacity of a people who have not only succeeded in preserving their ancient institutions, but have also maintained intact and secure against all the revolutionary up-heavals and fierce conflicts that have raged over the centuries the fundamentally liberal principles of their constitution. As one Englishman has written, 'When we seem to be respecting the dead, we are in reality respecting our fellow-citizens.' The survival of ancient institutions with their outward forms almost intact is evidence of the peaceable character of British constitu-tional history. It does not, however, tell us anything about how, behind the façade of pomps and ceremonies, these institutions really work. If the nation had been determined at all costs to adhere to its traditional forms, it would have ended by paralys-ing the government of the country. But although the British people have preserved the traditional framework of their institutions, they have been ready to adapt their political system in the light of changing circumstances.

THE COMPLETE ABSENCE OF DOGMATIC CONSERVATISM

No one would venture to claim that there has ever, even between 1945 and 1950, been any strong progressive movement in British politics, or that the British are temperamentally disposed to be constantly questioning the established order.

In the first place, as will become more apparent when we come to consider the electoral system, the British political system has only recently become democratic. Until 1883-85, birth and wealth were the keys to political influence. The first workman M.P. was not elected until 1874. Working-class representation in the House of Commons did not attain significant proportions until after 1906, and it was only in 1922 that the Labour Party became the official opposition. Harold Laski was able to write, without appearing unduly paradoxical, that between 1689 and 1945 the government of Great Britain was always in the hands of a single party whose two branches, first Whigs and Tories and later Liberals and Conservatives, succeeded each other in office without ever raising any question of basic changes in the constitution or even of any radical social or economic reform. The differences that divided Liberals from Conservatives were really no more than family quarrels that could always be settled by compromise.

The situation altered somewhat after the victory of the Labour Party in 1945, but the change was not so great as Laski both hoped and believed. The Labour movement remains decidedly non-Marxist and anti-Marxist. The British Communist Party is quite insignificant and secured only 2% of the total votes in 1945 and 0·19% in 1951.[1] One reason for the serious difficulties in which the Labour Party has found itself in recent years is that its leaders—Mr Bevan just as much as Mr Attlee or Mr Gaitskell—have had to take care not to alienate the middle-of-the-road voters upon whose support they rely. As a considerable proportion of those who vote Labour are persons of fundamentally moderate views, the Labour Party cannot go beyond a merely 'reformist' programme. It may even find it difficult to carry out its own brand of 'Liberal Socialism' that aims to combine individual liberty with a planned economy, and democracy—in the classic

[1] 0·19% in 1955.

political sense—with social justice. This forms an appealing
election slogan, but it may in fact be an attempt to square the
circle.

The British have an extreme aversion to any kind of revolutionary change. Although they elected a Labour government
in 1945, they did so only when its leader, Clement Attlee, was a
man they felt they could fully trust. Their motive in voting
Labour was to obtain greater social security and a higher
standard of living through economic planning, and they
certainly had no thought of bringing about a social revolution.
Mr Morgan Phillips, the General Secretary of the Labour
Party, has himself said that British socialism owes much more
to Methodism than to Marxism. The recent successes of the
Bevanites within the Labour Party tended to scare away the
middle-class electors and the floating voters who mostly belong
to the middle classes, and thus helped to produce the adverse
swing of Liberal votes that gave the Conservatives their
majority in 1951.

In addition to these political phenomena, a number of
psychological factors have also been important in frustrating or
considerably retarding many reforms.

The British always used to be criticised for their ignorance of
what was going on outside the British Isles and the British
Empire. Although things have changed in recent years, the
criticism is still not entirely without foundation. The British
have by no means lost that characteristic form of conceit which
leads them to believe, somewhat optimistically, that anything
British is bound to be unsurpassed, or at least quite good
enough as it is.

It has been said that an Englishman will never think about
anything if he can possibly avoid it. This is at least better than
failing to rise to the occasion in cases of absolute necessity,
which are now sufficiently numerous to keep the British capacity
for reflection quite adequately employed. It would be fairer and
more accurate to say that the British approach to politics has
always been one of extreme caution. It should also be remembered that the British have always valued character above
intelligence and experience above any abstract theory.

Their reluctance to embark into the unknown does not mean
that the British are necessarily opposed to any kind of reform,
but rather that, before implementing it, they want to consider

what effect it is likely to have and to be sure that the moment is opportune. They frequently demand that the people should first have an opportunity to make their views known. Their reforms, too, do not usually go beyond what is dictated by present needs or those of the immediate future, leaving any further changes to be made in the light of subsequent experience. The British have always shown a singular capacity for seeing what can be learned from experience and responding accordingly. Their aversion to abstract generalisations is matched by a readiness to recognise the truth when they see it, however unpleasant it may be. There is no need to elaborate on this aspect of British realism, of which there is abundant evidence in recent developments in her foreign economic and financial policy and in the evolution of the Commonwealth and the colonial empire.

It is indeed possible to go further and point out some important constitutional developments that have been possible only because the British are entirely free from any kind of dogmatic conservatism. The constitution is for the most part made up of customs, rules—generally unwritten—and conventions, which ensure that constitutional practice is kept in line with the theories commonly accepted at the time. Thus, while it is sometimes difficult to discover exactly how the constitution stands, it is always easy, when and to the extent that the country so desires, to adapt it to meet a new political situation or to reflect social change. 'It is the glory of our Constitution', said Mr Attlee when Prime Minister, on 15th August 1945, 'that changes which in other countries could only be realised amongst bloodshed and by civil war, can be realised through the peaceable instrumentality of the ballot box.' Behind the façade of apparently unaltered historic political institutions and traditional procedures there is an imperceptible process of change. The changes are usually not at all spectacular or even easy to detect, being merely slight adaptations such as are to be expected in a process of continuous evolution not governed by any *a priori* ideas.

The scope and objectives of even the most far-reaching reforms that have taken place in the British political system have always been extremely restricted.

Britain has never been a country for revolutions. Even when important constitutional changes have seemed called for, there has never been any question of setting up an entirely new system of government. Such a cautious approach used to be fairly widespread and was quite understandable in the days of absolute monarchy. In Britain there have never been any extreme movements of opinion to cause this attitude to be abandoned.

Magna Charta, though it touched upon a number of constitutional issues, was very far from being a comprehensive constitution.

The Revolution of 1688 and the Bill of Rights ultimately secured the people's right to govern themselves, but their immediate effects were merely a small number of limited reforms that did not represent any real break with the past. The supremacy of Parliament was confirmed as regards both finance and legislation, and a number of questions which had been disputed between the King and Parliament for several centuries were settled so as to curtail the powers of the Crown. The Revolution merely limited the powers of the monarchy by repudiating the Stuarts' claims to personal power and reaffirming the supremacy of Parliament and the Common Law. As on other occasions in British history, progress was achieved by adapting the existing institutions.

The Petition of Right, the Habeas Corpus Act, the Act of Settlement and the Parliament Act provide further examples of important reforms realised through measures of limited scope.

It was likewise by gradual changes, between 1818 and 1870, that the state came to assume responsibility for primary education. The state system of secondary education, inaugurated in 1902 and expanded in 1921 and 1936, is still by no means complete even after the Act of 1944.

The most revealing example of fundamental reforms cautiously introduced by gradual stages is to be found, however, in the history of electoral reform. The old aristocratic regime has now been replaced by a parliamentary democracy, but the necessary legislation was spread out over more than a century in a long series of measures from the Reform Act of 1832 down to the Representation of the People Act, 1948. Thereby the franchise was slowly broadened, free elections were established, corrupt practices outlawed, and a more equitable delimitation of constituencies and distribution of seats introduced.

Sweeping reforms and precipitate changes have no place in the constitutional history of Great Britain, where the political system is in a state of slow and almost continuous evolution.

The British system of parliamentary government is, of all political regimes, the most difficult to understand without constant reference to the history of the country. With each successive century it has acquired some new features and its character has been to some extent modified.

All through the seventeenth century, the major issue was the conflict between the prerogatives of the Crown and the doctrine of the supremacy of Parliament and the Common Law. Every phase in this struggle, until it ended with the victory of Parliament, was a major landmark in constitutional history, every new development opening the way to further reforms.

The eighteenth century saw the development of the party system and the principles and conventions of Cabinet government. This was just as continuous and imperceptible a process. It culminated in the nineteenth century with the recognition of the House of Commons, that is, the representatives of the people, as the supreme power in the constitution.

History provides abundant evidence of the continuity of British constitutional development.

Magna Charta is supposed to be a major landmark in the recognition of political liberty, but in fact it reaffirmed rather than altered the existing law. All that King John conceded at Runnymede in response to the demands of the barons, inspired by Archbishop Langton, had been granted in an earlier charter by Henry I more than a century before.

It is impossible to say exactly when the first Parliament ever met. The Model Parliament of 1295 followed a long line of precedents set by previous assemblies. Parliament is an institution founded upon custom that has only gradually acquired what are now its essential characteristics. Historians are equally hesitant about trying to give a definite date for the emergence of two distinct Houses of Parliament or for the disappearance of the King's power to legislate by ordinance.

Save for a few exceptional and brief interludes, the British constitution has never been static. It has gradually evolved in response to changing historical circumstances and continues to do so before our very eyes. The constitution may appear to be stable, but this is often only because it is so difficult to see when a recent precedent is going to become binding or how far an innovation is likely to become an obligatory practice.

When the King asked Mr Baldwin rather than Lord Curzon to form a government in 1923, it was not thereby ordained that the Prime Minister must always in future be a member of the House of Commons. Yet this has since become the universally accepted rule, Lord Salisbury's Ministry of 1900-02 being the last British government to be headed by a peer.

It is now generally accepted that the Queen cannot refuse to dissolve Parliament if the Prime Minister, on behalf of the Cabinet, asks her to do so. Until 1841, however, a dissolution used to be regarded as an appeal to the country by the sovereign as well as by the government. Even after that, some celebrated constitutional controversies arose between the Queen and Lord John Russell in 1851 and between the Queen and Lord Derby in 1858, as to whether she had the power to refuse a dissolution. Disraeli, in 1868, considered that she was constitutionally entitled to do so. George V in effect refused to dissolve Parliament in November 1910, and it is impossible to say categorically that this could never happen under any future sovereign. That the King granted a dissolution to Ramsay MacDonald in 1924 is in no way conclusive, since the political situation was then such that it would in any case have been quite impossible to avoid a dissolution. There are some strong arguments, to which we shall return later, to support the view that the sovereign could no longer refuse a government's request for a dissolution, but not so long ago some leading authorities still maintained that this was an instance where the royal prerogative could still be invoked in case of absolute necessity. The British have resolved the problem by saying that even though the prerogative may still exist in theory, it would be difficult to employ it in practice.

Any attempt to describe the main features of the British constitution is consequently bound to some extent to lack precision. As Stanley Baldwin once said, it is doubtless very easy for a historian to see exactly what the practice was at any given period in the past, but it is extremely difficult for a contemporary to say just how the constitution stands on any particular point at some particular moment in his own lifetime. A practice that is said to be 'constitutional' may always be on the point of being abandoned, while another is rigidly followed but could not yet be described as 'constitutional'.

Nevertheless, the doubtful points are not of major significance. Most constitutional rules, including all the most important, became generally accepted long ago. Whatever modifications may be taking place are usually comparatively limited in scope. Any reforms that have been introduced or appear likely in the future are not normally dictated by any abstract theories but designed to take account of what has been learned from experience or to secure greater practical efficiency. These two considerations determine whether there is likely to be any constitutional change and what form it may be expected to take.

It follows that, while not automatically prejudiced against reforms that can be justified by logical arguments, the British do not believe that these alone provide sufficient grounds for any reform. They are, on the contrary, much more concerned to see that their institutions will in fact work effectively, bearing in mind always the lessons that can be learned from the past, the political situation at the time, and the results that they hope to attain in the future.

Ever since the appearance of Montesquieu's writings on the British constitution, the separation of powers has been generally regarded as the essential basis of a liberal system of government. The British constitution has been held up as one whose direct object is political freedom. Yet British writers would be among the first to point out that, even in Montesquieu's time, the virtues of their constitution did not lie in any separation of powers, which might have proved extremely inconvenient in practice, but rather in that it 'provided machinery for free, public, and orderly controversy, and thus contained the means for its own amendment'. With a flexible constitution and no dogmatic preconceptions, it was not long before the executive and the legislature had come to work in close co-operation. They did so not in order to prevent arbitrary rule but in the interests of efficient government. In the light of experience they gradually evolved that working relationship now associated with Cabinet government.

K. B. Smellie has written that 'the Cabinet system was born when it was found from experience that the discretionary powers of the King necessary for the welfare of the State had to be combined with the legislative and financial supremacy of Parliament by the King taking as his advisers only those politicians who could secure the support of Parliament'. Its

origins were thus essentially empirical, and its present composition, its homogeneity and its political responsibility are
likewise determined by rules which have grown up in response
to purely practical considerations over the course of the
centuries.

The striking thing about the Cabinet is that, although it is
now undeniably the centre of gravity in the British constitution,
its composition, organisation and powers, and its relationships
with the sovereign and with Parliament, are still governed by
rules founded upon custom which have only very gradually
become at all clearly defined. Yet it has never been thought
necessary to set them down in writing. The main reforms that
have taken place in the Cabinet system have had the strictly
practical objective of improving its organisation and methods
of work so as to make it function more efficiently. Thus in 1916
Mr Lloyd George converted the secretariat of the Committee
of Imperial Defence into the Cabinet Secretariat, which first
appeared as an item in the estimates in 1917. Its value was
quickly recognised, but it was some years before its functions
became clearly defined. In 1938 the organisation and scope of
the Cabinet Office was revised and clarified and considerably
expanded, and this process continued during the second World
War. The war also saw a great development in the use of
Cabinet committees, both standing and *ad hoc*, on various
special topics, which did much to raise the efficiency of the
machinery of government. These, like the Cabinet Office, have
also been imitated in other countries.

The House of Lords provides another example of how the
success or failure of any constitutional reform depends on
whether there is any practical advantage to be gained thereby.
The question of reforming the upper House had been raised
long before the major crisis which, after a long struggle, was
finally resolved by the Parliament Act of 1911. Until the beginning of the twentieth century, however, the problem had never
been regarded as urgent because constitutional conventions had
grown up which offset the anomalous effects of the existing
system. In practice, the House of Commons controlled the
Cabinet, which was responsible only to the lower House. The
Lords had lost the right to initiate or amend money bills, and
in regard to all other bills it had become generally accepted
that they did not have an unrestricted right of veto. As early

as 1867 Bagehot had maintained, 'the House of Lords must yield whenever the opinion of the Commons is also the opinion of the nation, and when it is clear that the nation has made up its mind'.

This formula, albeit somewhat vague, was sufficient to cover all the usual run of political eventualities. It could not, however, resolve the altogether abnormal difficulties which arose after the Liberal victory in the general election of 1906, when the House of Lords tried to prevent the government from carrying out its programme. This upset the normal relationship between the two Houses. It seemed intolerable that Parliament should not be able to pass the legislation necessary to give effect to the measures for which the people had voted at the last general election. The clash between the Houses culminated in 1909 in an acute crisis that was finally settled, after a celebrated struggle involving two general elections, by the Parliament Act of 1911.

The Parliament Act was not itself designed to reform the House of Lords. On the contrary, the preamble stated, 'It is intended to substitute for the House of Lords as it at present exists a Second Chamber constituted on a popular instead of a hereditary basis, but such substitution cannot be immediately brought into operation.' The Act had the essentially practical objective of enabling Parliament to legislate in such a way that, no matter which party was in power, the government should always have the same power to carry through its legislative programme and thus give effect to the wishes of the electorate. All that the Parliament Act did was to lay down some brief rules of legislative procedure.

The reform of the upper House has remained pending ever since, but has never been taken up really seriously. The Attlee government decided that the Act of 1911 was no longer appropriate to the changed political situation, as it left the Lords still able to delay the legislative programme of a Labour government long enough to prevent its being carried through in its entirety. Their solution, however, was simply to amend the Parliament Act of 1911 so as to shorten the period of reflection that the Lords could impose upon the Commons and the people.

By such methods as these, reforms genuinely desired by the country as a whole have invariably been carried into effect without destroying the traditions that provide an element of political wisdom, restraint, and respect for the customary modes of political behaviour. It matters little that these reforms have not been prompted by ideological considerations. The important thing is that they have in fact brought about profound changes in the British system of government. This process of adaptation, sometimes speeded up under pressure of circumstances, has been going on for many generations and it is still continuing, in the middle of the twentieth century, with the same realism and lack of preconceived ideas and plans as in the past. Thus, as practically everyone who examines the system—most of all the British themselves—have agreed, 'the Constitution of William the Conqueror' has been able to survive over the course of the centuries and to remain or sometimes even become more closely attuned to the special needs of a strikingly stable political community and to the temperament of the British people. Yet at the same time it has succeeded in meeting all the demands that are placed upon a modern state.

The British constitution today can be compared to an old garment that is such a perfect fit for its owner, so eminently suited to his needs and practically indestructible, that he will go on wearing it for the rest of his days. This analogy helps to explain why the British constitution should be so difficult to reproduce in other countries.

The chief and irreplaceable merit of the British constitution is that it is so perfectly adapted to the needs of the country though, as we shall see, this is by no means its only virtue.

PART ONE

The Source of Power

THE POWER OF THE PEOPLE UNDER THE BRITISH POLITICAL SYSTEM

TO discover the source of power, we need to know where in theory political power resides and on what authority it is exercised. In Britain, unlike most other countries, the answer is not immediately obvious.

The British have never made the slightest attempt to shape their political institutions in accordance with preconceived theories or abstract general principles. The present parliamentary system is the outcome of a long process of evolution going back many centuries, and there have been few opportunities in the course of British political history to lay down any general principles like that of the sovereignty of the people. The country has gradually changed from an absolute monarchy into a democracy which is now a monarchy in form only, and in the process has experienced many different forms of government which cannot easily be classified. All that can be done is to distinguish a number of different phases in the development of her institutions and the accompanying gradual and often imperceptible shifts in the location of political power.

In these circumstances it is hardly to be expected that the British would have tried to give a definite answer to any purely theoretical questions concerning the source of political power, especially as they are a nation which does not believe that simple formulas necessarily provide the best solution to any problem.

In France, the Constituent Assembly declared in 1789 that sovereignty belongs to the people. This, from the legal point of view, was undoubtedly the great achievement of the Revolution. Constitutional lawyers consider it of fundamental importance to be certain where political power resides, because, once this is known, they can logically deduce the answers to many other important constitutional questions, which will of course vary according to whether sovereignty is held to belong to the people or to the nation.

The British, however, have shown little interest in such abstract questions concerning the source of power and have never found it necessary to make any formal declaration on the subject. They have generally been content to point out a number of historical and political considerations which lead them to conclude that Parliament is now the supreme power in the state. Parliament still, strictly speaking, means the sovereign acting with the advice and consent of the Lords Spiritual and Temporal and the Commons, although the latter are by now undoubtedly the dominant organ in the state.

Some writers indeed have drawn a distinction between legal sovereignty and political sovereignty, saying that the former belongs to Parliament and the latter to the people. This, however, is not so much a constitutional theory as simply a way of describing the facts of the present situation.

It is not at all certain whether the people can in theory be sovereign in a country which is a monarchy. The Belgian Constitution of 7th February 1831 asserted that monarchy and popular sovereignty are not incompatible, but most continental political theorists have found it impossible to reconcile the two. Where there is a hereditary monarchy and a sovereign who reigns by the grace of God, the people can hardly be sovereign, for this would imply that the political authorities were the delegates of the people who were given power for only a limited period at a time and were responsible to the people for all their actions. This, however, is a point in which British writers have never shown any interest.

There are admittedly a number of very old constitutional documents in which it was implicitly recognised, in terms appropriate to the circumstances of the time, that the people should in certain respects participate in the exercise of political power. In 1215 it was laid down in Magna Charta: 'No scutage or aid shall be imposed unless *per commune consilium regnis*, except in the three cases of ransoming the king's person, making his eldest son a knight, and once for marrying his eldest daughter. . . . In order to take the common counsel of the kingdom in the imposition of aids . . . and of scutage, the king shall cause to be summoned the archbishops, bishops, abbots, earls and greater barons, by writ directed to each separately. . . .' Magna Charta, however, was a mediaeval charter only concerned with the rights of the Lords Spiritual and Temporal, and its provisions are hardly very relevant to the present day. The Declaration of Right of 1688 declared, amongst other things, that the executive could not suspend or fail to carry out any law without the consent of Parliament, that it was illegal to raise or maintain a standing army in time of peace unless this had been authorised by Parliament, and that there should be free elections and freedom of discussion in Parliament. But nowhere in these historic texts was it ever laid down that sovereignty belonged to the people. All that we can really deduce from them is some idea of the historical importance of the limitations imposed upon the prerogatives of the sovereign by a Parliament which was growing more powerful but was still quite undemocratic.

Even in Britain itself these documents are regarded as of purely historical significance. What is much more important is to see how far the people today do in fact participate in the government of the country. Although their rôle has never been defined in general terms, this has not prevented the development of constitutional conventions that allow the people to play an important part in the political life of the country.

In so far as the government is in practice obliged to act in accordance with their wishes, sovereignty must clearly belong to the people. This is obvious from the laws, customs, precedents and practices which form the basis of the constitution. British political institutions are the product of a process of evolution in which the power of the monarchy and the political influence of the aristocracy have gradually declined over the course of the centuries, while the rôle of the people has steadily expanded.

The people are thus the source of political power. The fundamentally democratic nature of the British system of government can be seen by looking at the electoral system and the political parties.

Chapter One

THE ELECTORAL SYSTEM

FREE elections are the essential basis of democracy. In Britain, however, there are fewer elective offices than in many other countries, particularly in the United States.

In the first place, no one but members of Parliament and local councils are elected to office. There are no popularly elected judges, officials or other functionaries. Moreover, at the national level there is only one elective organ—the House of Commons—whilst the head of the state is a hereditary monarch and the upper House is an aristocratic body entirely composed of hereditary members and those who sit for life or for as long as they hold a particular office in the church. In these circumstances it might be thought impossible for the electorate to play any very significant part in politics.

In fact, however, the electorate has a rôle of fundamental importance. One reason for this is that today the hereditary elements in the constitution have relatively little influence. The sovereign has practically no discretion in the exercise of her functions, and the gradual self-effacement of the House of Lords has been quite as striking as the way in which the House of Commons has become to an ever-increasing extent the dominant organ in Parliament. Another factor which should not be overlooked is that in Britain general elections are usually held before Parliament has completed its full statutory term. This does not mean that the power of dissolution is very freely used or that it is necessarily as important under the British two-party system as it would be in some other forms of parliamentary government. Nevertheless, Parliament is often dissolved before the end of its term, and this means that elections occur considerably more frequently than would otherwise be the case. The main reason why the electorate is so important, however, is that a general election has exceptionally far-reaching significance. In Great Britain the people do not merely from time to time elect representatives to Parliament. They are actually able to say exactly what policy they think ought to be followed and give political power to one particular party. It is they who in fact select the Prime Minister in a way which, although indirect, makes it practically impossible for their wishes to be disregarded. This is much more than the people can do in many other democracies which have formally accepted the principle of the popular sovereignty. We shall try to show here how the British people do, to a very large extent, control the destinies of the country and should accordingly be considered to possess sovereign power.

Thus, in Britain even more than in other countries, we have to look primarily at the electoral system and the method of voting if we want to find out how much power the people do in fact possess. These are the essential bases of the political system without which it is impossible to appreciate the true nature of any system of government.

In this connection, it should be remembered that it was not until comparatively recently that Britain acquired a democratic electoral system. This was slow to develop on account of the somewhat unusual social structure, the lingering influence of the aristocracy which for many years encountered no widespread opposition, the conservatism of important sections of the ruling classes, the absence of revolutionary upheavals, and the moderate and cautious approach to politics which is a British characteristic. The electoral system evolved gradually in response to changing circumstances and alterations in the social structure, until eventually universal suffrage was achieved and elections came to be conducted in a free and impartial manner. The one thing which has remained unaltered right from the start has been the system of voting. Since the earliest days of the parliamentary system, elections have always been decided by a simple majority.

I. THE EXTENSION OF THE FRANCHISE

The establishment of universal suffrage in Great Britain has been the outcome of a very slow process of evolution. This is hardly surprising in view of the historical circumstances surrounding the origins and growth of Parliament and the distinctive way in which the political system has developed.

There is no necessary connection between the age of an elective assembly and the date at which democratic ideas begin to make themselves felt. There is no reason, therefore, why any extension of the franchise should have been demanded in Britain before it began to be sought in other countries.

So far as this was concerned, it was the great Reform Act of 1832 that marked the beginning of modern times. Before then, the composition of the electorate had been revised considerably, but certainly not in a democratic direction. On the contrary, whereas elections were originally able to produce an assembly which, in the circumstances of the time, could be regarded as something approaching a representative body, from about the end of the seventeenth or the beginning of the eighteenth century an election ceased to bear any close resemblance to the free expression of the will of the people. It is no use looking so far back for any sign of incipient democracy. The victory of Parliament in 1688 was a victory for the nobles and the wealthy and not for the people, who were no more sovereign after the Revolution than they had been before.

The Old Regime

All the changes which took place in the electoral system before the beginning of the nineteenth century were really a reflection of the changing nature of Parliament itself.

Parliament had developed out of the Concilium which mediaeval kings used to summon to assist them in governing the country. From among the very large number of Lords, the King used to select those with whom he wished to confer. Along with these peers, Simon de Montfort and Edward I decided to summon two knights elected by each county and two burgesses to represent each incorporated town. This did not, however, produce anything remotely resembling an assembly representative of the people. Electors voted as a matter of duty, and the franchise was certainly not a privilege to which they attached any value. The boroughs actually tried to rid themselves of the burden of separate representation in Parliament as this involved them in considerable expense. Members of Parliament were considered to be fulfilling obligations which they owed to the sovereign by assisting him in the transaction of his affairs, and knights chosen to represent their counties showed little eagerness to spend much time on their duties at Westminster. Parliament was at that time a purely advisory body with no political power, and it naturally had no control over the government.

Although the King's Council used to consult the representatives of the counties and boroughs, the latter did not take part in its deliberations but only communicated their views to the sovereign or expressed their approval of particular proposals through a Speaker appointed by the Crown. Most of the sovereigns of this period used to consult the Commons in this way because they wanted to make the heavy taxes that they already required somewhat more acceptable to the people. At times they also wished to acquaint themselves with the views of the freemen, and the poor communications of the period made it almost impossible to do this in any other way.

In these circumstances, there was no demand for the extension of the franchise, and the relatively democratic system of voting did not create any difficulties for the Crown or for the aristocracy. Until the middle of the fifteenth century there were no very stringent conditions limiting the right to vote, though the necessary qualifications varied somewhat as between the counties and the boroughs. In the counties, universal suffrage seems originally to have been the rule. Later the franchise was restricted to those who paid some kind of tax, but, by Acts of 1294, 1430 and 1432, anyone who possessed land worth 40s. a year had the right to vote. In the boroughs the qualifications for voting varied according to different local customs, but the most common was for every householder to be entitled to vote. Nor were the qualifications required to stand for election unduly severe. County members were generally large landowners, but boroughs used to choose tradesmen and artisans to represent them in the House of Commons.

It was not until after the middle of the fifteenth century that Parliament began to grow more powerful and its character gradually changed as a result of various political successes to which we must return later. The Commons ceased to be the tool of the sovereign, acquired leaders of their own, and began to oppose the policies of the Crown. The Hundred Years War helped to awaken the national and political consciousness of the people. The House of Commons increased in size and was able to take advantage of a number of weak kings in order to strengthen its position. Regular forms of parliamentary procedure were adopted, sessions grew longer and debates assumed greater importance. As a result, members were no longer elected unanimously. Elections developed into contests for a position no longer considered insignificant in which the aristocracy began to take an active interest. In the sixteenth century the boroughs began to elect sons of peers or wealthy landowners or men who had their backing, instead of the more humble citizens by whom they had formerly been represented, so that the more influential classes tended to gain control over the borough seats. In 1603 it was still possible to regard the House of Commons as simply a representative body, but as the seventeenth century advanced its ascendancy became more marked. It asserted its supremacy over the upper House, strengthened its control over finance and became able to exert considerable influence over the government, until with the Revolution of 1688 its supremacy was clearly established. Thereafter, as Pollard has observed, 'the Commons in Parliament enjoyed the fruits of their victory but had no desire to share them with the people in whose name their triumph had been secured'.

These changes brought about a gradual transformation in the methods of electing members of Parliament. Not only was the electorate reduced in size, but, in the boroughs at least, elections fell completely under the control of the aristocracy, the wealthy or the Crown, all of whom resorted to every kind of corrupt practice in order to maintain their hold over the electorate. The well-known techniques of electoral corruption which began to be adopted in the later seventeenth century were further developed in the course of the eighteenth century and had reached scandalous proportions before they began to be attacked by a series of Reform Acts, beginning with that of 1832.

Electoral corruption reached its zenith in the reign of George III. The electorate were pawns in an unprincipled struggle for power in which two main weapons were employed. First, the number of voters was reduced to a minimum to make it easier to control their votes. Secondly, every conceivable device was employed to ensure that the electorate would support a particular candidate.

Great importance was attached to keeping the number of electors as small as possible. No adjustments were made to take account of the growth of towns under the impact of the Industrial Revolution. Even great cities like Birmingham, Manchester, Leeds and Sheffield were left without any representatives in the House of Commons, while boroughs with hardly any inhabitants continued to send members to Westminster. There were 44 members from the county of Cornwall alone, and yet London, with three times the population, had only four. No new boroughs had been enfranchised since 1673, and those whose population had declined or become almost non-existent continued to elect the same number of members as before. Dunwich had been inundated by the sea, Old Sarum became entirely uninhabited, and Gatton was completely turned over to parkland, but they all continued to return their two members. The qualifications for voting varied between different boroughs according to their individual charters; sometimes the franchise was confined to the municipal corporation, sometimes it depended on membership of certain guilds or on property qualifications, and very often the sheriff had a large say in determining exactly who should be allowed to vote.

The franchise was less restricted in the counties and in some towns. Even so, immediately before the Reform Act of 1832 there was only one elector for every 35 inhabitants in the counties in England and Wales, and the total electorate in 1831 amounted to no more than 4% of the population. About half the constituencies had so few voters that they could easily be brought under the complete control of a particular interest.

Some 'rotten boroughs' were quite literally bought up. Anyone with enough money had only to purchase a majority of the houses to obtain with them the majority of the votes. Alternatively, if he could not buy the houses, he could buy up the municipal corporation or other persons who qualified for the franchise and were accustomed to sell their votes. Voting took place in public, so the electors were never free to vote as they thought fit, and as there was no serious attempt to regulate the conduct of elections, the result was to encourage overt corruption on a large scale.

Members of Parliament, once elected, were invariably subservient to those to whom they owed their seats. This was true regardless of the constituency they represented. The qualifications required for membership of the House of Commons were revised in 1710, and the conditions of eligibility were still further narrowed on several occasions in the course of the eighteenth century, until the House became the preserve of large landowners. In addition, there was a system of patronage which sometimes operated to the advantage of the Crown if the opposition were weak or had been temporarily silenced. Its chief beneficiaries, however, were the nobility and those with large fortunes who controlled a considerable number of seats and votes in the House of Commons, even though they might not themselves be members of Parliament. At the end of the eighteenth century, over half the borough seats were in fact controlled by 250 influential persons able to choose who should represent them in Parliament. Members of the House of Lords controlled the elections in constituencies which lay within their estates, and would either see that the candidates returned could be relied on to further the interests of their patron, or else sell the seats to anyone willing to pay.

These practices were carried on more or less openly and did much to create the reputation for corruption which was why the French at the time of the Revolution of 1789 had little faith in parliamentary institutions on the British model.

Britain was then quite clearly ruled by an oligarchy. Nevertheless, since the Reform Act of 1832, the forces of democracy have eventually prevailed.

The development of the British parliamentary system entered a new phase with the coming of the Industrial Revolution and the far-reaching social changes which this set in motion. These led to the extension of the franchise and so enabled the middle classes to play an active part in the political life of the country.

The Reform Act of 1832

When William IV came to the throne after the death of George IV in 1830, a new government was formed under the Whig leader, Lord Grey, whose Cabinet also included a number of Tories who were mostly progressive Canningites. Although the Whigs gained a majority in the ensuing general election, this did not automatically give them a mandate to reform the electoral system since election results did not then have the same political significance as they acquired after 1832. Before the Reform Act was eventually passed, there was a long struggle comparable to that which was later to take place over the Parliament Act of 1911. Grey's government was defeated and forced to fight another general election, after which it still met with unrelenting opposition from the House of Lords, and had to resign. Finally, Grey managed to persuade the King to create sufficient new peers to carry the bill. At this threat to swamp the upper House, the peers decided to give way, and on 17th June 1832 the Act received the royal assent.

The Reform Act of 1832 is widely held to be the most important Act ever passed by the British Parliament. It was certainly a measure of tremendous significance, both because it recognised the changed distribution of power in society and, above all, because it opened the way to further reform. That the Act itself introduced only a limited measure of reform will become clear if we examine the two principal topics with which it dealt.

In the first place, it provided for a redistribution of seats calculated to remove the more flagrant injustices in the old system which had not been revised since the reign of Charles II. The rotten boroughs were disfranchised and a number of seats were taken from the pocket boroughs, to give a total of 143 seats available for redistribution. Of these, 65 were allocated to towns in the north of England and 65 to counties which had hitherto been unrepresented or had had disproportionately few members in the House of Commons. Scotland received an additional 8 seats, and the remaining 5 were allocated to Irish constituencies. Nevertheless, many of the injustices inherent in the old system remained untouched, and the influence of the great landowners was still preponderant.

Their position began to be seriously threatened, however, by changes in the law which increased the numbers entitled to vote. The franchise was extended to all those who paid a rent of £10 a year in the boroughs or between £2 and £50 a year in the counties. The qualifying rent was still a considerable sum of money and did not indicate any revolutionary change. The number of voters increased by about 5% to a total of 653,000 in England and Wales and about 800,000 over the whole country. Nor was there at first any marked change in the type of persons elected to Parliament, although not only the aristocracy, large landowners and wealthy industrialists but also an increasingly influential group of small manufacturers and businessmen were now entitled to vote. The Whigs gradually identified themselves with the interests of this new class of voters, who became a powerful source of strength to the Liberal Party.

The Achievement of Universal Suffrage

The Conservatives also found themselves obliged to take up the question of electoral reform. In 1867 Disraeli continued the work begun in 1832 by taking over and gaining the credit for a Reform Act whose provisions had been largely devised by the Liberals. There was a further redistribution of seats whereby various insignificant boroughs were partly or wholly disfranchised and 52 seats became available for redistribution, of which 25 were allocated to the counties, 19 to larger towns, 7 to Scotland and 1 to the University of London. The most important part of the reform, however, was the extension of the franchise. Property qualifications, particularly in the boroughs, were lowered, and the vote was also granted to university graduates—clergymen, doctors and teachers—and anyone with an income from property of £10 a year or savings of £60 or more. Altogether the number of voters increased by over a million.

The Reform Act of 1884 made the franchise genuinely democratic. At the same time, a further 134 seats were taken from the boroughs and another 12 new seats were created for redistribution to the counties and larger towns. The traditional discrepancy in voting strength between town and country which the Conservatives had for many years been trying to preserve was finally brought to an end by a revision of boundaries designed to create approximately equal constituencies with a population of about 50,000 over practically the whole country. There was also a further important reduction in the qualifications for the franchise which was extended to the counties on the same terms as it had been given to the boroughs in 1867. The number of voters increased to about 4,500,000, and by 1915 the total had risen to 8,360,000. The secret ballot was instituted in 1872, and the Corrupt and Illegal Practices Act of 1883 ensured that elections could no longer be won by the power of the purse. The character of elections was thus gradually changed until they became the contest for power between opposing parties that they are today. The qualifications required to stand for Parliament tended to become assimilated with those for the franchise. This led to a marked change in the type of persons elected, and the introduction of members' salaries in 1911 still further broadened the social background of the House of Commons.

The introduction of conscription in the first World War virtually compelled the government to carry the process of electoral reform to its logical conclusion by granting universal suffrage. By the Representation of the People Act, 1918, the vote was given to all men over the age of 21 and to all women over the age of 30. The total number of voters was thus raised to over 21,300,000, of whom 8,500,000 were women. In 1928 women were granted the vote on the same terms as men, which meant that the number of voters rose to 28,000,000. Today the electorate numbers 35,000,000.

The second World War produced a final series of reforms designed to bring the electoral system still more into line with modern democratic principles. An Act of 1944 not only provided for another redistribution of seats but established statutory machinery for regular boundary revisions so as to ensure that an equal ratio between seats and votes would be maintained. Plural voting had already become comparatively insignificant, as the Act of 1918 had abolished the occupation franchise and required elections to be held on the same day throughout the country. The Representation of the People Act of 1948 abolished the last two surviving forms of plural voting—the business vote and the university vote. The business vote affected about 50,000 persons (48,974 were actually on the registers in 1945) who were allowed a second vote in a constituency other than that in which they lived because they occupied business premises valued at more than £10 a year. The only other people allowed to vote twice were university graduates, who retained the privilege originally granted to Oxford and Cambridge in 1603. In 1945, 116,647 university votes were recorded for the 12 special university members, who were usually extremely distinguished persons but whose political views always tended to be predominantly Liberal or Conservative. Many Conservatives would still like to restore the university vote which the Labour Party abolished, but it seems doubtful whether they could permanently succeed in setting aside the rule of 'one man, one vote' that is now the fundamental egalitarian principle upon which modern electoral systems are based.

Since 1950, elections have been fought on the basis of universal suffrage and a thoroughly democratic franchise. All British subjects, both men and women, over the age of 21 are now able to vote, provided that they have lived in their constituency for at least three months. Members of the armed forces can vote regardless of any residence qualifications. Only foreigners, lunatics, felons and peers are denied the franchise. Anyone qualified to vote is normally entitled to stand for election, subject to a few additional disqualifications similar to those that exist under most electoral systems.

Thus, by a gradual process of evolution over the past eight centuries, the House of Commons has developed into a lower House which is now the chief popular representative assembly of the country. Though it has never been expressly proclaimed that the people are sovereign, there can be no doubt that today political power rests ultimately with the British nation as a whole, who delegate their powers to other authorities by means of free elections.

II. THE CONDUCT OF ELECTIONS

For many years there were no definite rules governing the conduct of elections. Subsequently, for an even longer period, elections were largely controlled by a few powerful individuals or interests.

As the House of Commons grew more powerful, the electorate tended to become smaller and more easily manageable. At the same time, and for precisely the same reasons, elections continued to be conducted in such a way that there was absolutely no freedom of decision or guarantee of impartiality. The Reform Act of 1832 was again the first step in the creation of an improved electoral system.

The necessary reforms were introduced by gradual stages. The influence of the aristocracy declined and the power of the political parties steadily increased until the British electoral system—once the most corrupt in the world—has become singularly free from any vestige of corruption. The main features of the present electoral system, although now difficult to think of except as parts of an integrated whole, in fact evolved separately and empirically.

The Registration of Electors

The Act of 1832 was the first serious attempt to institute a proper register of electors, the absence of which had left the way open to all kinds of fraud. But the new system of registration was complicated and provided abundant opportunities for costly litigation. This put new and inexperienced electors at a disadvantage, while benefiting the aristocracy, who were still able to exercise predominant influence over the local party organisations. The latter made every effort to see that all their potential supporters were on the register while as many as possible of those likely to vote against them were struck off. The Acts of 1843, 1865, 1878, 1885 and 1895 put an end to the worst abuses in the registration system, but the compilation and revision of electoral lists were left under the control of the party organisations. This was at best only a lesser evil. There was no clear guarantee of impartiality until all responsibility for the registration of electors was transferred to the public authorities by the Representation of the People Act of 1918.

Since 1918 the state, through the Home Secretary, has assumed full responsibility for preparing the electoral register. Town Clerks in the boroughs and Clerks of the County Council in the counties are appointed Registration Officers, with power to add new names to the register and to remove any which are no longer valid. A statutory interval is allowed during which objections may be lodged regarding any name included in or omitted from the register, and any interested party has the right of appeal to the county court or, on a point of law, to the Court of Appeal, for a final ruling.

Corrupt Practices and Election Expenses

Corruption and intimidation long made a mockery of elections in Great Britain. It was encouraged by the fact that voting took place in public, the lack of any effective supervision of elections, the smallness of the electorate, the wealth of the land-owners, the average elector's ignorance of political affairs, and the deficiencies of party organisation. This unsatisfactory state of affairs improved somewhat as a result of successive electoral reforms, but did not finally come to an end until long after 1832. The Parliament elected in 1841 was described as 'the corrupt Parliament', and no less than £24,000 was paid out to the electors of St Albans between 1832 and 1854. Until 1868, the power to determine the results of disputed elections remained vested in a committee of the House of Commons, whose members could clearly not be impartial and found it impossible to take a stand against practices which, although corrupt, were employed by all the parties to further their own interests. Even after the introduction of the secret ballot in 1872, some abuses still continued. Sandwich and Macclesfield were both deprived of their seats after an inquiry revealed that over half the electors had sold their votes.

The only way to root out electoral corruption was by direct attack through special legislation. The first measure of this kind was the Corrupt and Illegal Practices Act of 1854, which attempted to define corrupt practices and imposed penalties on those accepting bribes as well as on those who offered them. It was fairly effective in suppressing corruption in the strict sense of the word, but did little to check the many other forms of intimidation that were employed.

In 1868 the power to adjudicate on petitions questioning the validity of election results was taken away from the House of Commons, which had shown itself thoroughly unfit for the task. Despite the objections of the judges, who were anxious not to become indirectly involved in politics, Disraeli succeeded in transferring this function to the Court of King's Bench, and the House was thus obliged to abide by the decisions of the court.

This was followed shortly afterwards by another and even more important reform. The revelation of other abuses in the general election of 1868 led to widespread demands for a secret ballot. The Conservative aristocracy, together with Lord Palmerston and a large section of the Liberal Party, had so far succeeded in resisting this proposal. In 1869, however, a committee was appointed to inquire into the question and reported in favour of a secret ballot for parliamentary and municipal elections. The House of Lords tried to oppose the reform, but in the end reluctantly gave way and the Ballot Act was eventually passed in 1872. It is still possible to identify individual votes if the result of an election is disputed, by means of the counterfoils corresponding to each ballot paper. Nevertheless, the Ballot Act was undoubtedly a vital reform. It meant that the electorate were at last really free to vote as they thought fit. One of its consequences was the emergence of the Irish Nationalist Party, which, according to many leading authorities, could never have come into being without it. The ballot did not put an end to electoral corruption, however, for it was still possible to influence the outcome of an election by spending even larger sums of money and canvassing individual electors.

The Liberal's Corrupt and Illegal Practices Act introduced by Sir Henry James in 1883 imposed more drastic restrictions which began to foreshadow the legislation in force today. Much more severe penalties, including heavy fines and in certain cases imprisonment, were imposed for corruption; corrupt practices were more stringently and narrowly defined; and intimidation became a serious offence. Any candidate found guilty of corrupt practices was disqualified from sitting in Parliament for the next seven years, and could never stand again for the same constituency. A second Act tackled another vital aspect of the question by imposing limits on election expenses. This not only assisted in checking corruption but helped to create a more democratic House of Commons. The employment of paid canvassers was forbidden, candidates were allowed only a limited number of committee rooms, it was made illegal to hire conveyances to take electors to the poll, no candidate was allowed to employ more than one salaried agent, his personal expenditure was restricted to £100, and all other election expenses had to be paid by an agent and not by the candidate himself. All these provisions remain in force today, and other restrictions of a similar character have been added by subsequent legislation.

The Act of 1883 is generally agreed to have brought about a considerable reduction in electoral corruption. There was an immediate decline in expenditure on elections, from about £1 for every elector in 1880 to £780,000 for an electorate of 5,670,000 in 1885.

The Representation of the People Act, 1918, and other more recent electoral legislation have proceeded further along the lines laid down in 1883. Many of the provisions of the Act of 1883, in particular those relating to the suppression of corrupt and illegal practices and the adjudication of election petitions, are still in force, having been interpreted and clarified by the decisions of the courts. The law relating to election expenses has been revised on several occasions, until they are now subject to very strict and minute restrictions. No candidate may spend more than £450, plus another 1½d. per elector in the counties or 1d. per elector in the boroughs, and another £100 for his own personal expenses. Other regulations govern methods of electioneering, the employment of agents and the use of buildings. After the election, each candidate has to furnish an account of his expenditure, and although it may not always be easy to make sure that he has fully complied with all the provisions of the law, the knowledge that any irregularities may give rise to a petition contesting the election result is a sufficient deterrent to prevent any really serious abuses. In the general election of 1951, the Conservatives spent £477,000, the Labour Party £406,000, the Liberals £53,000 and the Communists £6,000, making a total expenditure of less than £950,000 spread over an electorate of over 34 million, of whom nearly 29 million actually voted.[1]

With the development of party organisation, elections have become primarily a contest between the parties and are conducted in a completely different atmosphere which has helped to hasten the disappearance of the old abuses. The electorate may be subjected to new forms of political propaganda and sometimes to very pressing appeals from the candidates, but the age of corruption is past and the legislation penalising corrupt practices and guaranteeing free elections now has more of a deterrent than a repressive effect.

Nomination of Candidates

The Ballot Act of 1872 also introduced a new method of nominating candidates in place of the old procedure which had given rise to many irregularities and abuses. Candidates previously had to be adopted at a public meeting. If, as often happened, no one else came forward to stand against them, their adoption meant that they were automatically elected forthwith. Since 1872, however, nomination has been simply a matter of announcing one's candidature. When the date of the election is fixed, a nomination day is appointed on which each candidate has to deposit his nomination papers with the returning officer. The papers must be signed by the candidate, who has to be nominated and seconded by two registered electors and supported by another eight electors whose signatures must also appear on the nomination papers. If only one candidate is

---

[1] In the general election of 1955 the parties spent a total of £903,000 (Conservatives £458,000, Labour £379,000). This was only 76% of the statutory maximum.

nominated, the returning officer declares him elected. Otherwise, the list of candidates is published and the electors vote between them. In order to discourage frivolous candidatures, each candidate has since 1918 been required to make a deposit of £150, which is returned to him if he obtains one-eighth or more of the total poll.

The Poll

The organisation of the poll is governed by regulations relating to such matters as the day on which polling is to take place, the authorities responsible for making the necessary arrangements, and the actual conduct of the poll. Most of these regulations were laid down in the Act of 1918. It is only since then that all polling has had to take place on one day and on the same day throughout the country. This was an important change as, when voting used to be spread over more than a week, there was considerable scope for plural voting. People were then entitled to vote wherever they owned or occupied houses or business premises, so they could go round from one constituency to another using all their votes in turn. Plural voting was retained after 1918 in the case of occupiers of business premises and university graduates, but by an Act of 1928 no one was allowed more than two votes in all, and plural votes have since been entirely abolished. Polling day is always eight days after the issue of the royal proclamation summoning the new Parliament. It may not be a Saturday, a Sunday or a Monday, as this would mean intruding upon the Sunday peace of the voters or those responsible for organising the poll or counting the votes. Considering that voting always takes place on a working day, the number of abstentions is remarkably small—only 16% of the electorate in 1950 and 17% in 1951.[1] The vast majority of the electorate do in fact make use of their right to vote.

Polling takes place under the supervision of public officials. Each constituency has its returning officer, who is either the sheriff, the mayor or the chairman of the urban or rural district council, and he in turn normally delegates his functions to one of the registration officers in his district. The returning officer is responsible for announcing the date of the election, receiving nominations, deciding where the polling stations shall be

[1] 23% in 1955.

located, and making the arrangements for the actual voting, counting the votes and declaring the final result.

The procedure is very similar to what it is in France. The returning officer is in charge of the arrangements and there are ample guarantees that voting is always genuinely free and secret. The polling stations must be open between 8 a.m. and 8 p.m. and may be open from 7 a.m. to 9 p.m. if any candidate so requests, as is usually necessary in view of the fact that elections are always held on a weekday. Since 1918-20 it has been possible under British electoral law for most of those who have to be away from their constituency to record their votes in their absence. Anyone who can show that he is unable to vote in person because of his occupation or because he will be away from home on polling day can ask to be registered as an absent voter. He is then entitled to vote either by proxy in certain cases or, as is more usual, by post. Sailors and members of the armed forces also vote by post, and altogether about 500,000 postal votes were recorded in 1950 and 756,000 in 1951.[1]

Various public buildings are taken over to serve as polling stations. When he goes to vote, the elector is given a single ballot paper with the names of the candidates printed in alphabetical order. He puts a cross against the name of the candidate for whom he wishes to vote. When a ballot paper is issued, the number of the elector is recorded on the counterfoil, which is retained. This is intended to make it possible to identify individual votes in case of fraud, without in practice undermining the secrecy of the ballot. It is not so easy, however, to ensure that those presenting themselves are really registered electors as it is in countries where polling cards are issued. After voting, the elector folds his ballot paper in two and, without putting it in an envelope, places it straight in the ballot box. The candidates or their agents are present to see that there are no irregularities in the voting or during the count. The latter must begin as soon as possible after the close of the poll, and the votes for the whole constituency are counted in one central building, which is closed to the general public. If for any reason there is some delay before the counting can begin, the returning officer is responsible for seeing that there is no interference with the ballot boxes. In fact, such irregularities appear to be quite unknown in Great Britain today, even though it is still less than

[1] 526,000 in 1955.

a hundred years since all kinds of corrupt and dubious practices were rife.

The Election Campaign

The most striking features of the campaign which precedes each general election are its fundamentally democratic character, the spirit of fair play displayed on all sides, and the underlying patriotism and what might almost be described as restraint of all the parties.

The parties generally call a truce on the day before the royal proclamation is issued to summon the new Parliament. Before the elections of 1950 and 1951, the Prime Minister, the leader of the opposition, and the leader of the Liberal Party went with their wives and a large number of other members of Parliament to a special service of prayer and thanksgiving in St Paul's Cathedral, where the Archbishop of Canterbury gave an address emphasising the vanity of all human struggles and the grave responsibilities which power confers. Preparations for the election campaign always begin long beforehand in readiness against a dissolution, but the campaign itself does not officially open until the Queen has issued the traditional summons: 'We, being desirous and resolved, as soon as may be, to meet Our People, and to have their advice in Parliament, do hereby make known to all Our loving subjects Our Royal will and pleasure to call a new Parliament.'

All the usual techniques of political propaganda are employed in the course of the campaign, though its general tone is rather more restrained and serious than is generally the case in other countries. Each party is allowed a certain number of broadcasts, depending on how many candidates it has. The candidates work unsparingly, touring their constituencies and sometimes calling on individual electors and answering their questions. At their public meetings each side will denounce the other, but really violent controversy is unknown and the general atmosphere is not very different from that which prevails between the government and the opposition in debates in the House of Commons. Canvassers—the successors of those who in the days of corruption would try to buy electors or influence their votes by other kinds of pressure—nowadays go from house to house questioning the electors to see who is likely to vote for their party, and urging them to use their vote and to display window cards publicising their support for the candidate. Party slogans and election manifestos are proclaimed through loud-speakers. The press and the polls of the British Institute of Public Opinion make it possible to see what chances each party has according to the latest surveys, and how the general trend of opinion is moving. On polling day itself, there is more house-to-house visiting to urge all those who are believed not to have voted to exercise their right. Old people and invalids are taken to the polling stations and brought home again in cars provided voluntarily by party supporters.

The actual conduct of the campaign is largely in the hands of the various party organs—central offices, constituency parties and professional or voluntary election agents. The line which they follow in the campaign and the efficiency with which it is conducted obviously count for much in determining the final result of the election, but this also to a large extent depends on the work and effort they have put in during the years since the last general election. With the British system of voting, no party can ever afford to leave anything to chance.

III. PARLIAMENTARY REPRESENTATION

The system of parliamentary representation is undoubtedly the most remarkable of British political institutions and the one which has attracted most attention from foreign observers. Throughout history members of Parliament have been elected by a simple majority with no second ballot or alternative vote, and this is still the system today, although its merits and draw-backs have become the subject of what seems likely to remain an inconclusive debate.

As with many other aspects of British government, it is possible to make out a good case in favour of the traditional system of parliamentary representation in the context of con-temporary institutions and the two-party system. But it was never adopted as the result of any deliberate policy and it was certainly not because of any abstract theoretical considerations that it has remained unaltered over the course of the centuries.

As far back as the thirteenth century, members of the House of Commons were elected by simple majority whenever a constituency could not agree on a single candidate. The simple rule whereby whoever obtained the most votes was automatically elected seemed to work well enough in both boroughs and counties, which were alike small constituencies. It was never thought necessary to regard the electorate as a corporate body whose decisions could not be valid unless supported by an absolute majority of its members. Nor until recently have the British ever given much thought to the injustices which may result from such a crude representative system. They have still done nothing to eradicate them, but take their system of election by simple majorities for granted and have little faith in any of the alternatives that have been adopted in other countries.

The reason why the British have adhered quite unquestioningly to their traditional electoral system is because it has become so intimately bound up with other essential features of their political system. Among the most obvious is the close connection between the electoral system and the two-party system. A system of election by simple majority would clearly be incapable of creating a two-party system in a country where other fundamental causes gave rise to a larger number of parties. In Britain, however, it has, in conjunction with other factors, played an important part in producing the two-party system which could never survive under any other method of voting and which itself tends to discourage any departure from the simple majority rule. There is also a close connection between the electoral system and the power of dissolution. On the one hand, the power of dissolution makes the electoral system more equitable, because it means that if Parliament is not strictly representative of the country and consequently becomes out of touch with public opinion, it is not necessary to wait until the end of its full statutory term before there can be another appeal to the country. On the other hand, it is only because the British electoral system produces a clear majority for one party and leaves no doubt as to who should form the government that the power of dissolution is of any real value.

Apart from its relationship to these other aspects of British government, the representative system has two principal features—the size of the constituencies and the simple majority rule itself.

The Constituencies

Apart from the special university seats which were abolished in 1948, constituencies have always tended to be small.

Originally, each member was elected to represent a particular borough or county, and although successive Redistribution Acts have produced a more equitable distribution of seats in proportion to population, the constituencies have remained small. At present there are 625 constituencies in the United Kingdom, 357 being boroughs and 288 county constituencies.[1]

Small constituencies like these have the advantage, in theory at least, of enabling a personal relationship to develop between the member and his constituents. They can look upon him as their representative in Parliament, while he considers himself accountable to them for what he does. Furthermore, small single-member constituencies make it possible for independent members to be elected on the strength of their own personal qualities. In practice, however, the British system very seldom produces these results. Scottish and Welsh electors doubtless prefer to have Scotsmen or Welshmen to represent them in Parliament, but in most constituencies this is not a decisive consideration. The average elector knows very little about the candidates for whom he has to vote except the parties to which they belong. A candidate who has the time and the means may, with great skill and pertinacity, manage to win a few hundred extra votes by means of personal contacts, and an outstandingly popular or able figure or a respected former trade union leader may gain a few thousand supporters on the strength of his personal reputation. Such factors might be decisive in a marginal seat, but in the vast majority of cases a candidate's fate depends on the party to which he belongs. It is still not compulsory for candidates to belong to a political party, but in fact elections in Britain have been almost exclusively a party affair for even longer than in other countries. The smaller constituencies do not make the rôle of the parties in Britain substantially different from what it is elsewhere. In a safe seat, the member is in effect chosen by the local committee of the dominant party. In a marginal constituency, the outcome of an election depends on the local parties' choice of candidates, in conjunction with other general or local considerations which help to determine public opinion. Thus there is clearly a strong incentive for local party committees to select good candidates, but even so their personal qualities have very little effect on the

[1] As a result of further recommendations by the Boundary Commission in 1954, the number of seats was increased to 630.

result. This was proved by what happened in the constituencies which used to elect two members where, however great the disparity between the personal merits of the two candidates put up by any one party, they almost always finished within a few hundred votes of each other in the final poll. There does not therefore seem to be any special advantage in the small constituencies. These have been retained simply because they were part of the traditional representative system that has never been substantially altered except to create exclusively single-member constituencies and to install a more equitable distribution of seats.

Originally each county was represented in Parliament by two knights, each borough by two burgesses and each enfranchised town by two of its citizens. This was how the Model Parliament was composed in 1295. The representation of the counties remained unchanged for many centuries. The first redistribution measures only affected the towns and boroughs, between which there was some attempt to re-allocate seats more evenly in proportion to population. By the Reform Act of 1884, however, the whole country was divided into single-member constituencies on the basis of one member for every 54,000 inhabitants. This was advocated by Gladstone on the ground that it would provide a representative system which was both simple and economical, and at the same time would not leave minorities totally unrepresented in Parliament. Single-member constituencies were retained under the Act of 1918 except in the case of 10 English boroughs, the City of London, Dundee, the universities and three Irish counties, each of which elected two members. The last surviving two-member constituencies were finally abolished by the Representation of the People Acts of 1948 and 1949, which divided them into separate single-member constituencies.

In 1918 special non-partisan boundary commissions, from which politicians were strictly excluded, were set up to decide what would be a fair distribution of seats. It was laid down that as a general rule each single-member constituency ought to have a population of approximately 70,000, but boroughs and counties with less than 70,000 but over 50,000 inhabitants were not to lose their seats. For Northern Ireland, a separate Act prescribed a ratio of one seat to every 43,000 inhabitants. The ensuing boundary revisions did not entirely destroy the old pattern of constituencies or produce an absolutely uniform ratio between seats and population. The new boundaries in fact tended to favour the Conservatives, but this was purely accidental and the commissioners were not in the least swayed by political motives. There have since been several further boundary revisions and, by the House of Commons Act of 1944, provision has now been made for regular revisions of boundaries to take account of shifts in population. The Labour Party benefited from the changes which took place in 1945, but the advantage returned to the Conservatives after a further large-scale revision in 1948, in which only 80 constituencies were not affected. It would never be possible to have exactly equal constituencies. Successive boundary revisions correct some discrepancies only to create others. The important point about the British system, however, is that such inequalities as do arise are never the result of gerrymandering deliberately designed to strengthen the position of a particular party.[1]

Election by Simple Majority, and its Effects

Each constituency votes for a single member, who is elected by simple majority in accordance with the traditional British practice whereby the candidate who obtains the most votes is elected whether or not he secures an absolute majority. A similar method of election by a plurality of votes exists in the United States, which also has a two-party system, although there the machinery of government and the general tenor of political life are very different from what they are in Britain. Election by simple majority is a crude representative system, the implications of which have been so widely discussed by political scientists that it is unnecessary to recapitulate here the familiar theoretical arguments as to its advantages and disadvantages.

Such a system cannot function properly without well-organised political parties able to maintain firm control over their supporters. The British parties do in fact fulfil these

---

[1] The boundary revisions of 1954 appear to have had little effect on the results of the general election of 1955: the new constituencies mostly elected Conservatives, but the changes in existing constituencies mostly favoured the Labour candidates. It was estimated that with the 1951 boundaries the Conservative majority would have been somewhere between 62 and 67; in fact it was 67.

criteria and the electoral system itself has helped to bring this about. A general election is normally a struggle for power between the two main parties who are contending for the right to govern the country and are therefore obliged to put up candidates in practically every constituency in order to have any prospect of being able to form a government. An election is thus a contest between the candidates and, even more, between the programmes of the different parties. The issues are much the same over the whole country, which means that the electorate are faced with a simple choice which it is perfectly well within their power to make. All the voter has to decide is whether the party at present in power should continue to govern the country or whether the opposition should be called upon to take its place. A general election consequently involves much more than merely electing representatives to Parliament. This is a point to which we shall have to return later in the section on Cabinet government. For the moment we must confine our attention to the effects of the simple majority rule, which can be conveniently summarised under five main heads.

1. In the first place, a general election in Britain usually leaves one party with an absolute majority of seats in the House of Commons, so that it is automatically able to form a government. This does not always happen when elections are decided by a simple majority, but it is almost bound to be the result when the simple majority rule operates under a two-party system. This ensures stable governments. A British Cabinet can rely on being able to remain in office until the next election, while the opposition has no chance of overthrowing the government unless there is a split in the majority party, which is something that its leaders will always try their hardest to avoid.

The only circumstance in which an election may not result in an absolute majority of seats for any party is if there are more than two parties seriously aspiring to office. This was the position while the Liberal Party was declining and the Labour Party steadily gaining strength. Even then, however, the Conservatives succeeded in obtaining an absolute majority in 1924, when they secured 68% of the total seats. The elections of 1923 and 1929 are in fact quite unique in British political history in that there were three parties seriously contending for power, each of whom put up a sufficient number of candidates for the party which won the election to be left with less than half of the total seats. In 1923 the Conservatives were the largest party but had only 42% of the seats, while in 1929 the Labour Party had the most votes but only 46.9% of the seats. Under the British electoral system, a third party always tends to be worsened in a general election, so that if there are more than two parties, the weakest is eventually forced out of existence. Either it becomes merged in one of the other two parties, or else it ultimately fails to attract any appreciable amount of popular support. The eclipse of the Liberal Party is thus becoming steadily more pronounced. It obtained only 9 seats in 1950 and 6 in 1951. There are few independent candidates, and hardly any are ever elected (none in 1950 or in 1951). There have been no Communists in the House of Commons since 1950, although two were returned in 1945. In the vast majority of constituencies (497 out of 625 in 1951) an election is a straight fight between two parties, so that one of them is bound to secure an absolute majority of seats.[1]

It is of course possible for a party to win an election but have only a small majority of seats in the House of Commons. In 1847 the Liberals had 329 seats to the Conservatives' 327, giving a majority of only 2. In 1852 the Conservatives, with 331 seats, had a majority of 8 over their opponents. In 1950 the Labour Party had 315 seats to the Conservatives' 298 out of a total House of 625, while in 1951, again out of a total of 625, the Conservatives had 321 and the Labour Party 295. It has been quite common for a government to have a parliamentary majority of less than 50, as was the case with the Liberals in 1837, 1854, 1892 and in January and December 1910. Where the largest party has only a small majority, it has sometimes proved difficult to form a government, as Lord Derby found in 1852. A party with a slender majority can sometimes strengthen its position by obtaining the support of some smaller party. In this way the Liberal Party was able to remain in power for some years after 1910 because it had the support of the Irish Nationalists. Without such additional support, a Cabinet with a tiny majority may find itself in a very delicate position where any division in Parliament, even on a comparatively minor

[1] In 1955 the smaller parties secured a slightly larger proportion of the total votes, but the two main parties still won all but 9 of the 630 seats: only 6 Liberals, no Communists and 3 others were elected.

issue, can become a serious threat to the government. If circumstances are favourable, a weak government can sometimes increase its majority by appealing to the country. But there is always the possibility, by no means remote, that the party which wins an election may not have a sufficient majority to form a strong government. This makes the parties plan and direct their election campaigns with a view to securing the maximum number of votes for their candidates, paying particular attention to those electors who are uncertain how to use their votes.

2. The second point to note about the British system of election by simple majority is that the outcome of a general election really depends on the behaviour of a comparatively small number of voters. Each of the two main parties has a number of safe seats where it can count on heading the poll, as the electors tend to support the same party with remarkable consistency. Consequently, both parties devote their main efforts to securing a majority in the marginal constituencies. In London, for example, the City and the West End are safe Conservative seats and in the East End there are invariably Labour majorities, so the result ultimately depends on what happens in the northern and southern suburbs. Similarly, in each constituency the electorate can be divided into two distinct categories—those who are firm supporters of one party, and others who appear to shift their allegiance from one party to another in the light of changing circumstances, the records of the parties and their personal hopes and fears. In 1935, for instance, Labour could have won the election had it secured only 3,000 extra votes in each of the constituencies where National or Conservative candidates were elected by a majority of less than 6,000. The result could thus have been reversed if only 750,000 people had voted for the other side. Moreover, the constituencies where National candidates were elected by small majorities were lower middle-class districts where the vital floating votes appear to be concentrated. In these circumstances, it is easy to see how canvassing may affect the result of an election and why, while naturally trying not to offend their traditional supporters, the parties always make a special effort to attract lower middle-class votes.

It is almost impossible to make any really reliable estimate of the total number of these floating voters who, by transferring their support from one party to another, virtually determine the outcome of elections. So far as can be deduced from the votes which the parties have obtained in each constituency in successive general elections, there would appear to be no more than three million floating voters in the whole country. This may well be an overestimate, but if there were an exceptionally large number of candidates, the number of floating voters would probably be much less. In the general election of 1951, for example, it appears that by comparison with 1950 and over the country as a whole, slightly more than 1% of the electorate must have voted differently. Most of these were Liberals in constituencies where there was no Liberal candidate in 1951. It is difficult to say just how far these Liberal votes were responsible for giving the Conservatives their slender majority over the Labour Party, but in view of the fact that in 1950 Labour won 25 seats by a very few votes and held 85 others by extremely small majorities, it seems reasonable to suppose that it needed only a very small number of voters to transfer their support to the Conservatives to give them a majority in the House of Commons. In fact, 20 of the 23 seats gained by Conservatives appear to have been won with the help of Liberal votes.

The situation in 1951 was somewhat unusual, since the Liberals only contested 108 seats compared with 475 in 1950, leaving about two million Liberals with no Liberal candidate for whom they could vote. The Labour and Conservative parties both made great efforts to secure these Liberal votes, and the Conservatives were decidedly the more successful of the two. What happened in 1951 does not, however, tell us very much about the floating voter in general or the kind of people who, in more normal circumstances, would come into this category. It is sometimes argued that, as they may be presumed to be the people who learn by experience, they must represent the most active and enlightened and possibly the most politically mature sections of the population. This, however, seems extremely improbable. Several other relevant considerations, some peculiar to Great Britain and others of a more general character, point in quite a different direction. In the first place, though die-hard obstinacy may be undesirable, this does not make opportunism the highest of all political virtues. A person who changes his party between one election and another may be a man with a mind of his own who is able to learn from experience, but he could equally well be someone without any definite personal convictions who is ready to follow the prevailing currents of public opinion and is easily carried away by momentary mass emotions because he has never learned to think for himself. Vacillation between the parties is relatively easy to explain in countries where there are large numbers of parties and the distinctions between them are not always very obvious, but it is more difficult to account for such shifts in party allegiance under a two-party system, even if the differences between the two party programmes are not always very profound. If we maintain that the floating voters must be the most politically mature and enlightened, it would seem that we ought to say the same of members of Parliament who change their party, but few would care to endorse the second proposition. Moreover, if we consider the type of candidate who used to be elected for the university seats, we shall find another reason why the British floating voter should not be credited with outstanding personal qualities. It is fair to assume that university graduates belonged to the best informed and politically mature section of the community, yet they were remarkably consistent in always electing Conservatives or Liberals or Independants with Conservative inclinations, and never by any chance a member of the Labour Party. The fact that the university members were generally men and women of high calibre is clearly not the only reason why the Conservative Party has advocated the restoration of the university vote that was abolished by the Labour government in 1948.

Furthermore, all the studies which have been made of electoral behaviour in various constituencies seem to indicate that floating voters are mostly found in the lower middle classes, notably among salary earners, white-collar workers and some of the best-paid manual workers. Many of those in this group are trade unionists who automatically vote Labour, but others are more hesitant and tend to think more of how far each party is likely to advance their own personal interests. Their tendency to transfer their allegiance from one party to another is not a sign of any exceptionally keen political judgment, but simply the natural consequence of the fact that their social status is somewhat uncertain and they do not readily identify themselves with any particular social class.

There can be no doubt, however, that this system of election by a plurality makes the outcome of an election dependent on the behaviour of a few thousand voters who are neither active nor even nominal members of any political party. It only needs somewhere between 1% and 3% of the electorate to vote for the other side to produce a sufficient swing over the country as a whole to give the opposite party a majority in the House of Commons until the next general election. This phenomenon has largely determined the character of the British party system.

3. Thirdly, the party which wins an election generally has a majority of votes as well as a majority of seats. The House of Commons may therefore be tolerably well representative of the strengths of the parties in the country. The large number of constituencies means that the injustices which arise when members are elected by a simple majority tend to cancel one another out, and the minority party is unlikely to find itself very seriously under-represented in the House of Commons.

All the same, under the British electoral system, there is nothing to stop a party with less than half the total votes winning an absolute majority of seats.

Without going back beyond 1910, there are several cases in which a party has won an election when it has only had a minority of votes. The Liberals and Irish Nationalists together won 53·3% of the seats with 45% of the votes in January 1910, and in the following December 53% of the seats with 48% of the votes. In 1918 68·3% of the seats went to the government coalition although it had only 48% of the votes. The Conservatives won 56% of the seats with 38·2% of the votes in 1922, and 68% of the seats with 48·3% of the votes in 1924. In 1945 the Labour Party emerged victorious with 62·4% of the seats although it had only 48·9% of the total votes. In 1950 it still secured 50·4% of the seats although its share of the poll dropped to 46·5%.

These exaggerated majorities involved less injustice than might be supposed, for in all the above instances the party which won the election did in fact obtain more votes than its main rival. A more unusual situation arose in 1951 when the Conservatives were returned to power with 51·36% of the seats but only 47·96% of the votes. This was less than the total number given to the Labour Party, which had only 47·20% of the seats. Labour with 48·78% of the total poll actually had more votes than the Conservatives and more than they had obtained in the previous year when they had won the election. In most other countries, such a situation would put the government in a practically untenable position, but under the British system the Conservative government had no difficulty in remaining in office provided that it showed itself responsive to the changes in public opinion, to which it naturally tended to become increasingly sensitive as the next general election approached.[1]

The Cabinet is never under any illusions as to the true nature of the political situation, and fully realises that its strength in the House of Commons is not an accurate reflection of the support it commands in the country. The main parties are ready to accept the injustices which they know may result from election by a plurality of votes because they regard these as an established feature of their political system, and the party which benefits from an exaggerated majority is always conscious that this phenomenon may well operate against it in the future. If a party manages to win a majority of seats with only a minority of the total votes, this probably means that its supporters are well dispersed over the country so that it wins many of its seats by a comparatively small majority while its opponents pile up very large majorities in a smaller number of constituencies which do not suffice to give them a majority in Parliament. Even if this is not always the explanation, it is clear that a party which manages to secure only a little less than half the total votes stands to gain from the tendency of the British electoral system to produce inflated majorities.

4. When elections are decided by a plurality of votes, it would obviously be an extraordinary coincidence if the number of seats won by the different parties ever corresponded exactly to their respective shares of the total votes. Under the British two-party system, however, the electoral system has almost invariably resulted in exaggerated majorities, until it has even been thought possible to predict the result of an election by means of a mathematical formula. In 1909 Sir J. Parker Smith

---

[1] In 1955 the Conservatives won 54% of the seats (344 out of 630) with 49·7% of the votes, while Labour secured 46·4% of the votes but less than 44% of the seats (277).

attempted to explain the relationship between the proportion of votes and seats won by each of the two main parties by saying that if the ratio between their total votes were A : B, then the ratio between their shares of the total seats would be $A^3 : B^3$.

It could hardly be expected that every election result would conform to so simple a formula. In fact it was proved wrong in 1950 and again in 1951.[1] This should give no cause for surprise, since the total number of votes obtained by each party is by no means the only factor that determines the outcome of an election. It also depends on how far the supporters of each party are well dispersed over the country or heavily concentrated in certain constituencies, on the number of 'three-cornered fights', and on how many candidates are elected unopposed. It would be wrong to conclude that the relationship between votes and seats in any election is purely a matter of chance, but the cube law is far too simple a formula to be valid without further qualification. Mr David Butler and other psephologists have tried to make some allowance for the way in which, with the present distribution of seats, election by simple majority without a second ballot results in one party wasting a disproportionately large number of votes by piling up large majorities in a few constituencies. At the moment, the Labour Party is at a disadvantage in this respect. To allow for this, its total number of votes should be reduced by 4%. The cube law would then be found to hold good for the relationship between the votes and seats obtained by the two main parties in 1950 and 1951.

Whatever one thinks about the cube law, there can be no doubt that election by simple majority tends to produce a disproportionately large majority for whoever wins the election and leave the main opposition party relatively under-represented in the House of Commons. This distortion of public opinion can sometimes be very great, and any smaller third parties are likely to be even more seriously under-represented. The British representative system is certainly not without its good points: in normal circumstances it does genuinely allow the people to decide how they want the country to be governed; it enables the power of dissolution to be used to good effect; and,

[1] In 1955 the discrepancy was even greater: according to the cube law the Conservative majority should have been 101 seats—34 more than they actually obtained.

above all, it helps to ensure strong and stable government by producing a clear majority for a single party. Nevertheless, it is no use trying to pretend that it does not result in considerable injustices or cannot seriously distort the wishes of the people.

It is sometimes argued that although the electoral system exaggerates the effect of any swing in the country, the result at least reflects the direction if not the precise extent of any shift in public opinion. Yet this overlooks the fact that, when there is no very sharp swing in votes, the result does not depend solely on the number of votes cast for each party but also, to an even greater extent, on how their respective supporters are distributed over the country. It is not necessarily a serious weakness in an electoral system that it should give a party with a clear majority a larger proportion of seats than of votes. The trouble is rather when neither party has a substantial majority of votes and the result of the election depends on factors from which no party ought to be able to gain an advantage, such as the distribution of seats and the behaviour of minority parties, both in individual constituencies and over the country as a whole.

Admittedly, in British experience, election by simple majority has seldom brought to power a government to which the majority of the electorate were opposed. But there is nothing in the nature of the system to prevent this happening, and it did in fact occur in both the general elections of 1910, in 1929, and—most strikingly of all—in 1951.

Most British writers do not attempt to deny that election by simple majority produces these inequitable results, but they maintain that it has other advantages which more than compensate for its shortcomings in this respect.

5. That is why, although there have been some inquiries into the question of electoral reform, it is not regarded as a matter of high priority or even as a practical possibility.

This does not mean there has been no criticism of the most flagrant injustices of the present system, such as have been outlined above, nor of the arbitrary way in which, by distorting the relative strengths of the parties in the House of Commons, it may enable a government with an artificially large majority to follow a policy which would have been difficult or impossible for them to pursue had they had only as many seats as their share of the votes would have justified. In 1900, for example, the Conservative majority was 134 when it should only have been somewhere between 15 and 20. In 1918 the majority of the Lloyd George-Bonar Law coalition should not have been more than 84 but was actually inflated to 344, and this probably had a marked effect upon the proceedings at the peace conference. If seats had been distributed strictly in proportion to votes in 1931, the Conservatives would have had 270 instead of 473, the Liberals 110 instead of 68, and National Labour 50 instead of 13. In 1935 the Conservatives would have had a majority of only 41, whereas in fact they obtained 235 more seats than their opponents, and this, indirectly at least, was one of the chief reasons why the foreign policy of the Baldwin and Chamberlain governments was not discarded before 1940.

These inequitable consequences of election by simple majority without a second ballot are nothing new. Only comparatively recently, however, has any serious consideration been given to the possibilities of electoral reform. It was originally thought that the system of single-member constituencies introduced by Gladstone in 1884 would suffice to ensure that minorities were not too seriously under-represented in Parliament. The problem became more serious with the rise of the Labour Party after 1906 and the increasing number of three-cornered fights in which a candidate was often elected by a minority of votes. This led to the appointment of a Royal Commission on Electoral Systems in 1908. Two years later, the Commission produced a report which, while recognising that a transferable vote would have certain distinct advantages, expressed a preference for the alternative vote, even though this was open to the same criticisms as election by simple majority with a second ballot, a system for which the British have never shown much enthusiasm on account of the way in which it has operated in France.

In 1918 there was an attempt to introduce a single transferable vote for the university constituencies, and it was intended to apply the same system experimentally in a hundred other constituencies. This was a development of the modified form of proportional representation originally proposed by Hare in 1859. The idea is that each constituency should elect several members, each elector only being allowed to vote for one candidate, but having the right to place the other candidates in order of preference on his ballot paper. If the candidate he places first has more votes than are needed to secure election or too few to remain in the running, his vote is transferred to the next candidate on his list. After the necessary calculations have been made and the votes redistributed accordingly, the number of seats allotted to each party should correspond to its share of the total poll. The result will thus be an accurate reflection of the clearly expressed wishes of the people. This system has been adopted in Tasmania and in Eire, where it is generally considered to work satisfactorily.

There has been little criticism of the basic principles of the single transferable vote. It has one great advantage over other forms of proportional representation in that it does not give the party organisations the same hold over the candidates who do not need to have the backing of a party, or over the electorate who can vote and express their preferences for the candidates as individuals and not as representing any particular party. Nevertheless, nothing came of the proposal to introduce a single transferable vote experimentally. The necessary legislation was passed by the House of Lords but subsequently rejected by the Commons on 13th May 1918.

Since then, nothing more has been done towards reforming the electoral system. There have been some attempts, mostly inspired by the Liberal Party, to secure a measure of electoral reform, but there has never been any sign that the country generally would be in favour of any change. Neither of the two main parties would support a single transferable vote. This has been advocated by some individual members of both the Labour and Conservative parties, but the general opinion appears to be against any alteration of the present electoral system.

Although no one seriously pretends that this produces a strictly representative House of Commons, it is thought to have other advantages too precious to sacrifice for the sake of a more equitable form of parliamentary representation. Three main arguments are commonly advanced against the introduction of proportional representation.

With proportional representation, the state of opinion in the country and any changes therein would be accurately reflected in the House of Commons, but the shifts in the balance of power between the parties would be far less marked than they normally are when members are elected by a simple majority. The general elections of 1950 and 1951 did not, admittedly, result in a substantial majority for any party. Judging by past experience, however, it seems as if these will remain exceptions to the general rule unless public opinion were to become permanently divided into two evenly balanced groups. There have usually been marked swings in the balance of power between the parties at regular but not too frequent intervals. These have had a salutary effect on British politics as a whole, for they make the power of dissolution and the threat of using it an effective political weapon. Still more important, they make it possible to avoid the stagnation which would set in if one party remained in power for too long, while still avoiding all the evils associated with government instability.

Another strong argument against proportional representation is that it would destroy the traditional clear division between the government and the opposition in the House of Commons by giving rise to new blocs and splinter parties which would lead to weak coalitions and short-lived governments.

Above all, any change in the electoral system would almost certainly mean the end of the two-party regime that is now one of the essential bases of British government. This is why the Labour and Conservative parties are both opposed to any electoral reform likely to benefit only the Liberals or other minority parties. It would certainly not be in the interests of the two main parties to introduce any measure of proportional representation, for at the moment each in turn stands to gain from the exaggerated majorities which result from elections by simple majority. The survival of the two-party system is thus to a large extent dependent on the maintenance of the present electoral system. It would almost be true to say that the electoral system is just as vital a part of the British political system as the two-party system itself.

Chapter Two

POLITICAL PARTIES AND THE
TWO-PARTY SYSTEM

GREAT BRITAIN is ruled by party government.
The rise of political parties and the expansion of their
functions is one of the outstanding developments of our age.
This has been going on all over the world, and it is possible to
trace the development of political parties in the modern sense
of the word in Great Britain during the last hundred years.
There, however, the principle of party government and the
division of the country into two main groups of opinion dates
from the constitutional conflicts of the seventeenth century and
has been the basis on which the whole of the present machinery
of government has been erected. Of all the classic examples of
democratic government, the British parliamentary system might
be described as the one whose functioning is most dependent
upon the party system. The conduct of elections, the formation
and survival of Cabinets, and the activities and the very existence of Parliament, have always been almost completely under
the control of the political parties. Yet they have never en-
croached upon the liberties of the individual, and the struggle
between the parties has remained entirely free from the bitter-
ness and violence often created and fostered by party 'machines'
in other lands.

In this connection, the influence of history has again been
important. The political parties and the two-party system, like
the constitution which they have done so much to shape and
which could not now function without them, have a long
history. Their evolution has been a slow and steady process in
which the Reform Act of 1832 forms an important landmark.
The reform of the electoral system has led the parties to assume
their modern characteristics in order to attain empirical
political objectives.

The Restoration of 1660 and the accession of Charles II is
usually said to mark the emergence of the divisions of opinion

which were to find their expression in political parties. In fact, however, these divisions date back to the Reformation and the deep-rooted religious differences which appeared at the end of the sixteenth century. During the reign of James I, the Puritans were already active in Parliament, where they attacked the established church and the retention of Roman practices and defended the supremacy of the law against the Divine Right of Kings. On the other side were the more conservative elements, the court and the supporters of the King, who favoured one national established church instead of an anarchy of sects, and maintained that the royal prerogative could override the privileges of Parliament. These remained the traditional positions of the Whigs and the Tories during the succeeding centuries, although their viewpoints were somewhat modified as the religious controversy lost its original intensity.

The earliest approach to an organised party appears to have been the meetings held outside Parliament to bring together men of like minds when the opposition to the King was gaining ground in 1640. Government supporters as well as those on the opposition side held many such meetings in the years which followed, and from 1660 onwards it is possible to speak of embryonic parties. Their formation was originally inspired by the passions aroused in the Civil War, which was considered less as a revolution than as a conflict between two parties. On one side were the Cavaliers, the forerunners of the Tories, who took their name from the rebels who attacked the Protestant colonies in Ireland; these were the men with secret leanings towards Rome, the aristocracy and landowners, and supporters of the King and the established church. On the other side were the Roundheads—Puritans and Dissenters, who cropped their hair as a gesture of defiance against the wigs of the courtiers. They acquired the name of Whigs, taken from a group of Presbyterian crofters in the west of Scotland, and stood for Parliament against the King, for religious toleration for everyone except Roman Catholics, and for the liberties of the subject. They included some of the more liberal-minded aristocrats and landowners, and the businessmen and City merchants.

The general election of 1679, the first for seventeen years, was conducted under conditions that foreshadowed those under which a modern Parliament is elected. Once elected, the members tended to group themselves into parties, and a variety of corrupt practices were employed to produce greater party cohesion. After 1714 the King, with the assistance of the Political Secretary to the Treasury, who was known as the Patronage Secretary, could dispose of sufficient patronage to give him a powerful means of controlling and preventing defection among his supporters, and to enable him to support these 'King's men' in general elections. The opposition was thus forced to adopt similar methods. Parties began to take an active interest in elections, and early in the eighteenth century they began organised electioneering. By 1807 the Whigs were raising a fund to pay for future election campaigns, and about this time a central fund was established to assist candidates who undertook to support electoral reform. The Tories had consequently to resort to similar tactics.

The evolution of political parties was also closely bound up with electoral reform. The party system as it existed before 1832 had developed out of very long-standing differences of opinion within the country. These had temporarily abated in the period of common hostility to the Papacy, but were again exacerbated by the events of 1642 and 1688. The traditional bases of the opposition were somewhat altered by the impact of the French Revolution. With the Reform Act of 1832, however, the very foundations of political power were shifted. The scope of political controversy broadened and the parties were led to take a greater interest in general elections. As in other countries, the parties set up electoral committees in order to win supporters and strengthen their party organisation. In Great Britain, the Act of 1832 precipitated this process by instituting a system of registration of voters that made it practically essential for organised political groups to take the lead in compiling and revising the electoral lists. The Conservatives and Liberals each set up local committees which for many years endeavoured to exploit the electoral law—in particular the provisions regarding registration and disqualification of electors—in the interests of their own party. Peel regarded the registration of voters as a new source of political power which might become more important than the House of Commons. Since then, the parties have acquired other important functions in seeking out sympathisers and potential supporters and in canvassing at election times. The Labour Party has developed much more recently and quite differently from any previous political party, but it has been ready to learn from Liberal and Conservative experience. Meanwhile the growth of political democracy has forced the older parties to undertake new and different tasks that have led them to assume the features characteristic of the modern party system, which may be examined from several different aspects.

I. THE TWO-PARTY SYSTEM

The two-party system has probably attracted more attention than any other aspect of parliamentary government in Great Britain. It is even more important there than in the United States, on account of its relationship to the system of Cabinet government.

Ever since the seventeenth century, when it was already possible to speak in terms of parties, there have never, except for a few brief intervals, been more than two major parties in Great Britain. Until 1906 either the Liberals or the Conservatives, the successors of the Whigs and the Tories, were always in power. The Labour Party began to gain in strength after 1906, until it has now supplanted the Liberal Party, which has been on the decline since 1924, and become the second major political party.

Besides these major political groups there have of course always been some minority parties—Radicals, 'Peelites', Liberal Unionists, Liberal Nationals, National Labour, the Co-operative Party, the Communists and the Commonwealth Party, to name only a few.

At some periods, moreover, Britain has had a three-party system. Between 1874 and 1922 the political situation was considerably complicated by the presence of a substantial body of Irish Nationalists, who usually occupied over eighty seats in the House of Commons. Between 1910 and 1935 the Labour Party and the Liberals in turn constituted a third political party.

These interludes, however, have only been temporary departures from the two-party system which has alone remained an outstanding and enduring feature of British politics. The Whigs and 'Peelites' combined to form the Liberal Party, into which the Radicals were later absorbed; the Liberal Unionists joined forces with the Conservatives; and only the second World War prevented the Liberal National and National Labour groups from being very speedily absorbed into the Conservative Party. During these periods of three-party government the political system has functioned somewhat differently from usual. There have been alliances between the parties in Parliament, if not at general elections; difficulties have sometimes arisen over the choice of a Prime Minister; coalition governments have been formed; and minority governments have been more common than at other times. All the same, these interludes have been quite exceptional. In Britain, as in the United States, third parties have either been unable to survive or else have gained in strength until they have supplanted one of the major parties which had been losing ground. Today, the two-party system is more firmly established than ever before, as the even balance between Labour and the Conservatives makes it particularly imperative for the electorate not to waste their votes by giving them to any other parties. In the general election of 1951 nearly all the votes and seats (96·74% and 98·50% respectively) went to one of the two main parties.[1] If it is possible to speak of 'natural law' in politics, it might be said that there is a natural tendency in Britain for parliamentary government to be conducted on the basis of a two-party system.

Reasons for the Two-Party System

The two-party system is too vague a term to throw much light on the true causes of this important phenomenon. It can only be understood if we put aside all idea of finding a simple explanation or even a small number of decisive factors. The two-party system has become firmly established in Britain as the result of many different influences, some of which have also been operative in other Anglo-Saxon countries and in the United States in particular, while others are peculiar to Great Britain. It is impossible to point to any one of these as the sole determining factor, and it is always possible to find another country where some of the same conditions exist without having given rise to a two-party system. Nor is it even possible to give any clear and definite indication of the relative importance of the great variety of factors whose coexistence and combined influence is what has made a two-party system inevitable in Great Britain.

---

[1] The same occurred in the general election of 1955, when the two main parties won 96·1% of the votes and 98·50% of the seats.

We have already pointed out how in Britain, as in the United States, historical factors have played a leading part in the development of the two-party system. It originated because, at a very early stage, the country happened to become divided into two main bodies of opinion over religious issues which soon became inextricably bound up with politics. Thereafter, partly by sheer chance and partly because of the Anglo-Saxon temperament, other issues emerged on which all the opinions voiced fell into one or other of two main categories. Such issues included the contest between Parliament and the King; the struggle to prevent the spread of French Revolutionary doctrines and later against continental despotism; the opposition to conservatism and imperialism; the question of whether to preserve the existing basis of the political system or to reform the electoral system to reflect the changed social structure; free trade versus protection; Home Rule or preservation of the Union with Ireland; socialism or conservatism in economic and social policy; a foreign policy of appeasement or active defence of the established international order; the preservation of capitalism or socialistic reforms of the structure of society. Each of the two main parties have advocated distinct solutions to these major issues, and the electorate have never put much faith in any other proposals, which they have usually regarded as, at best, ineffective.

This is not really surprising if we remember that the homogeneity of the British nation has long been one of its most outstanding characteristics, and that until 1924 the government invariably consisted of either Liberals or Conservatives who were not separated by any differences of fundamental political philosophy so that the basic economic structure of society was never called in question. As Harold Laski put it, 'The principles of Gladstone always started from the same premises as those of Disraeli; so did those of Mr Asquith and Mr Lloyd George start from premises which, in broad substance, Lord Balfour or Lord Baldwin would have been willing to accept.'

For many years neither of the two main parties had any distinctive social policy. The same interest groups—the aristocracy, the landowners and the wealthy—were predominant on both sides. It was no more dishonourable for an English gentleman to be a Whig than for him to be a Tory, and long before 1832 members of the opposition had come to be treated with the same respect as those who belonged to the government party. Divergent economic and social interests within the parties were not sufficiently strong to create internal divisions such as have arisen in the United States, where different interest groups still demand equal representation within the party organisations. Another factor which tended to prevent internal divisions within the parties, with the notable exception of the split over Home Rule for Ireland, was the absence of any serious conflict between the fundamental beliefs of those who belonged to the same party. The result was that electors who differed from their party on secondary questions confined their opposition to pleading their cause within the party organisation, in order that the party with which they had become associated through traditional or family links or through their own personal preferences should not suffer a reverse on any major issue. Thus it has been said that during the period of rivalry between Gladstone and Disraeli the differences which divided them were undoubtedly not so great as those which separated the extreme wings of each of their respective parties.

Since the Labour Party succeeded the Liberals as the principal opponents of the Conservatives, the differences between the two parties have, on the surface at least, become more pronounced, and the parties are now more nearly representative of different class interests. Yet there has never in fact been any very radical difference between Labour and Conservative programmes. On many fundamental issues the nation as a whole is in agreement, and in addition the electoral system forces both parties to appeal to the same group of floating voters. The similarity of the two party programmes in the general election of 1951 was much more striking than any differences between them, though for reasons of electoral strategy the latter were constantly stressed and sometimes artificially over-emphasised by the party leaders.

In these circumstances it is quite easy to understand why there should be a two-party system. Whether the government be Labour or Conservative, its policies are to a large extent conditioned by circumstances beyond its control, if not completely dictated by the needs of the moment and by current economic, financial, social and international developments. As one Englishman said some time ago, 'We're all socialists now.' Some things are bound to happen in any case. Frequently the only question which the parties can put before the country is not so much what policy to adopt, as by what means and how quickly the policy already agreed upon ought to be carried out. Such an issue can be resolved into a simple choice between two parties, one composed of Conservatives and moderates, and another, originally Liberal and later Labour, of those who favour bolder policies and reforms. This would normally be a valid description of the relationships between the parties, although these may be modified should unusual circumstances or political developments arise.

Election by simple majority is clearly essential to the maintenance of the two-party system in Great Britain, just as it is in the United States. This is the factor to which other writers have given particular attention, although it seems doubtful whether, even in Britain, this method of voting would alone have been sufficient to produce a two-party system. Its introduction would probably not be enough to do away with a multi-party system where there was not the same division of opinion into two basic groups. So far as Great Britain is concerned, however, it may be said that with election by simple majority, a general election always tends to re-emphasise the division of the country into two main parties should it ever show any signs of disappearing.

There is no need to dwell at length on the way in which sooner or later minority parties are inevitably eliminated. The same happens in the United States. The electorate are anxious not to waste their votes, so they will not give them to a party which commands little support because it is either on the decline or is newly established and has not yet proved that it represents any broadly based or lasting current of opinion. Voters consequently do not look beyond the candidates of the two main parties, of whom they select the one who seems most nearly to represent their views. Most of the votes given to a minority party are wasted, as these very seldom succeed in winning any of the seats for which they manage to put up a candidate.

Another relevant consideration is that a general election in Great Britain decides which party shall be asked to form the new government. As there is no proportional representation, the electorate tends to vote straight away and in an organised manner for one or other of the only two parties which usually have any hope of being able to form a government. It is of very little importance who takes third place. A minority party in that position might be able to hold the balance between the two main parties in the House of Commons, but that would hardly be an enviable position, least of all for the middle-of-the-road party. It would then be faced with four alternatives. It might invariably support the same party in Parliament, in which case the electorate would eventually decide that it ought to share in the fortunes and responsibilities of that party and was no longer entitled to a separate existence. If, on the other hand, it were to vote sometimes with the government and sometimes with the opposition, it would only be attacked for vacillation and opportunism. Alternatively, it might abstain, but if it did so too often it would give the impression of not having any policy of its own. Lastly, it could divide its votes and let some of its members support each side, but if this happened it would be criticised as not being a real united party. Thus whatever course it takes will damage its prospects of being returned to power in the future. It will doubtless make great financial sacrifices in its efforts to contest as many seats as possible, as the Liberals did in 1929 and in 1950. Very soon, however, it will find itself without the necessary resources: it will be difficult to find candidates because few will be prepared to lose £150 in an unequal contest or to share in the expenses of a campaign that is doomed to failure; the party will be unable to obtain propagandists for its cause; and will find it impossible to raise funds because people will not give money to a party that has no prospect of being able to carry out its policy. No party can go on contesting 500 seats in every general election if it wins only a few dozen, but as there are over 600 members of the House of Commons it is essential to put up at least 500 candidates in order to have any hope of wielding any substantial influence in British politics.

The history of the Liberal Party illustrates how the decline of a major party gathers momentum once it has begun to lose ground. The break-up of the coalition government left the Liberals divided, and in the general election of 1922 they obtained 29·1% of the votes but only 18·5% of the seats. In

1923 the reunited party scored its last major success by winning 25·86% of the seats with 29·7% of the votes. Since then the system of election by simple majority has invariably operated to its disadvantage, and with every general election its decline has become more pronounced. In 1929 it won 23·4% of the votes but only 9·6% of the seats. In 1931, when the Liberal Nationals allied with the Conservatives, the Liberals and Liberal Independents secured only 7% of the votes and 6% of the seats. In 1935 they had 6·6% of the votes and 2·7% of the seats, and in 1945 9% of the votes and 1·87% of the seats. After making a great effort in 1950, they secured only 9·1% of the votes and 1·44% of the seats. In 1951 they only put up 109 candidates, of whom 6 were elected. Altogether they obtained only 730,556 votes or 2·56% of the total poll, a result which left absolutely no doubt as to the totality of their eclipse.[1] Any smaller party has been even more swiftly and relentlessly eliminated.

The rise of the Labour Party, on the other hand, shows what conditions have to be fulfilled and what difficulties overcome before a newly formed party can have any chance of success. The Labour Party was established in 1900, and from 1906 onwards it began to put up candidates in general elections. It gradually gained ground until in 1918, when it still had only 63 seats, it became recognised as the official opposition to the coalition government. It finally obtained office, though only for a brief interval, when Ramsay MacDonald was asked to form a government in 1924. Until 1922 it had always suffered from the system of election by simple majority, and it rose to power only after carrying on a continuous struggle for twenty years and proving that it did indeed represent a powerful body of opinion. It only succeeded in becoming one of the two major parties because of the eclipse of the Liberal Party, which it has gradually supplanted, thus forming a new two-party system.

The connection between the two-party system and the electoral system is just as close in Great Britain as in other Anglo-Saxon countries. The desire to preserve the two-party system has also been the main reason why the British have always rejected any form of proportional representation. Yet although the party structure has been greatly affected by the

[1] In 1955, with 110 candidates, the Liberals secured 722,405 votes (2·7%) and the same 6 seats (0·95%).

electoral system, it should not be forgotten that this is only one of a number of factors. Although it is difficult to consider any of these in isolation, it is important that none should be overlooked.

One important reason for the survival of the two-party system is that Parliament can be dissolved if the Cabinet loses its majority. It has become customary to appeal to the country whenever a difference arises between the Cabinet and the House of Commons. The issue before the electorate thus resolves itself into a clear choice between the government and the opposition. Any third party is therefore at a great disadvantage. Electors would really be wasting their votes if they gave them to a party which is neither the majority nor the opposition, and the younger voters at least are not likely to have anything to do with it. It has nothing to offer to anyone with political ambitions, and is opposed by at least one, if not both, of the two main parties, who will be hoping to win over some of its supporters. The power of dissolution consequently favours the two main parties. Even if it is not very often used, its existence is sufficient to discourage party splits and encourage dissident groups to return to the fold of one of the main parties. A coalition government is also in a very weak position to obtain popular support for its policies in a general election, especially if this follows a dissolution. Whenever coalition Cabinets have been forced to dissolve, there has tended to be a return to the normal two-party system, so that it has again been possible to have a single-party government with a majority in the House of Commons.

This brings us to another important reason for the survival of the two-party system. A general election in Great Britain has long been an extremely democratic process in which a perfectly clear issue is placed before the electorate. Its main purpose, as we have seen, is to choose a new government, and the choice naturally lies between the two major parties. The voters are simply called upon to decide whether the government should remain in office or give way to the opposition. The British have come to expect an election to take this form and are now deeply attached to the present system. The rôle of the electorate in Britain is, in its different way, quite as important as in other countries where they can often do no more than subscribe to some set of abstract political principles which have no particular likelihood of ever being put into practice. Without a two-party system it would be almost inconceivable that the government should be chosen by the electorate. If there are more than two parties, this power is more or less openly transferred from the people to the lower House of the legislature. In this respect, therefore, the British attachment to the two-party system is a reflection of their wish to preserve the democratic basis of their constitution. There can be no doubt that the nation is united in its desire to be able to exercise in practice the sovereignty which belongs to it in theory. The decline of the Liberal Party has been largely due to these considerations.

The architecture of the House of Commons has been another important influence on the two-party system, as British writers and politicians are wont to emphasise. The Chamber is rectangular, with a gangway down the middle, and the Speaker sits at the far end, with the government benches on his right and the opposition benches on his left. Thus the two parties sit facing each other across the gangway which marks the division between them. Members of minority parties naturally have places set aside for them, and if there is any difficulty the Speaker decides where they should sit. But the House differs from the semicircular chambers of most legislatures, which, if not alone sufficient cause for the emergence of a large number of parties, certainly encourages their formation. The Commons' Chamber is really only designed to accommodate two parties. This helps to keep the two main parties together, as every member has to show, by where he sits, which side he is on. To change one's party means moving to the other side of the House, and this is a spectacular proceeding which can easily ruin a man's career. According to Sir Winston Churchill, who has twice crossed the gangway, it is not a step that anyone would be likely to take without having carefully considered all the implications of his decision.

These may appear to be no more than secondary considerations, but, particularly in Great Britain, they ought to be regarded as important factors. The existence of a two-party system in the United States, where there are semicircular chambers in Congress, proves no more than the obvious truth that the American two-party system, like the British, depends on many other factors apart from architecture. It does not mean that architecture is wholly without significance, least of all in a country where the present practice of placing the government and the opposition on opposite sides of the House dates back to the sixteenth century and was unquestioningly accepted in the time of Walpole when parties began to assume an important rôle in politics.

Finally, it must be remembered that once a two-party system has become established, it is obviously in the interests of the two main parties and of their leaders to see that it is not destroyed. They will try to win over as many as possible of the supporters of any third parties or minority groups and, at the same time, endeavour to preserve the unity of their own party by averting party splits and framing their policies so as to take account of the views of any powerful section of their members. Thus Lord Salisbury carried on negotiations with Lord Randolph Churchill until it was quite certain that he would resign from the Conservative Party. When the break came, Churchill did not carry any of the rest of the party with him, and actually formed his own 'Fourth Party' with three of his personal friends. The Liberal split over Home Rule appears to have been due to Gladstone's miscalculations as to the attitude of Joseph Chamberlain. During the South African War the Liberal Party was kept together by the great dexterity of Sir Henry Campbell-Bannerman, and its final split in 1931 was really one of the principal causes of its eclipse. In our own time the Labour Party has often appeared threatened with schism, but has displayed an equally striking readiness to modify its policies in order to preserve the unity of the party.

Thus the existence of two strong and well-organised parties, the discipline which they impose on their members and the authority wielded by their leaders, all tend to preserve the existing pattern of government. British institutions have assumed their present form because of the two-party system, and many of their characteristic features are now closely bound up with the party system and help to ensure that there shall never be more than two main parties.

Evaluation

To assess its merits and drawbacks, the two-party system must not be considered in abstract isolation, but as one element in a system of government in which all the constituent parts are closely interrelated. It is also important not to be misled into thinking that it would necessarily have the same advantages and disadvantages if it were to be introduced in any other country.

Apart from a number of secondary advantages, there appear to be three main points in favour of the British two-party system. In the first place, it makes the parliamentary system democratic by allowing the electorate to choose their government. Secondly, it makes for stable governments that can normally reckon on remaining in office for the full term of a Parliament. This means they have no great difficulty in carrying through the legislation necessary to give effect to their programme, and are in a strong position to act quickly and to govern as firmly and efficiently as would ever be tolerated in a democracy. Thirdly, the two-party system normally rules out alliances between the parties in Parliament or at elections, together with coalition governments and bargaining between different political groups. It is thus quite clear where political responsibility lies, and there are adequate sanctions to ensure genuine public accountability.

Yet these advantages have only been acquired at the price of a number of weaknesses. The most serious is the injustice of the two-party system. It is inherently conservative and, together with the system of election by simple majority, favours the maintenance of the status quo. There is nothing to stop anyone founding a new party, but it will never be able to survive or play any significant part in politics unless it represents some exceptionally lasting and deep-rooted movement of public opinion. This would never happen without virtually a revolution. The British, with their empirical approach and dislike of drastic upheavals and hasty innovations, have been quite prepared to accept the injustices of the two-party system because this has been largely responsible for the stability of their political life.

The two-party system is also criticised as too crude to be appropriate to the complexities of modern politics. However vague and subject to modification the party programmes may be, they only allow the voters a very limited choice between alternative policies, especially as on many issues there is very little difference between the main parties. An Elector can very seldom vote in a way which exactly expresses his own personal convictions. If he disagrees with the foreign policy of one party and the domestic policy of the other he is in a dilemma, because if he gives his vote to any third party it will be as good as wasted. The fact that many of the electorate were in such a quandary in 1923 and 1935 would explain why such a high percentage abstained from voting in those years. Yet the British consider this disadvantage of no more than secondary importance, for it could only be avoided by having an absurdly large number of parties. Besides, it is doubtful whether the average British voter is greatly interested in the details of political issues except in so far as they affect him personally. He is used to the system that lets him express a preference for a certain general line of policy without giving much thought to what this implies as regards the solution of any particular problem, or else leaves it to the party organisations to work out the best possible compromise.

The British are thus hardly aware of the drawbacks of the two-party system. Its advantages, on the other hand, make it appear quite indispensable, particularly as it is now so firmly entrenched as to be essential to the proper functioning of the machinery of government which has gradually developed over the course of the centuries.

Many different and almost irresistible factors help to preserve the two-party system. Perhaps the most important of all is the political homogeneity of the British people, to which they owe their unfailing facility for finding compromise solutions. This national trait shows, more clearly than anything else, the difference between the two-party system and multi-party regimes, and explains why the former can only really exist in Anglo-Saxon countries.

In countries where public opinion is divided in many different ways over a large number of issues and people tend to adhere firmly to definite sets of political principles, differences of opinion tend to result in party splits. Moreover, if the electoral system is such as to give every different school of thought some hope of being represented in Parliament, this again encourages the establishment of new parties and stops those on the decline from disappearing completely. If the parties refuse to come to terms and each retains its own identity, the compromises which are the essential basis of any political activity, especially under a parliamentary system, will not be achieved until it becomes necessary to form a Cabinet. Even then, the government will be founded upon alliances for limited purposes that make for heterogeneous and unstable majorities.

British experience has been diametrically opposed to this. On most major political issues there are no really fundamental differences. Even if any do arise, the British are still content to keep to two parties corresponding to the two main trends of opinion. In the course of the centuries they have learned to be tolerant, and they do not attach much importance to abstract general principles.

The party organisations themselves are a powerful influence in reconciling differences within the party and maintaining a united front. Party splits are usually averted, as members are generally ready to compromise on secondary issues so as not to endanger the main points in their programme or to deprive themselves of any hope of attaining office. Once a party has a majority in Parliament, its task is even more straightforward— to form a Cabinet and support its policy. The opposition is also a united party that succeeds in fulfilling a useful purpose, and its unity means that it is always a possible alternative government.

There is consequently a close connection between the number of political parties in Great Britain and their principal characteristics.

II. THE CHARACTERISTICS OF THE PARTIES

This is a subject worthy of extensive study, but here it is only possible to give a brief account of the distinctive features of the main political groups and point out the principal characteristics which they have in common.

The Main Political Parties

The Conservatives are the successors of the old Tory Party, and still wont to assert their affinity with the historic figures from whom some of their traditions and political ideas are derived. Nevertheless, as is only to be expected, there is only a very remote connection between the party of Sir Winston Churchill and Sir Anthony Eden and that of Sir Robert Filmer or Sir Robert Peel or even that of Disraeli.

When political parties originally emerged in Great Britain after 1660, the Tories were mostly nobles, landowners and country clergy who remained loyal to the established church.

The Puritans and all who favoured religious toleration, together with many of the aristocracy and richer landowners who had become associated with the dissenters or acquired business interests, were all on the side of the Whigs. After the Revolution of 1642, support for the church became associated with championship of the monarchy. The Tories were consequently left in a weak position after the victory of Parliament in 1688. Their loyalties were divided between the Stuarts, whom they still considered entitled to rule by Divine Right, and the Hanoverians, who upheld the established church. Moreover, they were not so wealthy as the Whigs. They were therefore excluded from the government for the greater part of the eighteenth century, until they finally attained office under the younger Pitt. They then remained in power almost without intermission until 1830, as the Whig opposition was weakened during the period of the wars against France, which was also a period of resistance to all ideas of social reform.

The Reform Act of 1832 was a triumph for the Whigs, but Sir Robert Peel thereafter succeeded in changing the formerly reactionary attitude of the other party, which henceforth became known as the Conservative, and later the Conservative and Unionist Party. Disraeli made even greater efforts to broaden the basis of the party by demonstrating that respect for tradition and for the monarchy were not necessarily incompatible with far-reaching political and social reforms. Under Disraeli's successor, Lord Salisbury, the Conservatives were more concerned with opposition to Home Rule and with the imperial policy upon which the country had, at first cautiously and later more vigorously, embarked. Nevertheless, the party was never allowed to stagnate owing to the influence of Joseph Chamberlain, the former Radical who had joined the Liberal Party and later went over to the Conservatives. After the Balfour government was defeated in 1905, the Conservatives did not return to office until they entered the war-time coalition government ten years later. In 1922 they again became an independent party. During the ensuing period of three-party government they were led by Bonar Law and Stanley Baldwin, and endeavoured to tackle the problems of the inter-war years. They returned to power after the resignation of Ramsay MacDonald in 1935 and stayed in office until the outbreak of war. Though defeated in 1945 and again in 1950, they regained power in 1951, when they obtained 13,717,538 votes to Labour's 13,948,605.[1]

In the course of time, and since the middle of the nineteenth century in particular, the distinction between the parties has gradually come to correspond to economic distinctions, if not actually class divisions within the country. The Liberals used to look for support to the manual workers and industrialists, while the main strength of the Conservatives lay with the nobility, landowners and capitalists. With the development of industry and the growing importance of forms of property other than land, employers and businessmen tended to become Conservatives while the wage-earners and white-collar workers mostly supported the Liberals. These divisions became more pronounced after the Liberal Party split over Home Rule, when a number of the leading Whig families went over to the Conservatives. The South African War had a similar effect. The rise of the Labour Party, coupled with the Liberal policy towards Labour in 1924, left the Conservatives as the only party really opposed to Socialism, and it became increasingly clear that the Labour Party was the only possible alternative to Conservatism.

The outlook of the modern Conservative Party is still coloured by the views which it has advocated at earlier stages in its history, as can be seen in its attitudes towards the church, Ireland, the tariff question, the House of Lords, the empire and fiscal policy, and its cautious approach to economic and social reform. It still relies on the support of the aristocracy, in so far as they can still exert any influence, the wealthier classes, big businessmen and those engaged in agriculture and some of the liberal professions. Certain areas of the country might be described as Conservative strongholds, unaffected by any swings in votes (swings may be highly influential where elections are decided by simple majority) which may be caused by the unpopularity of a particular policy or by the behaviour of Liberals. The safe Conservative areas include Northern Ireland, rural constituencies apart from the Celtic fringe in the north of Scotland, North and West Wales, and Cornwall which never can be counted upon to remain loyal, the City of London,

---

[1] In 1955 the Conservatives were again returned to power with 13,286,564 votes and 344 seats, as against 12,404,970 votes and 277 seats secured by the Labour Party.

Westminster, parts of Holborn, Chelsea and most of the wealthier suburbs, and the city centres and more prosperous residential areas in the larger towns.

With the two-party system and the simple majority rule, the outcome of an election is often decided by middle-class votes. Conservative programmes therefore tend to be framed in moderate terms. Although firmly opposed to any unduly socialistic measures, they can never be truly reactionary.

The reason for this can be found by examining the sources from which Conservative supporters are drawn. In 1951 the party stated that it had 2,793,968 members, but it obtained 13,717,538 votes in the general election, so it is especially important to see what kind of people vote Conservative without actually belonging to the party.[1]

Such persons are to be found all over the country, even in the most solidly Labour regions. Labour members of Parliament for the industrial constituencies of South Wales never obtain more than two-thirds of the total votes. In 1951 Labour secured only 60% of the total poll in the solidly Labour area in Durham, while in Yorkshire it had little more than an absolute majority. Thus there is often considerable doubt as to the outcome of an election and the Conservatives contest practically every seat in the hope of gaining the extra few thousand votes they need to carry the constituencies where there is the smallest adverse majority. Uncontested elections have become increasingly rare. Neither in 1950 nor in 1951 was any Labour member elected unopposed.

Conservative supporters are drawn from a wide variety of different social backgrounds. An inquiry carried out by the British Institute of Public Opinion, the results of which were published in the *News Chronicle* in 1950, showed that 53% of all Conservative voters were women. During the eleven years after women were enfranchised every government showed Conservative inclinations even when the Conservative Party was not actually in office. Although the Conservatives were defeated in the first general election after women received the vote on the same terms as men, the enfranchisement of women appears to have operated to their advantage, in just the same way as it has benefited moderate parties in other countries. The age distri-

---

[1] In 1955, with about 2¾ million party members, the Conservatives obtained 13,286,564 votes.

bution of Conservative voters was much as might have been expected. They included relatively few younger people, only 18% being between 21 and 29 while 41% were over 50. Nevertheless, only 10% were over 65, which was no more than the proportion of Labour voters in that age group. This suggests that, above a certain age, the tendency to become Conservative as one grows older is counterbalanced by the change in outlook which results from a lower income. As regards income levels, 9% of the Conservative voters were from the wealthiest class, 31% from the middle class, 48% from the working class and 12% from the poorest classes. The comparable figures for Labour supporters were 0%, 9%, 65% and 26%. Thus the middle class is still predominantly Conservative, but the Conservative Party also derives considerable support from the working class, and it has more voters among the very poor than Labour has among the very rich. Many agricultural workers vote Conservative, as do some manual workers in industrial and mining areas. Even though the Labour Party was originally based upon the trade unions and is still dependent on their support, 15% of all trade unionists vote Conservative. The Conservative working man in Great Britain is a social phenomenon which would merit a special study. The Conservatives are by no means an exclusively upper-class party. If they were, the two-party system could never survive. The gradual breakdown of class divisions within the country has made the Conservative Party increasingly democratic, as has become especially marked in recent years. This growing sense of national unity has greatly strengthened the position of the Cabinet, which on many important issues can now rely on the support of the whole country and not merely of its own party. Today, however, the lack of fundamental differences between the parties is not so pronounced as it was when the Liberals were the main opponents of the Conservative Party.

The Liberals, successors of the Whigs, were primarily a party of a section of the nobility, and the higher clergy and the rich City merchants who opposed the Stuarts because of their lack of religious toleration and their claim to rule by Divine Right. They secured the recognition of liberal principles in such constitutional measures as the Habeas Corpus Act, the Bill of Rights of 1689 and the Toleration Act. Apart from a single break of one year, they were in power continuously from

1715 until 1770. During this time, thanks to the less active rôle assumed by the monarchy under the Hanoverians and the personalities of Walpole and the elder Pitt, they succeeded in consolidating the privileges of Parliament and the powers of the Prime Minister. Religious toleration and the expansion of foreign trade were outstanding features of this period, but it was also the age of electoral corruption which saw the development of an oligarchy based on wealth. During the wars with France the Whigs suffered an eclipse, but as Liberals they returned to power during the reign of William IV, when Lord Grey formed the ministry of Whigs and Canningites who carried through the reform of the electoral system in the face of strong opposition. Thereafter, Liberal and Conservative governments held office alternately, the Liberal ministries being headed by Lord Melbourne, Lord John Russell, Lord Aberdeen and Gladstone—the most distinguished of them all—who was four times Prime Minister. Liberal policy in the nineteenth century was largely shaped by the delayed influence of the ideas of the French Revolution and of the Revolution of 1830. The Liberals were responsible for humanitarian reforms in the colonies, the development of factory legislation, the recognition of the rights of trade unions, the electoral reforms of 1872 and 1885, and the championship of Home Rule for Ireland. They returned to power again in 1905 under the leadership of Campbell-Bannerman, who was later succeeded by Asquith as Prime Minister. During this term of office they had to deal with many serious issues, including the strengthening of the Anglo-French Entente, Lloyd George's 'revolutionary' budget, the curtailment of the powers of the House of Lords, Home Rule and social unrest. Subsequently they had to assume heavy responsibility for the conduct of the war, although they formed a coalition government with the Conservative and Labour parties in May 1915, Lloyd George later replacing Asquith as Prime Minister. The Liberals fell from power in 1922, and they have never again held office, except in so far as a few Liberals or Liberal Nationals were included in Ramsay MacDonald's coalition government and in the War Cabinet of 1940 to 1945. Liberalism belongs to an age which is past, and it is doubtful whether there can be any future for the party. The reasons for its eclipse and the nature of its present position can both be easily explained.

The extent of its eclipse can be seen by comparing the results of the general elections of 1906 and 1951. In 1906 the Liberals won over three million votes and 401 seats, to which should be added another 83 held by Irish Nationalists and 29 held by Labour members who normally supported the Campbell-Bannerman government which thus had an overall majority of 354. By 1951, when the electorate was much larger, the Liberals obtained only 730,556 votes and 6 seats. The reason for their decline, already marked by 1935, is inherent in the philosophy of Liberalism itself. Though supposed to be a 'party of movement', they have in fact followed a very moderately progressive policy not unlike that which the Conservatives have been forced to adopt except that the Liberals have been prepared to go rather further and faster. Liberalism has very little to offer by comparison with the socialism that the trade unions have been ardently propagating since the beginning of the twentieth century. The Liberal Party has a glorious past, but most of its programme has now been carried into effect. It has been left in a position somewhere midway between the Labour and Conservative parties, and it is becoming increasingly difficult to see that it has any distinctive policy of its own. It has been forced to become a party of the centre in a country where the electoral and political systems do not favour any third parties, least of all parties of the centre.

Its eclipse is due to several causes, most of which are obvious. In the first place, many of its doctrines are no longer at all original or else not really relevant to modern conditions, since the questions at issue are now not so much whether to have any restrictions on free trade or state control generally, but merely how much of each is desirable. When new problems arose in the inter-war years, the traditional doctrines of the Liberal Party prevented it from taking up many of the proposals which were gaining the support of a growing section of public opinion and which the Labour Party had no hesitation in recommending. Another factor which should be emphasised in this connection is that a number of important reforms carried through under Liberal or predominantly Liberal governments since 1905, such as the Parliament Act of 1911, the Trade Union Act of 1913 and the reform of the electoral system in 1918, upset the pre-existing political equilibrium and introduced immense new imponderable risks which the Liberals were exceedingly ill-equipped to face. Asquith and Lloyd George had to lead a coalition in which the Liberals were still held responsible for any failures or unpopular measures of the government, although its policies and action were in fact largely controlled by the Conservatives. The electoral system has also operated to the disadvantage of the Liberals, whom the electorate have considered as mainly to blame for the three-party system. In an effort to conserve their position as far as possible, they made an alliance with the Conservatives in the general election of 1924 which had disastrous results. They fared better from their alliance with the other parties in 1931, but this brought them no lasting benefits. Indeed, these alliances led the opponents of the Labour Party to regard the Conservative Party as the only alternative, a tendency which has become more marked the more the Liberals have tried to dissociate themselves from the Conservatives. Divisions within the Liberal Party, and in particular the split between the Liberals and Liberal Nationals, were fostered by the differences between Asquith and Lloyd George and by the appointment of Lloyd George as Prime Minister when he was not the leader of the party and disagreed with the official leadership on many important points. The Liberals suffered their first major defeat in the general election of 1922, when they obtained only 117 seats (64 being held by independent Liberals and 53 by Liberal Nationals), whereas the Conservatives won 347 seats, and the Labour Party, who defeated Liberals in 108 constituencies, 142. The electorate had thus chosen to vote for the Labour Party in preference to the Liberals as the alternative to a Conservative government. The general election of 1923 did not provide conclusive proof that this represented a permanent shift in public opinion, but the election of 1924 confirmed that it was no passing phenomenon. The Conservatives won the election with 415 seats and 7,054,000 votes, Labour had 5,489,000 votes and 152 seats, and the Liberals were left with only 2,925,000 votes and a mere 42 seats. Any remaining illusions of the Liberals were destroyed in the general elections of 1929 and 1931. In 1935, when Labour obtained 8,236,000 votes and 154 seats, the Liberals secured only 2,309,000 votes and 54 seats, and 33 of these were held by Liberal Nationals who were becoming increasingly difficult to distinguish from Conservatives.

The Liberal Party today is a minority party. It still has a number of supporters in intellectual, upper middle-class and

non-conformist circles, and is especially strong in rural areas of
Scotland and Wales. But the system of election by simple
majority invariably operates against it. Until 1950 it always
managed to secure a fairly appreciable number of votes, the
exact number at different elections varying from 1,400,000 to
5,000,000 and often being somewhere around two and a half
million. It was still a party of some significance, especially as
the third party in general elections, and also as the centre party
in the House of Commons, where the Labour governments of
1924 and 1929-31 were dependent on Liberal support. Since
the general election of 1951, however, there have been only six
Liberals in the House of Commons and the party has had only
a very small amount of indirect influence in Parliament. Its
position in the country is no better, for its doctrines are not
sufficiently inspiring or relevant to contemporary problems to
command any wide measure of popular support. Its decline has
increased the number of floating voters and thus helped, in 1950
and again in 1951, to produce a more marked swing of the
pendulum in favour of the Conservative Party. Many Liberal
electors had to choose between abstaining and voting for one of
the two main parties. Three-fifths of these Liberal votes appear
to have gone to the Conservatives and two-fifths to the Labour
Party. This is much as might have been expected, since Labour
had already gradually absorbed the more progressive elements
in the Liberal Party and become the principal advocates of the
chief reforms that were originally part of the Liberal programme.

The history of the Labour Party has naturally been different
from that of the older political parties. It started as an extra-
parliamentary party, and was a direct offshoot of the trade
union movement. Trade unions had begun to develop as early
as 1825, as a result of the Industrial Revolution. Chartism and
Christian Socialism helped to produce the beginnings of a
working-class movement in the nineteenth century, but it was
not until about sixty years ago that this began to participate in
an organised fashion in the political life of the country. Towards
the end of the nineteenth century, two groups of particular
interest were formed: the Social Democratic Federation, which
had only a limited following on account of its Marxist doctrines;
and the celebrated Fabian Society of Bernard Shaw, Sidney and
Beatrice Webb and H. G. Wells, who advocated a reformist

brand of socialism and gained considerable influence in intellectual circles. Under the inspiration of Keir Hardie, a working-class trade unionist party was established in Scotland. In the general election of 1892 this succeeded in securing the election of fifteen working-class M.P.s, all of whom stood as Liberals. When the Trade Union Congress met at Bradford in 1893, it agreed to form an Independent Labour Party. This, with help from some of the Fabians, put up a number of candidates in the general election of 1895, although none were elected. Nevertheless, as a result of the efforts of Keir Hardie, the Trade Union Congress agreed in September 1899 to summon a conference to meet in London in the following year at which the trade unions, the Independent Labour Party and the Social Democratic Federation would be represented. The S.D.F. subsequently withdrew, but despite the opposition of one of the leading trade unionists, John Burns, the T.U.C. decided to form a working-class political party. To this end they set up the Labour Representation Committee, which in 1906 became known as the Labour Party, as it has been ever since. In 1906 it contested its first general election, putting up 50 candidates, of whom 29 were elected. These, together with other trade unionists who had been elected as Liberals, tried to bring pressure to bear on the Liberal Party in favour of social reform. The *Daily Herald* was founded by the Labour movement in 1911. The Labour Party began as simply an association of trade unions, socialist trade councils and co-operative societies, but individual membership has been possible since 1918. During the war Labour came into the coalition, but there was a split in the party after the armistice. The Independent Labour members, although few in number, then became the official opposition to the coalition government which the National Labour group continue to support.

The establishment of the Communist Party in 1920 did nothing to undermine the growing strength of the Labour Party, which secured 191 seats in the general election of 1923. In the following year it was given an opportunity of proving itself in office. Mr Baldwin's Cabinet was defeated by a combination of Liberal and Labour votes, and Ramsay MacDonald was asked to form a government. This first Labour Government soon ran into difficulties in Parliament and over its general policy, and was forced to ask for a dissolution, which resulted in the Conservatives being returned with an overwhelming majority. In 1929 Ramsay MacDonald again became Prime Minister. In 1931, however, the economic crisis and the serious social problems which it created forced him to form a national government with the Conservatives and Liberals, and this soon fell from power.

The Labour Party nevertheless recovered from the setback which it suffered in 1931. Under the leadership of Mr Attlee, Mr Morrison and Mr Bevin it advanced from strength to strength. After participating in the War Cabinet from 1940 to 1945, it gained an unprecedented victory in the general election of 1945, when it won nearly 12 million votes and 394 seats. Although defeated in 1951, it still had a larger share of the poll than the Conservatives, who won the election with 13,717,538 votes compared with Labour's 13,948,605. With 298 seats as against the Conservatives' 321, the Labour Party, despite its internal divisions, remained an extremely powerful opposition in the House of Commons. The party is still predominantly composed of 'indirect members', though the individual membership is by no means insignificant. In 1951, out of a total membership of 5,937,000, there were 876,000 individual members compared with 4,937,000 members of affiliated trade unions.[1]

The Labour Party is not only able to rely on exceptionally powerful support from the trade unions, but it also maintains close contact with the trade union movement, and especially with the T.U.C., outside the formal channels of the party organisation. The Attlee government always had the firm backing of the T.U.C., and when the Labour Party is in opposition it can still exert considerable influence through the trade union representatives who sit on many government committees.

If the Labour Party had remained exclusively a trade union party it could never have reached the stage of being able to form a government. It originated as a working-class party and subsequently became a socialist party, but it could not be considered as a possible alternative to a Conservative government until it had acquired some middle-class support and ceased to be the party of any one particular social group. The

---

[1] In 1955 the Labour Party had a total membership of 6,483,994. The number of individual members has declined from 1,014,524 in 1952 to 1,004,655 in 1953, 933,657 in 1954 and 843,356 in 1955.

Labour Party has managed to do this because it embraces two distinct wings, such as have normally existed, in a less marked form, in major political parties in Great Britain. The party itself is only kept together through constant efforts to reconcile its internal differences, its leaders having to resort to mediation, threats and expulsions in order to prevent party splits.

Labour has never been a revolutionary party. It still follows a comparatively moderate policy in the hope of winning as much support as possible among those voters who are not firmly committed to either party. In the past some left-wing movements have developed within the Labour Party, such as the campaign for a Popular Front led by Sir Stafford Cripps and Mr Bevan in 1937, Mr Bevin's foreign policy, and the episode which led to the expulsion of Mr Zilliacus and Mr Solley in 1949. Mr Aneurin Bevan's resignation from the Labour government in 1951 and the growing strength of the extremist elements among the Bevanite rebels highlighted the clash of views within the party, and the moderate policies of Mr Attlee, Mr Dalton and Mr Morrison were strongly criticised at a number of party conferences. On several occasions a complete party split was very narrowly avoided, and the party has sometimes been driven to abstain from voting in the House of Commons as the only way of covering up its internal differences.

The Labour Party has thus inevitably been forced to adopt a middle-of-the-road policy. Its 'democratic socialism' does not necessarily imply unrelenting opposition to all Conservative policies. Conscription, for instance, was introduced by the Attlee government. Over the question of denationalisation, a truce was soon concluded between Labour and Conservatives, and in the autumn of 1953 the T.U.C. declared that it was not in favour of any further nationalisation.

The moderation of the Labour Party is not really surprising if we remember that it has long since ceased to be a class party and become a national party from which no section of the population is excluded.

Its greatest strength naturally lies in districts where social distress has been particularly acute and Labour policies have led to an improvement in working-class conditions. East, north-east and south-east London are predominantly Labour, and elsewhere nearly all Labour seats are in industrial regions. Its only successes in the counties are usually in the industrial areas

of South Wales, Durham, Staffordshire, Derbyshire, Lanca-
shire and Cumberland.

Labour supporters are drawn from several different sections
of the population. First, there are the wage-earners and manual
workers, who are generally affiliated to the party through their
trade unions. According to the most reliable estimates, only a
little over half of this group actually belong to the Labour
Party, but these include a high proportion of the most active
trade unionists, whose voluntary services are extremely valuable
to the party at election times. The Labour Party also has some
middle-class members, by no means all from the lower middle
classes, who include salaried workers, small shopkeepers and
businessmen, farmers and agricultural workers. In addition,
the party can generally rely on the firm support of the Co-
operative Party.

What is particularly striking about the Labour Party is its
reluctance to have anything to do with any group or party
which has or looks as if it might have extremist tendencies. The
Co-operative Party, which is essentially moderate in its outlook,
has been allowed to enter into a special relationship with the
Labour Party, and National Labour members who wished to
rejoin the party after 1931 had no difficulty in gaining re-
admission. But all the Communist Party's requests for affiliation
between 1920 and 1925 were firmly refused, and since 1924
Communists have not been accepted as individual members.
The Labour Party also took steps to protect itself against
penetration by other groups clandestinely inspired by the Communists. The National Executive Committee was empowered,
after holding an inquiry, to disaffiliate any Communist-inspired
groups, and a list was drawn up of 18 different organisations
regarded as ineligible for affiliation. Any co-operation between
the Labour Party and these groups was also banned, and their
members are not allowed to join the Labour Party in an
individual capacity. It should be added that the Communist
Party does not represent any significant political force in Great
Britain, and obtained only 21,640 votes in the general election
of 1951, when not a single Communist candidate was elected.[1]

The future of the Labour Party will depend on whether it
can overcome its serious internal differences and remain a

[1] Communist candidates in 1955 secured 33,144 votes (0·1%), and none
were elected.

united party. The electoral system and the internal discipline of the party both help to hold it together, and successive compromises between the extreme wings have produced a brand of socialism which has not in the least disrupted the balanced and tolerant atmosphere of political life in Great Britain. Labour and the Conservatives can succeed one another in office without this involving any very drastic change, and the differences which divide them are kept within bounds because of certain general characteristics that they have in common.

Common Characteristics of Political Parties

One striking feature of both the principal parties is that, while they have clearly not gone so far in this direction as the two main parties in the United States, they each include representatives of many different sections of public opinion and a wide range of social and economic interests.

This tendency was noticeable even in the days of the Whigs and the Tories, when the distinction between the parties sprang from the political and religious differences which had emerged during the Civil War and did not in any way correspond to conflicting economic interests. Nobles, landowners and men of property were well represented on both sides. Businessmen and industrialists tended on the whole to support the Whigs, but the Whig Party drew its supporters from many different sections of the community which could hardly be said to form one distinct social class. In the seventeenth and eighteenth centuries the Whigs were always the wealthier of the two parties, but the aristocracy was equally well represented among the Tories, and both parties supported measures to increase the incomes of landed proprietors.

The position was somewhat altered in the nineteenth century when, as has already been mentioned, the wealthier classes tended to become Conservative while the working classes supported the Liberal party. Thus the distinction between the parties became to some extent a reflection of social and economic differences, though it still could not be said that any particular interests were exclusively represented by either party. Despite the differences between their programmes, Liberals and Conservatives both shared the same fundamental beliefs regarding the general economic and social structure of society.

Nor is it surprising that they should have agreed on these basic principles when, even though they may not have represented exactly the same interests, they both included representatives of a wide range of different interest groups. As Laski put it: 'The men who directed the destinies of both circles came, broadly, from the same social environments; they spoke the same language; they moved in much the same circles; they depended upon the same common stock of ideas. They thought in the same way because they lived in the same way. . . . A Tory democrat like Disraeli could be more advanced in matters of social legislation than a Liberal like Gladstone or a Radical like John Bright. A Conservative aristocrat like Lord Cecil could have more cosmopolitan conceptions of foreign policy than a Radical man of the people like Mr Lloyd George. . . . A Conservative like Lord Baldwin . . . had a much higher conception of the responsibility of capital than a Liberal businessman like Viscount Runciman.'

Laski, in 1938 at least, considered that the situation changed completely after the Labour Party replaced the Liberals as the second major party, when the party system began to operate 'in an atmosphere different from anything known in the two and a half centuries of its history'.

This would appear to be a mistaken view. In the inter-war years, a party founded as an offshoot of the trade union movement and professing socialist doctrines may have been regarded as revolutionary, but today such a view could not be seriously maintained even in Great Britain. The Conservatives have found that it is no longer possible to take a firm stand against everything that savours of socialism, especially when it is socialism of the strictly reformist British variety. On the other hand, the Labour Party, never a revolutionary party, has tempered its doctrines as it has grown more mature. The influence of the former Liberals who have joined the Labour Party, and its anxiety to appeal to large numbers of voters who are neither wage-earners nor trade unionists, have encouraged it to follow a moderate policy. In a large country with many different interests to be represented, it would be impossible for the characteristics of the two main parties to be any different from what they are. Their size and scope are too great for them to be homogeneous parties. In 1951 many Liberals with right-wing tendencies voted Conservative and many others whose sympathies were with the left voted Labour, yet there can hardly have been any very fundamental difference between those who, in 1950 and previously, had all supported the Liberal Party. The Conservative Party does not consist solely of 'die-hard Tories' who speak of Mr Bevan in tones of horror. It also includes advocates of a form of 'Tory democracy' that embraces many ideas which, apart from certain overtones inspired by sentiment or tradition, are not substantially different from the tenets of the more moderate elements in the Labour Party. Occasionally, a permanent split has occurred in one of the major parties, as among the Tories in 1846, among the Liberals in 1886, and in the Labour Party in 1931. Such party splits, like the differences which for some years now have been clearly apparent within the Labour Party, serve as a reminder that party cohesion can never be taken for granted and that, in Britain as in the United States, the two-party system could not survive without constant efforts to reconcile opposing points of view within each party.

The all-embracing character of the parties has inevitably affected their political outlook. Invective against 'Tory warmongers' and 'socialist totalitarianism' is invariably heard in every general election campaign. Nevertheless, the programmes of the parties and their policies when in office cannot be otherwise than moderate because they have to try to satisfy a very mixed group of supporters and to win over floating voters. Although British foreign policy has never been 'bipartisan' in the strict sense of the word, it has always followed very much the same lines no matter which party has been in power, and on major issues there is, generally speaking, no essential difference between the Labour and Conservative points of view. The Attlee government was responsible for the conciliatory policy towards Communist China, which it later dropped, but it was Mr Churchill who first launched the sensational proposal for a meeting with Stalin, which was rejected at the time but taken up again afterwards. In the field of domestic policy the left wing of the Labour Party and the right wing of the Conservatives clearly have very little in common. These extreme wings are not, however, in a position to dictate the policy of their parties, which always follows a more moderate line. Mr Churchill's government managed to denationalise the iron and steel industry, but it was quite impossible for them to do away with the system of 'planning' established under the previous government or to reopen the debate on the basic principles of the new system of social security that had been introduced. They were able to make some slight reductions in the burden of progressive taxation on large incomes, but any interference with the basic principles of the fiscal system was out of the question, and all Conservatives were fully aware that their party would not be able to effect any drastic cuts in taxation. A Conservative Cabinet might press forward rather more rapidly with rearmament, but it could never carry this so far as seriously to reduce the living standards of the wage-earners or of the middle classes. Mr Butler's financial policy was in fact strikingly reminiscent of the famous 'austerity' programme of Sir Stafford Cripps. The lack of fundamental differences between Conservative and Labour programmes at general elections is often no less striking than the similarity between Liberal and Conservative programmes in the past. After the general election of 1951, when the common ground between the two parties was exceptionally extensive, the Conservatives were extremely circumspect about trying to execute any part of their programme with which the other party was not in sympathy.

This restraint and moderation of political parties in Great Britain is particularly vital to the effective functioning of the parliamentary system. It is clearly not a natural phenomenon but one born of constant efforts at mediation and compromise between opposing points of view on the part of the party organisations.

III. PARTY ORGANISATION

Party organisation in Great Britain, like most other aspects of the political system, does not correspond to any general classification based on rational principles. The present arrangements are largely the outcome of history, chance, tactical considerations and the quest for efficiency. It would be quite arbitrary to say that they belonged to any recognised types of party organisation.

Party organisation in Britain tends on the whole to be less flexible than in the United States. This is quite easily explained by the differences in the way politics are conducted and in the size of constituencies in the two countries, by the fact that

Britain is not a federal state, by the greater homogeneity of British parties, and by the important place occupied by the party leaders under the parliamentary system.

Origins and Development of Party Organisation

Although the division of opinion in the country into two main sections dates from very early times and the party system itself was already in existence several centuries ago, it was not until the nineteenth century that party organisation really began to develop. The parties do not appear to have adopted any very definite system of organisation until after the Reform Act of 1832.

Previously, the Whigs and the Tories had both held meetings of members of Parliament, and larger gatherings which included other persons, to decide on party policy, to try to analyse public opinion and to see how they could influence it and use their patronage to the best advantage and secure electoral successes for the party. But there was no permanent organisation with power to enforce any kind of party discipline. Anyone who stood for election was substantially free to express his own views or those of his patron, and the cost of the campaign had to be met by the candidate out of his own pocket or with help from his patron. Members of Parliament were still to some extent allowed to vote according to their own personal judgment, and debate in Parliament could materially affect the outcome of a division. Aspiring politicians thought less about joining a party than of securing the support of some prominent or influential patron or 'friend'. The importance of such political 'friendships' in this period has given rise to the custom whereby members of Parliament still refer to other members of their party as 'my honourable Friend'. Both the Whigs and the Tories were primarily parliamentary parties, composed of members of the House of Commons and the peers and other 'friends' to whom they owed their seats.

In the course of the nineteenth century, however, the major parties adopted a definite system of party organisation. They did so for a number of reasons, the most important being the electoral reform of 1832, which, as we have seen, broadened the franchise and provided for the registration of electors. This forced the parties to pay much more attention to electioneering.

Local associations sprang up all over the country to supervise the registration of voters. They were largely autonomous organisations, mainly concerned with finding the best possible candidates, canvassing, and organising party propaganda and election campaigns. Subsequent electoral reforms broadened the scope of their activities, and their functions gradually became more clearly defined.

Another factor that undoubtedly promoted the development of party organisation was the personal prestige of such leaders as Gladstone and Disraeli. Just at the time when the electorate had been enlarged by the Reform Act of 1867, the parties were led by such outstanding personalities that people tended to vote for a candidate less because of his own personal qualities than because he undertook to support the policies of his leader. The party leaders, for their part, tried to improve the organisation of the party in order to increase their chances of electoral success, and consequently began to wield considerable influence within the newly established central party organisations. The work of Disraeli was particularly significant in this respect.

Another consequence of the extension of the franchise was to make local associations require more and more financial support in order to carry out their functions. The parties were therefore obliged to set up national campaign funds and co-ordinate the activities of the local organisations. Annual party conferences were held to agree upon the general lines of party policy. These also helped to preserve the unity of the party and to improve the morale of its members. The party headquarters grew more powerful as the local associations became increasingly dependent upon them for financial assistance. If they could do nothing else, they could at least influence constituency parties in their choice of candidates and exercise a certain amount of control over the way members voted in Parliament.

Central and Local Party Organisations

An important landmark in the development of party organisation in the Conservative Party was the formation of the National Union of Conservative and Unionist Associations very shortly after the Reform Act of 1867. After the Liberal victory in the general election of 1868, Disraeli went a stage further, and 1870 saw the creation of a Conservative Central Office under his direct personal control. In 1872 agreement was reached on the distribution of functions between the National Federation and the Central Office, the latter being left in charge of the party finances for which it was directly responsible to the leader of the party. In 1886 intermediary organs between the National Union and the local associations were established, and in 1906 the Central Office was strengthened by the introduction of representatives of the constituency organisations. Since then, the organisation of the party has remained substantially unchanged. Local associations continue to be responsible for the selection of candidates, though if they require financial assistance, they must be guided in their choice by a special standing advisory committee at the Central Office. Constituencies receive help and guidance from central organs of the party which supply them with information and organise general election campaigns. The Central Office undertakes the recruitment and training of the paid agents employed by the constituency parties as their permanent operational staff. It is also responsible for ensuring that seats are not 'bought up' by candidates making unduly generous contributions to the party funds. The amount which any candidate may donate is governed by regulations laid down in 1944 and enforced by the standing advisory committee which approves candidatures on behalf of the party. The functions of the annual party conference are far less specific than those of the Central Office. The conference provides an opportunity to review and reaffirm the party policy and it is also a means of publicity and of value in maintaining the unity of the party.

In the Liberal Party, organisation developed in much the same way as on the Conservative side. Sometimes the Liberals were in advance of the Conservatives, and on other occasions they followed their lead. The Birmingham Liberal Association was the pioneer in this field. It was reorganised after 1867. Further reforms introduced by Joseph Chamberlain and his lieutenant Schnadhorst after 1873 made it an outstanding model of an efficient and democratic party organisation which was widely imitated in other parts of the country. After the Conservative victory in 1874, a National Liberal Federation was set up in 1877 at the instigation of Joseph Chamberlain in order to co-ordinate the activities of the party through an annual conference and a national committee that could meet more frequently. Chamberlain was a leading figure in the Federation, which was responsible for some notable developments in the party organisation, in particular the establishment and central direction of a large number of local associations. Another important landmark came in 1891, when the National Federation unanimously adopted the famous Newcastle Programme, a detailed political programme embracing a large number of reforms advocated by the party which all Liberal candidates were expected to support. This appears to have been the origin of the well-known 'theory of the mandate', whereby the party which gains a majority is now held to have received a mandate from the electorate to carry out its programme. After undergoing some vicissitudes while Lloyd George was Prime Minister, the organisation of the Liberal Party was revised in 1936. It is now more democratic than that of the Conservative Party, notably in so far as many functions corresponding to those of the Conservative Central Office are exercised by a national body based on the local associations.

The organisation of the Labour Party was bound to be somewhat different from that of older parties that had evolved empirically and owed much to the personal influence of a few individuals. The Labour Party was founded by the trade unions and socialist societies, and the unions played a leading part in shaping its organisation. Local constituency parties were not established until 1918, and there are still more trade union than constituency representatives on the National Executive Committee of the party. This has 25 members, of whom 12 are elected by various groups of trade unions, 7 by constituency parties and regional Federations, and 1 by socialist and co-operative societies; the remaining 5 are women chosen to represent the women's sections of the party.

The annual conference has supreme control over all the activities of the Labour Party, but no means of exercising any direct influence over the parliamentary party and no authority over the Cabinet when the party is in power.

The party conference is made up of delegates from the trade unions, constituency parties, regional federations, and socialist and co-operative societies. There are also a number of *ex officio* members, including members of Parliament, prospective candidates, members of the National Executive and local agents of the party. It is the annual conference that determines the party's general policy. Its procedure ensures that trade union influence is always dominant, though the parliamentary party and the National Executive Committee are allowed some say before any election manifesto is adopted.

The National Executive Committee consists of the leader and deputy leader of the party, *ex officio*, and other members elected by the annual conference, who always include a high proportion of members of Parliament. The National Executive Committee is the chief administrative organ of the Labour Party, charged with maintaining liaison with the parliamentary party, supervising the local associations, managing the party finances and enforcing party discipline.

The party itself is made up of 11 regional federations and a fairly elaborate system of constituency parties.

There is also a National Council of Labour composed of seven representatives each of the Labour Party, the trade unions and —since 1941—the Co-operative Union. Before the second World War, this enabled the various organisations in the Labour movement to formulate a common policy. Today, however, it does no more than maintain liaison between the constituent groups.

The organisation of the Labour Party seems on the whole to be less flexible, more closely linked to the parliamentary party and more democratic than that of the other parties, and the leader of the party does not appear to have assumed such a dominant rôle. Nevertheless, the parliamentary party remains an autonomous group. The real purpose of party organisation in the Labour Party is just the same as in the Conservative Party—namely, to ensure a maximum of popular support for the party in Parliament.

The Party Leaders

In every political party, the party leader is bound to occupy an important place. As he will become Prime Minister if his party wins an election, the choice of leader is a matter of vital interest to the whole country and not merely to his own party. The outcome of a general election has sometimes in fact been decided by the personalities of the respective party leaders.

For many years, however, there was no definite procedure

for appointing party leaders, who in most cases virtually appointed themselves by becoming indispensable to the party. The Prime Minister is always the leader of the party in power. This at least has never been seriously questioned, but a delicate situation can still arise if a Prime Minister resigns or dies in office. When Gladstone resigned in 1894, the Queen tried to get over the problem by personally selecting Lord Rosebery as his successor. This automatically made him leader of the Liberal Party but created serious difficulties within the party, and it would now be quite inconceivable for the sovereign to try to impose a leader in this way. Nowadays leaders are chosen either by the Cabinet or else by the parliamentary party, or some other organ of the party.

Until 1942 the leader of the majority party was always leader of the House of Commons, but in recent years the Prime Minister has usually appointed one of his colleagues to the latter post. The duties of the leader of the House have become so much greater that they would be a very heavy additional burden for the Prime Minister, and party discipline is strong enough for him to find it quite easy to delegate the leadership of the House to some other minister.

When a government is defeated, the late Prime Minister normally becomes leader of the opposition unless he specifically declines that position. In the nineteenth century, it appears to have been considered that, in the absence of a former Prime Minister, an opposition party had no leader but merely a parliamentary leader in each house. Today, however, the House of Lords is no longer of equal importance with the Commons, and it is apparently recognised that the leader in the House of Commons should be regarded as the leader of the party as a whole. In the Conservative Party, an important precedent in this connection was set in 1923 when Mr Stanley Baldwin was chosen to succeed Mr Bonar Law. Lord Curzon, who might have been thought a more likely candidate, was rejected because he sat in the upper House. Although the *de facto* supremacy of the House of Commons is thus acknowledged, party leaders are still formally elected by the parliamentary party as a whole, including the peers. In the Conservative Party, prospective candidates and members of the executive of the National Union of Conservative and Unionist Association are also allowed to vote for the leader.

The Conservative Party apparently takes the view that, once appointed, a leader retains his office until he chooses to lay it down. In the Labour Party, on the other hand, the leader has to be re-elected every year by the parliamentary party, which has successively chosen Mr Clynes, Mr MacDonald, Mr Henderson and Mr Attlee as its leaders and thus also designated them as prospective Labour Prime Ministers. Since 1924 the leader of the Liberal Party has been similarly elected.

When the leader of the party is Prime Minister, he is assisted in the exercise of his functions by the other members of the Cabinet and, indirectly, by the subordinate organs of the party. When in opposition, the leader normally acts in consultation with other former ministers. In either case, meetings of members of Parliament are sometimes held to decide what course of action the party should adopt on some particular issue.

In the Conservative Party, there are no formal limitations on the powers of the leader, provided that he can defend his policy effectively at the annual conference of the party. The Liberals, however, have now introduced more democratic arrangements whereby all statements of policy on political issues have to be approved by a representative conference of the party, and the leader has been deprived of most of the powers which he used to possess over the central organisation. The leader of the Labour Party appears to have even less discretion. He can do little without the approval of the parliamentary party and is also virtually compelled to take account of the views of the National Executive Committee and the annual conference. If the party is divided, as in recent years when its unity has been severely strained, the leader may find himself in a very difficult position. Even in the Labour Party, however, a great deal still depends on the personality of the leader himself.

Finance

Another aspect of party organisation is the party finances, of which it is rather difficult to give a very clear account. As in other countries, local associations and sections of the parties have some revenue of their own from annual subscriptions, donations, proceeds of dances and bazaars and similar sources. Sometimes a candidate contributes towards his election expenses, but not all are able to do so—even in the Conservative Party—and their contributions are very seldom sufficient to cover the entire cost of the campaign. The central organisations of the parties have therefore been obliged to build up national funds. These they either spend themselves in ways best calculated to further the interests of the party as a whole, or else redistribute in the form of grants to the local associations, whose expenditure is then closely supervised by headquarters.

The Conservative Party is at a decided advantage in so far as it can rely on a substantial backing from the wealthiest classes, big business and industrial and commercial interests. Even so, it is not so well off as it used to be. As the party has become more democratic, it has been forced to increase its expenditure. Until comparatively recently it could cover all its requirements from funds obtained from a few hundred supporters. In 1947, however, an appeal for a fighting fund of £1,000,000 was launched by Lord Woolton, then chairman of the party. The Liberals, now that they are a party of the centre, have found it increasingly difficult to raise funds, and their steadily worsening financial position has undoubtedly helped to precipitate their decline. The present income of the party is barely £50,000 a year.

The Labour Party has extensive financial resources, thanks to its large membership and the powerful and well-organised support it receives from the trade union movement. There has been great controversy as to whether trade union funds could be used for political purposes. The question came before the courts in the Osborne Case in 1907-09, and the position has since been regulated by the Trade Union Act of 1913, the Trade Disputes and Trade Union Act of 1927, and finally by the Act of 1946. The latter restored the system of 'contracting out', first introduced in 1913, whereby unless he has specifically 'contracted out' of the political levy, a proportion of a member's union subscription may be given to Labour Party funds. In 1927 the Conservatives succeeded in imposing the alternative system of 'contracting in', which remained the rule until 1946. Union members had then to make an express declaration of willingness to contribute to the party funds before any part of their subscription could be used for political purposes. In fact, only 45% of all union members 'contracted in', whereas today

91% have tacitly agreed to pay the political levy, the proceeds of which have risen from £51,000 to over £124,000 a year. The total annual income of the Labour Party in 1950 was about £232,000, and to this must be added the general party funds, special funds for general elections and by-elections, and capital funds which together brought the financial resources of the party up to £689,615, according to the official figure published by the party. The Conservatives, however, maintain that the Labour Party really has far larger resources than this and that there is nearly £1 million at the disposal of the national party organisation alone.

Doubts have been expressed in some quarters as to whether the party in power may not at times have taken advantage of the desire of certain wealthy men to obtain honours, by giving them peerages or decorations as a reward for particularly generous contributions to the party funds. It is certainly true that the number of peers has greatly increased since party organisation became a more important and onerous task. Nevertheless, governments have shown such great discretion in recommending for honours only men and women whose personal merits are so obvious that there is little point in pursuing this delicate question any further.

All the same, the establishment and maintenance of the vast political machine which any major party now requires is bound to be an exceedingly expensive business, and it would be inadvisable to rely entirely upon the figures published by the parties themselves to find out how much they really spend. They also incur expenditure under other heads such as women's sections, youth groups, political education and publicity, day-to-day party propaganda, and the services of local agents, of whom the major parties employ large numbers and whose salaries and expenses must add considerably to the expenditure they incur in fighting elections. In 1951 the latter alone cost each of the two main parties somewhere between £400,000 and £500,000. No amount of money, however, can create an efficient party organisation in a party which does not also possess organising ability, determination, experience and initiative. Nor are British parties in the same position as those in the United States, which have a regular breathing space between Presidential elections when they do not have to maintain their party organisations in full fighting order. In Britain,

Parliament can be dissolved at any time, so the parties must always be ready to fight an election campaign. This is one reason why so few Independants are ever elected to Parliament (none in 1950 or 1951), and why those not satisfied with either of the two main parties are extremely unlikely to succeed in forming a third party which will have any chance of prevailing over the established parties.

Party organisation is nevertheless essential to enable the parties to fulfil their allotted functions.

IV. THE FUNCTIONS OF POLITICAL PARTIES

The Rôle of Political Parties

In Great Britain, as in other countries, the functions of political parties have been steadily expanding throughout the past century. With the democratisation of the parliamentary system, parties have had to make far more energetic and sustained efforts in the sphere of political education and electioneering. They are now actively concerned with many matters quite outside the field in which personalities, wealth, and connections with peers, great landowners or businessmen were the determining factors before the Reform Act of 1832. The functions of political parties have developed in much the same way as elsewhere, although their activities are still less extensive and more restrained than, for example, in the United States: public authorities assume full responsibility for the organisation of elections, there are fewer elective offices, elections are not so frequent, the techniques of political action and propaganda are not so spectacular or highly developed, and pressure groups and canvassing are relatively less important.

The party organisations have endeavoured to take the greatest possible advantage of new developments in the techniques of political education, publicity and propaganda. The Conservatives are greatly helped by the press, which is very highly concentrated under the control of a few big chains of newspapers with enormous circulations. Apart from the *News Chronicle* and the *Star*, which are traditionally Liberal, all these daily papers present some shade of Conservative opinion. The Conservatives also have the backing of the employers' associations and of the various economic interest groups that play an active part in politics. The latter often represent *de facto* monopolies, such as Tate and Lyle in the sugar industry who carried on a campaign in favour of free enterprise as opposed to nationalisation in which the symbol of 'Mr Cube' appeared on all their packets of sugar and on posters put out by Lord Lyle. On the other hand, the Labour Party can always rely on a substantial measure of support from the political activities of the trade unions, who provide a well-organised body of voluntary workers for the party cause. Although they employ different techniques, the Labour and Conservative party machines really serve the same purpose in keeping the country constantly informed of public affairs, moulding public opinion and forcing the people to make up their minds on current political issues. They also help to preserve the serious and objective approach to politics, the mistrust of generalisations and extremist points of view, and the respect for the freedom of every citizen regardless of his opinions, that have become outstanding characteristics of political life in Great Britain.

Their Electoral Functions

It was the electoral functions of political parties which originally led to the development of modern party organisation. The importance of these functions is now in some ways greater and in other ways less than it was in the nineteenth century. They are less important, in so far as many of the corrupt practices employed to win votes have either fallen into disuse or been forbidden by law. Public authorities play a larger part in the organisation of elections, and now that the electorate are better informed and more mature politically, it is generally recognised that they should be left free to vote as they think fit. In other respects, however, the parties are now more significant than ever before. This is due to the growth of party organisation and because, even in a highly individualist society, many problems can only be tackled by the combined efforts of many individuals and groups. Political parties have also come to play an ever-expanding part in the government of the country as a whole.

In the first place, the parties choose the candidates in parliamentary elections. In theory there is nothing to stop anyone standing as an independent candidate. In practice, however, such candidatures are becoming increasingly rare. Altogether there were 104 in 1945, but only 56 in 1950 and 23 in 1951.[1] Only in quite exceptional circumstances does an independent candidature have any real political significance or any chance of success, since an election is really a contest between the two main parties and no one wants to waste his vote on an isolated individual who could never accomplish anything if he were elected. It is consequently usual for candidates to have been adopted by a party. Local associations have a large amount of discretion in selecting their candidates. Even where these have to be approved by the party headquarters, the latter practically never turn down anyone put forward by the local association, which is in a better position to judge the needs of its own constituency. If, as often happens, a local association cannot find a suitable candidate, it applies to the party headquarters, and Abbey House or Transport House will supply them with a list of persons having the requisite qualifications. If a candidate fails to secure election, that may be the end of his political career. If he has created a good impression, however, he will be asked to stand again at the next election, and he may eventually be given a chance to move to a constituency where there are better prospects of a majority.

The parties can also decide whether they will contest any particular seat. The main parties are both obliged to put up candidates in practically every constituency, as an election is basically a struggle for power between the two. A minority party, however, or any third party that has not yet entirely withdrawn from electoral contests, has to concentrate its limited financial resources on a smaller selection of constituencies and the outcome of an election may be considerably affected by which seats it chooses to fight. In many constituencies Conservative and Labour supporters are approximately evenly balanced, and if there is no Liberal candidate the Conservative will normally be elected, as the majority of the Liberals generally vote Conservative while the rest either vote Labour or abstain. In some constituencies the Labour Party has been strengthened by the fall in the number of Communist candidates (100 in 1950 and 10 in 1951), but Communist voters (102,000 in 1945 and 91,000 in 1950) have never been sufficiently numerous to have

[1] In 1955 there were 13 independent candidates plus 12 Sinn Fein candidates in Northern Ireland and 11 Welsh Nationalists.

any effect on the overall result of an election.[1] On the other hand, we have seen how the Conservative victory in 1951 was to a large extent due to the fact that the Liberals only put up 109 candidates, compared with 305 in 1945 and 475 in 1950. In certain cases, therefore, a party's decision to contest or refrain from contesting any particular seat may have far-reaching political repercussions.

In the actual conduct of an election campaign, the rôle of the party organisations is always of fundamental importance. Candidates are dependent on the support they receive from their local association and on the funds and means of publicity that it is able to supply, either from its own resources or with the help of grants from the party headquarters. Moreover, the campaigns in the constituencies are closely bound up with the national campaign, which has sometimes been carefully and elaborately planned in advance. A candidate always stands to gain if any third party happens to be favourably disposed towards his own, or from the popularity of the party leader, or from any general movement of opinion which, quite regardless of his personal merits, would like his party to form a new government or to remain in office.

The Parties in Parliament

This brings us to the rôle of political parties in parliamentary government. As they have come to play an increasingly active part in the political life of the country, their traditional functions have gradually been supplemented by others that have given the British parliamentary system some of its most distinctive characteristics.

In the first place, parties provide the raw material from which governments are formed. A general election normally leaves one party with an absolute majority in the House of Commons, which means it has a mandate from the country to carry out its programme and will remain in office until the next general election. This is one of the most fundamental conventions of the constitution, reflecting the democratic basis of the political system and the rules of parliamentary procedure. Nevertheless,

[1] In 1955, 17 Communist candidates secured 33,144 votes. The result of the general election of 1955 does not appear to have been appreciably affected by the presence or absence of Liberal candidates, of whom there were 110.

once the country has given its verdict, it is the party organisation that determines the composition of the government.

The Prime Minister is in theory chosen by the Queen, who is above party. So long as one party has a clear majority, however, the sovereign could not in practice send for anyone other than its leader. Sometimes in the past the majority party has had no recognised leader, but, in view of the development of party organisation, it is extremely unlikely that such a situation would ever arise under modern conditions. In any case, if there is any doubt, it has become customary to let the party decide who should be Prime Minister and not to leave the choice to the sovereign. This follows the precedent set in 1880 when Gladstone, who had resigned from the leadership of the Liberal Party in 1874, was reappointed Prime Minister on the advice of the parliamentary leaders of the party after one of them, Lord Hartington, had been asked to advise the Queen. If a Prime Minister resigns or dies in office, his place will be taken by the Deputy Leader of the party, who is the recognised heir-apparent. Even when there is a coalition government, the parties still decide who shall be Prime Minister. When Mr Churchill replaced Mr Neville Chamberlain in 1940, he was not chosen simply because of his personality or from considerations of national policy, but also to meet the wishes of the Labour Party. The choice of the Prime Minister invariably rests with the party or parties to be represented in the government, irrespective of what form this may, in exceptional circumstances, assume. Normally he will already be well known as the leader of his party and, in particular, will be a familiar figure to the electorate, since they will have cast their votes for or against him as the head of the party he leads.

The choice of other ministers rests indisputably with the Prime Minister, who advises the Queen as to whom to appoint. Here again the party organisation is influential. Although, just as in other countries, there is naturally a variety of other political considerations to be taken into account, the positions which the Prime Minister's colleagues have held in the party leadership while in opposition will largely determine their offices in the government.

British political parties are so organised that they can always offer a possible alternative government. When a party attains office, it inevitably has to make some changes in emphasis in its policies, which will be modified in the light of new developments or new ideas that emerge during the life of a Parliament. All the same, governments are spared the incessant bargaining between different groups which is a necessary accompaniment of other political regimes. The policies of the Cabinet are the policies of a single party, put before the country at the general election when the people gave it a mandate to carry them out. Under the British system a party is in fact able to do so.

One of the main functions of the majority party in Parliament is to enable the Cabinet to remain in power by supporting it in carrying out its programme. Trevelyan has described 'The secret of the English constitution' as 'the steady confidence reposed by the Parliamentary majority in the Cabinet of the day . . . obtained . . . through the bond of a party loyalty held in common by the Cabinet and by the majority of the House of Commons'. That is the essence of Cabinet government. Election by simple majority tends to produce exaggerated majorities in Parliament, so the majority is usually perfectly well able to give the government all the support it requires. It is generally ready to do this because of its very close ties with the government. The Cabinet is nothing more than a small group of men through whom the party exercises the power which it has won in a general election. The Cabinet and the party will both be held responsible for the government's policies and the extent to which it has fulfilled its mandate. It is usually quite impossible for them to evade this responsibility to the electorate because it will generally have been quite clear from the result of the previous election that power was given to one party and one party alone.

The parties can only fulfil this function by imposing fairly strict discipline upon their members. Whenever a candidate is nominated and supported in his election campaign, it is always more or less understood that he will loyally uphold the rules and constitution of his party and follow the general line of party policy.

How far a local association can control its member of Parliament has always been a subject of some controversy. Its powers are closely circumscribed by the influence of the party headquarters in the selection of candidates. A local association can always refuse to renominate a sitting member, but it is difficult for it to force him to resign if he does not adhere to the programme in consideration of which he was elected. When members have changed their parties, they have sometimes offered themselves for re-election, but it has been equally common for them simply to continue to occupy their seats until the next general election.

It is within Parliament itself that party discipline is strongest. The general rule is that a member is free to vote as he thinks fit on questions that do not raise any issue of party policy, and if he disagrees with his party he can normally abstain from voting even on a matter of policy. On the other hand, the whips —whose name is derived from huntsmen and the whips which they carried—are always there to try to keep the party together and see that its members vote in divisions. If a member fails or appears reluctant to fall in with the rest of his party, the whips will either bring pressure to bear on him themselves or else ask the leader or general secretary of the party or some other influential person to intervene. The government and the opposition each have their own whips. Government whips hold public offices, generally as Parliamentary Secretary to the Treasury, a Junior Lord of the Treasury or an officer of the Royal Household. In November 1953 they included three officers of the Royal Household—the Controller, the Secretary and the Vice-Chamberlain—and five Lords Commissioners of the Treasury. The chief government whip is even provided with an office, which is within easy reach of the Prime Minister at number 10 Downing Street. The chief whips are the normal channels of communication between the parties in Parliament, known in parliamentary terminology as transactions 'through the usual channels'.

Members are generally ready to accept party discipline. They do so because they are anxious to retain the support of their party at the next general election, as it is unlikely that they could fittingly go over to the opposite party and there is no third party with any appreciable following. Persistent refusal to bow to party discipline may result in expulsion from the party, whereas by submitting to it a member will be able to wield some influence, at least in one of the two wings of the party. In extreme cases, a threat to dissolve Parliament is a practically sure way of reuniting the majority. A member's political career is far too dependent on his party and on the influence of the whips for him to be much disposed to rebel against their discipline.

The opposition is in a minority and generally has no prospect of being able to break up the government's majority. Nevertheless, as we shall see later, it has an essential place in the machinery of government. By its questions and criticisms it keeps the Cabinet constantly on the alert. The presence of a united opposition reminds the government that it will ultimately have to pit its strength against those who represent views opposed to its own which it must always take into account in framing its policies since they may command far more support in the country than might be thought from the size of the opposition in the House of Commons. The minority party also makes every effort, both in the country and in Parliament, to convince the nation that its policies are superior to those of the majority and that it ought to be returned to power in place of the existing government.

V. THE 'SWING OF THE PENDULUM'

The two main parties hold power alternately. This 'swing of the pendulum' became noticeable as soon as the characteristics of the two-party system were at all clearly defined and even before it had assumed all its present features. Apart from War Cabinets and coalition governments, no party since the Reform Act of 1832 has ever won more than two general elections in succession. The 'swing of the pendulum' does not of course operate with the certainty of a statistical law, but it seems to be an almost inevitable phenomenon in British politics. It occurs so regularly that it cannot be explained simply by saying that a government always tends to lose vitality after it has been some time in office.

It appears to be the outcome of a combination of institutional and political factors.

From the institutional point of view, election by simple majority tends to exaggerate any shift in public opinion. This means that a change in the allegiance of only a comparatively small number of floating voters may be enough to give the opposition a majority of seats in the House of Commons.

From the political point of view these fairly regular shifts in the balance of power between the two main parties do not appear to be due to any vacillation on the part of a particular group of voters but to two other factors. These both help to show how the British political system actually operates. The first, which has already been mentioned, is the absence of fundamental differences of opinion on major issues. This is still an outstanding feature of British politics, even though the Conservatives are now opposed by a nominally socialist party. Labour has its more extreme left wing and the Conservatives include some 'die-hard Tories', but the vast majority of British voters are basically agreed on the policies they wish to see adopted. Such differences as do exist are generally concerned with the way to carry out these policies or how quickly to seek to attain common objectives. It is only in these latter respects that there are any real differences between the two party programmes. Some voters therefore think it perfectly justifiable to give each party in turn a chance to prove the merits and effectiveness of its proposals. The better-informed sections of the electorate would probably not share this view, but it is certainly quite an understandable attitude for those without any definite ideas of their own, who tend to judge the parties by their past records, believing that their relative merits can only be assessed by looking at what each has managed to accomplish in the past. As there is no very clear distinction between the two party programmes, this attitude is not so inconsistent as it might otherwise appear.

Another reason for the regular shifts in the balance of power between the two parties is that, although obviously anxious to win or to retain the support of the electorate, they normally refuse to employ any dubious methods in order to attain this end. They make no attempt to interfere with the 'swing of the pendulum' in ways which would conflict with their idea of 'fair play'. The struggle between the parties may not be carried on in a spirit of complete disinterestedness, but each party respects those who do not share its views to an extent which is seldom encountered elsewhere. The majority does not try to crush the opposition, since it is always conscious that it may become the government of the future. The minority criticises but does not indulge in obstructive tactics, as it is aware that it may one day be in the position of the government and itself be faced with a parliamentary opposition.

One remarkable feature of British politics is that a party which has a majority does not exploit all the means at its disposal in order to keep itself in power. This is partly, though not entirely, due to the sporting instincts of the British people and to the fact that public opinion would react very strongly against any breach of the 'rules of the game'.

It generally seems to be considered undesirable in principle for any party to remain in power for too long. The British are fully aware that periodic changes of government have their disadvantages and that the advent of new men and new policies and changes in the administrative system is bound to cause some dislocation. Nevertheless, the disruptive effects are lessened by the similarity between the programmes of the two parties, and in any case changes of government are not sufficiently frequent to result in unduly weak or unstable governments. It is therefore considered desirable for the two main parties to hold office alternately, so that each general election gives one of them a chance to put its programme into practice. It is thought that each party should sometimes be put to the test of governing the country and that, when in opposition, it should be compelled to consider alternative policies and not confine itself to purely negative criticism. The British voter has little time for general principles and prefers to judge a party on its record of concrete achievements. On the other hand, he prefers that no party should have too long an uninterrupted term of office. Power tends to exhaust, and may also corrupt, those who have to exercise it, until their programme is no longer relevant to current problems and they lose vitality and become set in their ways. A period in opposition enables a defeated party to recover its strength and regroup its forces. It is compelled to look at political problems from a new angle and to revive its critical faculties, which may have fallen into disuse. It can also make its influence felt through criticism of the government until such time as it is once again able to change places with its opponents.

The British people have never known what it is to have irreconcilably opposed parties. Their belief that the two parties should hold office alternately implies that they do not think any policy can be wholly good or bad. They know that they will, in time, be able to judge from experience whether the programme for which the majority voted has merit enough to outweigh its disadvantages. Pressure from the opposition in Parliament and from public opinion helps to ensure that the most serious weaknesses in government policy are rectified. If they are not, the people have a chance to change their government and choose a different programme at the next general election. This programme, like that of the previous government, will be largely a compromise between divergent points of view, but it will introduce some new lines of policy and different means of realising its objectives, and there will be a different team of men to carry it out.

Thus it would be true to say that in Britain the people are the real source of political power. What is even more important is that the people participate in the exercise of power more directly than in many other countries where the electoral system produces a legislature far more accurately representative of public opinion than the British Parliament. Free elections and a secret ballot will always be essential prerequisites of democratic government. British democracy, however, goes a stage further than this. It is a genuine instance of government by the people, since the result of a general election determines the composition and policy of the government throughout the life of the ensuing Parliament. Every five years at least, and usually at more frequent intervals, the British people can choose what kind of government they want, and they do so in a manner which leaves no possible doubt as to their wishes. Rousseau maintained that the British were totally mistaken in thinking that they were free. In fact, however, they enjoy far greater freedom than many other democratic nations, since they have a form of semi-direct democracy which largely counteracts any oligarchical tendencies in the representative system. Parliament was originally a feudal institution and later an organ of the aristocracy. Today, however, it is an instrument of democracy. The people as a whole play an active part in the political life of the country through the two highly organised political parties, other currents of opinion being disregarded as of only secondary importance. The people decide which of the two main parties is to form the government. Each party in turn has to assume full responsibility for governing the country and is held responsible for the results of its policy. Normally, it is the people who decide when a government should remain in power and when it ought to give way to the opposition.

These special features of the parliamentary system in Great Britain have resulted in a unique form of parliamentary government, which we can now examine in greater detail.

PART TWO

The Organisation of Power: Cabinet Government

THE PREPONDERANCE OF THE EXECUTIVE

GREAT BRITAIN was the original home of parliamentary institutions. Here was first developed the system of government which has since been taken as the model for the constitutions of other Commonwealth countries and been imitated in so many and varying forms in other parts of the world outside the British family of nations. The essential characteristics of parliamentary government are very simple: a politically irresponsible head of state, a Cabinet which is politically responsible to Parliament and must resign if it fails to command a majority, and the power of dissolution. The essential point is that the government must always act in accordance with the will of the people, expressed directly in general elections and indirectly through Parliament in the intervals between elections. As the Cabinet is responsible to Parliament, it cannot act in defiance of the wishes of Parliament or of the electorate on any matter of importance. If such differences do arise, it becomes necessary to find a new government whose policy is in accordance with the wishes of Parliament and of the country.

Parliamentary government is based upon collaboration between different organs with independent powers. It cannot exist where all the functions of the state are concentrated in a single body or where there is a rigid separation of powers. But the requisite balance of power need not always take the same form. There are many possible types of parliamentary government, the form of which varies considerably from country to country.

It would be conceivable for the legislature and the executive to have approximately equal powers. It would not normally be possible to maintain such an equal balance for any length of time, however, even if it could ever be realised in actual practice.

In many parliamentary regimes the legislature has become the dominant organ. The logical justification for this is that the Cabinet is merely an emanation of Parliament which is itself the more representative body, and there can be no genuine democracy unless the lower House of Parliament, directly elected by universal suffrage, always has the last word. This form of parliamentary government has been adopted in France since the establishment of the Third Republic. It sometimes, though not necessarily, leads to government by assembly.

Parliamentary government may also develop in the opposite direction. The Cabinet can become the dominant political organ, able to control the government of the country and direct the work of Parliament which assists it in the execution of its programme. A dominant executive can also be defended on theoretical grounds. The Cabinet, no less than Parliament, comes into being as the result of an election which more or less determines its composition. Under certain electoral and party systems the electorate may be able to give a direct mandate to a particular team of men pledged to carry out a definite policy. The party which has a majority forms the government, and at the next general election has to answer for the way in which it has carried out its mandate. Members of the majority party in Parliament support the Cabinet and accept its leadership because they recognise that the source of its power is thoroughly democratic, being founded upon the will of the people, and because they know that unless they do so there is no prospect of the promises which they made to the voters when they were elected being carried out during the life of that Parliament.

Every system of parliamentary government naturally has its own distinctive features, resulting from a complex combination of many different factors. History, the national temperament, beliefs and ideologies, conventions of political behaviour, the electoral system, political parties, attempts to imitate a particular model or to avoid certain dangers, and sometimes sheer chance, all play their part.

Thus in Great Britain the relationships between the Crown, Parliament and the Cabinet have gradually developed to produce a unique parliamentary regime in which the executive is now the dominant organ. The Crown has had to withdraw from active participation in politics. Parliament remains legally sovereign and in theory the supreme organ in the state, but it is no exaggeration to say that effective political power is nowadays concentrated in the small group of men who constitute the Cabinet.

The supremacy of the Cabinet has never been declared in any written document. In Britain few constitutional principles have been laid down in writing, and the true nature of the political system cannot be discovered from any legal texts. But this does not make 'Cabinet government' any the less a reality. It should not be taken to imply simply parliamentary government, as it has been by some continental writers. It has a more specific and restricted meaning. The British Cabinet has more freedom and more power than any other democratic executive except possibly the President of the United States.

In studying the British political system, it is generally unwise to try to trace out any systematic line of development, and any summary description is bound to be misleading. Nevertheless, it is necessary to show how the executive has acquired and consolidated its dominant position and how this has been reconciled with the principles of democracy. This can be explained by considering the Cabinet from two different points of view: first, as the heir to the prerogatives of the Crown, and then as a government deriving its political authority from the people.

Chapter One

THE CABINET AS HEIR TO THE PREROGATIVES OF THE CROWN

THE continued and uninterrupted existence of the monarchy and the respect in which the Crown is held in Great Britain can only be explained in the light of the history of the supreme organs of the state. We must therefore see how parliamentary government has developed, imperceptibly influenced by a number of factors peculiar to Great Britain.

Originally the King not only reigned but really ruled the country. This remained true until the seventeenth century. The King had some advisers, but he was under no obligation to act in accordance with their recommendations. Charles II ruled as an absolute monarch with complete control over the executive. But his powers of decision meant that he was held responsible for policy, and the people, in so far as they had any coherent opinions and were able to voice them through the aristocratic and unrepresentative Parliament, demanded the right to make their views known. So long as the King kept the government of the country in his own hands, criticism of his policy meant revolution. In 1649 and in 1688 the British people did resort to revolutionary methods, and by this means a constitutional monarchy was established.

It was not by revolutionary means, however, that the British gradually evolved a system which ensured that, although the monarchy remained, the government was dependent on popular support. The origins of the Cabinet are to be found in the increasingly important part played by the personal advisers upon whom the King relied to obtain the support of Parliament, especially when he wanted it to vote him money. One of these advisers, usually the First Lord of the Treasury, would be a leading member of Parliament who acted as an intermediary between the King and the parliamentary majority. In some cases such persons assumed a more important rôle, and although the office of Prime Minister was slow to emerge, it became customary for the King to consult those who could command a majority in Parliament and to act as they advised.

The accession of the Hanoverians facilitated the transition to a system in which the King still reigned but no longer actually took decisions or assumed responsibility for policy, which was henceforth determined in accordance with the wishes of Parliament. The monarchy was thus placed above criticism, rebellion and revolution. Once it ceased to wield any effective authority, it had no longer to fear any attack on its prerogatives. Its powers—and its fear of losing power—both passed to the Cabinet and to its leader, who became known as the Prime Minister.

The legal position of the Crown remains unchanged. The people are still in theory the Queen's subjects; Parliament owes its very existence to the sovereign by whom it is summoned, prorogued and dissolved; ministers are the servants of the Crown; money paid into the Treasury is the Queen's revenue; and the land itself is her royal domain.

All this now refers, not to the Queen personally, but to an abstract legal concept of the Crown that embraces all the powers, prerogatives and sovereign rights exercised in the Queen's name by the Prime Minister and other members of the Cabinet.

The Cabinet is almost entirely a customary and not a legal institution. It has been moulded by historical events, by empirical measures taken to meet the needs of particular political situations, by the gradual growth of the party system, and by the way that the country has become progressively more democratic without abandoning its traditional institutions. These forces have gradually determined the composition of the Cabinet, perfected its organisation under the Prime Minister's leadership, and strengthened its influence and power.

I. THE COMPOSITION OF THE CABINET

The rules governing the composition of the Cabinet combine respect for the past with a realistic effort to face up to the political needs of the present.

The Origins of the Cabinet

The origins of Cabinet government are well known. It developed out of the practice, not at all peculiar to England, whereby the King used to surround himself with a group of advisers. The King's government included the holders of certain offices under the Crown and, in addition, a Privy Council very similar to the King's Council in France. Under Henry II, the Council and the Courts of Common Law became distinct emanations of the King's *curia*. The Privy Council had political and administrative functions, and during the fourteenth and fifteenth centuries it was the deliberative body within which royal decisions were taken. Under the Tudors, the Privy Council was itself divided into an executive and a judicial branch, the latter being the famous Court of Star Chamber which remained in existence until 1641. Meanwhile the Privy Council gradually increased in size until the King began to select a few of its members to form a Committee of State or Cabinet of particularly trusted advisers whose existence and proceedings were more or less secret, to whom he would confide the most important affairs of state. This had become a firmly established practice by the beginning of the seventeenth century, as the executive had to deal with many complicated questions which could not be discussed at the meetings of the large Privy Council. A notable example of such an inner committee was the Cabal formed by Charles II after the fall of Clarendon, the name of which was derived from the initials of its members— Clifford, Arlington, Buckingham, Ashley and Lauderdale. The British Cabinet is now an emanation of Parliament whose members are drawn from the party that the people have chosen to form a government. Nevertheless, the modern Cabinet is in the direct line of succession from what was once the instrument of personal rule.

The Privy Council

The Privy Council remains in existence, and this antiquated institution is still the official council of the sovereign. It has several hundred members, who have the title of 'Right Honourable' and must take a special oath of obedience and secrecy. They include all present and former ministers, the Prince of Wales, the Royal Dukes, the Archbishop of Canterbury, the Archbishop of York, the Bishop of London, the Speaker of the House of Commons, the Lords Justices of Appeal, the Lord Chief Justice, retired diplomats, judges, and leading figures in the fields of literature, science and the arts. Anyone who is not a member by virtue of his office may be summoned to the Privy

Council by a declaration of the Queen in Council, and members may be excluded from the Council by the same procedure. This occurred in the case of Fox in 1798 and of Sir Edgar Speyer in 1921. The Lord President of the Council, who presides over the Privy Council and is in charge of the Privy Council Office, is a Cabinet minister and usually one of the leading members of the government.

Individually, members of the Privy Council have a number of traditional prerogative rights. They can, in theory, exercise all the powers of a justice of the peace anywhere in the country. They are also in theory entitled to participate in the proceedings of the House of Lords, though in practice they hardly ever make use of this privilege.

The Council itself has not been altogether deprived of its corporate functions. These, however, have gradually become almost entirely a matter of form. The only occasions when the whole Council meets as a body is on the marriage of a King or Queen and after the death of the sovereign, when the Council, together with the Lords Spiritual and Temporal of the Kingdom and 'numbers of other gentlemen of quality', proclaims the accession of the successor to the throne.

On the other hand, there are frequent informal meetings of the Council, when only a very small number of members are present. These are held for the purpose of receiving oaths of office, appointing and removing holders of posts in the appointment of the Crown and receiving homage from bishops. The Council's most important functions are to issue orders in council and to make certain types of proclamations, such as those summoning, dissolving or proroguing Parliament, or declaring war, neutrality or a blockade. The Council does not deliberate on these matters, but simply gives its formal assent to executive acts already decided on by ministers or by the Cabinet. Orders in council are used by the government to give effect to its policy whenever it does not need to seek new powers from Parliament. The historic Privy Council has thus become the normal means of making statutory instruments for enacting the 'delegated legislation' which is now the subject of so much comment and criticism in view of its rapid increase following the recent growth in the powers of the executive. The quorum at these informal Council meetings is three. The Secretary of the Council usually summons four or, more often, six privy councillors, all of whom will be Cabinet ministers. The minutes of the meetings signed by the Secretary give authority to its proceedings. The Council meets in the presence of the Queen. Without her there can be no Privy Council, but only a committee meeting.

The Privy Council is also, in effect, a list of persons from amongst whom the members of certain committees must be selected. These vary greatly in importance. Most were once executive organs, all the effective powers of which have now passed to some government department. The best known is the Board of Trade, established in 1706, which has not met since the end of the Napoleonic Wars, the President of the Board of Trade being today no different from any other departmental minister. The Ministry of Health, the Ministry of Agriculture and Fisheries and the Board of Education (which became a Ministry in 1944) each took over executive functions formerly vested in a committee of the Privy Council. A few of these committees still exist, such as those which have advisory functions in respect of Jersey and Guernsey, the universities of Oxford and Cambridge, the Scottish universities, and the charters of municipal corporations. One committee of real importance is the Judicial Committee of the Privy Council, membership of which is confined to judges, former Lord Presidents and Lord Chancellors, and two other persons appointed by the Crown. It was constituted in 1833 as a supreme court for the British Empire over which the King in Council retained the jurisdiction which he lost in respect of England at the time of the Long Parliament. The subsequent development of the Commonwealth, however, has not left the Judicial Committee any substantial power in regard to those Commonwealth countries which are now virtually sovereign states.

One other committee of the Privy Council must certainly not be overlooked as it occupies the key position in the whole of the British system of government. This is the Cabinet itself, which has acquired all the main political functions formerly vested in the Privy Council and which have now been greatly expanded.

The Cabinet, as we have seen, was originally an emanation of the Privy Council. Cabinet government came into being through the efforts of Parliament to ensure that it should be clearly known who were the King's advisers and that they should be held publicly responsible for their advice. Parliament repeatedly demanded—in 1341, in 1376, under Richard II, and subsequently under the Lancastrians until 1437—that the King should choose his councillors from among members of the two Houses. By the end of the reign of Charles II, the King had a distinct body of intimate advisers, but decisions were still taken by the Privy Council and the emerging Cabinet was generally regarded with suspicion. This mistrust was reflected in two provisions of the Act of Settlement, designed to restore the old advisory functions of the Privy Council and to make it illegal for a member of the House of Commons to hold any office of profit under the Crown. In 1705, however, these clauses were repealed. Had they remained in force, parliamentary government could never have developed as it has, and the House of Lords would have been bound to assume a much more influential position. As it was, a Cabinet system began to develop in the reign of Queen Anne. The functions of the Council increasingly tended to become a mere formality, while important decisions were taken by the chief ministers meeting in the presence of the Queen, and their collaboration gave rise to a growing sense of ministerial solidarity.

Another major development took place after the Hanoverian accession. As George I did not speak English, the sovereign ceased to be present at Cabinet meetings. The governmental responsibilities of the Crown consequently diminished, and those of the Prime Minister were correspondingly enlarged. George II, like his father, was more interested in Hanover than in Britain, where Sir Robert Walpole came to power in 1721 and steadily increased his influence. His opportunist devices and corrupt practices enabled him to secure and retain the support of a majority in Parliament. He surrounded himself with a group of ministers who were all of the same party and resigned when they lost the confidence of the House of Commons instead of when they fell out of favour with the King. After Walpole's time, ministerial solidarity disappeared again until 1782, when Lord Rockingham formed a government based upon the same principle which subsequently became the generally accepted rule. With the appointment of the younger Pitt in 1783, there was once again a Prime Minister who was unquestionably the leading figure in the government. The changes wrought in the political system by the Reform Act meant that in 1834 Sir Robert Peel occupied a position not fundamentally different from that of a modern Prime Minister. After 1841 it was definitely accepted that the Cabinet was politically responsible to the House of Commons.

The Cabinet Today

It would certainly be an exaggeration to say that the Cabinet is still no more than a committee of the Privy Council. Every Cabinet minister must be a privy councillor, but the Council itself has no authority over the Cabinet. Nevertheless, the special features characteristic of the composition of modern Cabinets—now the intermediary between the sovereign and Parliament—and the development of the Cabinet in response to the establishment of constitutional monarchy and the democratisation of the House of Commons, are best explained in the light of its origins.

In the first place, the sovereign relies upon the Cabinet in order to obtain parliamentary support, so that Cabinet ministers have to be in close touch with both Houses and able to speak and reply to criticism in Parliament. Ministers must therefore be chosen from among the members of the two Houses. The appointment of peers has never created any difficulty. Members of the King's Council were more often than not members of the upper House, and for many years there were always a large number of peers in the Cabinet. On the other hand, we have seen how the House of Commons at one stage tried to make its members ineligible for ministerial office in the belief that such appointments would weaken their control over the executive. Nowadays, however, it is a firmly established rule that Cabinet ministers should sit in one of the two Houses of Parliament. There have been some departures from this rule: Gladstone, General Smuts, Ramsay MacDonald and Mr Malcolm Mac-Donald were all at one time in the Cabinet without having a seat in Parliament. But these were quite exceptional instances, all of short duration, and have not encouraged any repetition of the experiment. Such appointments would be frowned upon by Parliament, and a minister without a seat in either House would be a very heavy burden for a Cabinet which has to govern in conjunction with Parliament and in accordance with parliamentary conventions and procedures. It is now almost inconceivable that anyone should be in the Cabinet without being a member of Parliament, except possibly if he were in the process of trying to find a seat. Any minister who failed to secure election and was not willing to accept a peerage would have to resign his office.

As the House of Commons has grown more influential, it has naturally become usual for the majority of ministers, including the holders of the most important offices, to sit in the lower House. Labour governments have hardly ever included more than the minimum of three peers other than the Lord Chancellor prescribed by the Ministers of the Crown Act, 1937. The special powers of the lower House in regard to finance make it essential for the Chancellor of the Exchequer, the Financial Secretary to the Treasury and the Financial Secretary at the War Office to be in the Commons. Otherwise, the Prime Minister is free to decide which ministers should sit in each House. This will depend on the attitude of the opposition and the extent to which any particular department requires a spokesman of Cabinet rank to defend it in the House of Commons. In any case, it is seldom politically desirable for a government to have an unduly large number of ministers in the House of Lords.

Ministers not only have to have a seat in Parliament, but are actually selected for office on the basis of their performance as private members. Once a member is elected, he must first prove his worth before he has any hope of promotion to one of the front benches—the Treasury Bench if his party is in power, or else the opposition Front Bench. According to Gladstone, Sir Robert Peel first made it a rule that no one should be admitted to the Cabinet until he has had previous experience of government office. This is still the accepted general principle, although not always rigidly adhered to in practice. The usual ladder of advancement for a successful member of Parliament is, after some years on the back benches, to become parliamentary private secretary to a minister and thence to progress to a minor post in the government before being placed in charge of a department.

Cabinet Homogeneity

Another characteristic feature of the Cabinet is its homogeneity. We have already seen how the party structure and the electoral system result in power alternating between the two main parties, one of which always has an absolute majority of seats in the House of Commons. It follows that Cabinet government is usually government by a single party which has been returned to power by popular vote. Here again the present position is the outcome of a series of historical events. Before 1688, the King's Cabinet was composed of privy councillors chosen primarily because they commanded the confidence of the sovereign himself. Although possibly selected because of their influence with Parliament, they did not necessarily all belong to the same party. The five ministers of the Cabal government, for example, had really no common policy. After 1688, however, Parliament had succeeded in asserting its control over the prerogatives of the Crown, and could prevent the King from governing otherwise than in accordance with the wishes of the parliamentary majority. It became recognised that the close link between the government and Parliament—now a well-established feature of the British political system and the key to the power of the Cabinet—would most easily be achieved if the entire Cabinet was appointed from the parliamentary majority. The first politically homogeneous Cabinet was formed in 1695 when William III, probably on the advice of the Duke of Sunderland, decided to exclude the Tories from his government and have a Cabinet entirely composed of Whigs. This Cabinet, however, lasted only four years. In the following century, after Walpole's time, there were some very heterogeneous ministries. As late as 1782 it was still possible for former ministers who had fallen from power to be included in the new government along with their political opponents, the latter being the true Cabinet which alone had any real power.

After 1782, however, the idea of party government was generally accepted. Some critics pointed out how a considerable number of the political leaders of the country would always be excluded from office, but little weight was attached to such arguments, the fallacy of which had been demonstrated by Chatham's government of 1766 which was a non-partisan ministry embracing the most able men from every political group. In Britain, as in other countries where there is no proportional representation, coalition government would almost certainly lead to difficulties in parliamentary elections. Besides, strong and efficient government would be impossible without a stable and united Cabinet, untroubled by any hard bargaining and transitory compromises between rival political groups. The political homogeneity of the Cabinet produces that close relationship of mutual confidence between the government and the parliamentary majority which Trevelyan has described as the secret of the British constitution.

This does not mean that Britain has never had a coalition government. War Cabinets were formed at times when it was necessary for the whole nation to unite in the struggle against a common enemy, and that of 1940-45 appears to have proved quite as efficient as any politically homogeneous Cabinet. Nevertheless, the Labour Party annual conference in 1944 decided to appeal to the country with an independent'programme as soon as it was possible to hold a general election, and the coalition government only lasted fifteen days after the end of the war with Germany.

There had previously been other coalition governments at times when the political situation made one-party government impossible, chiefly when there was no single party with a clear majority. The governments of 1852-55, 1895-1905, 1915-22 and 1931-40 are generally regarded as coalitions, but it is doubtful whether this description is appropriate to them all as the parties which combined to form the government often became completely united shortly afterwards. Thus the Unionist government of 1900-05 was not a true coalition, and the 'National' governments of 1935-40, if not those of 1932-35, were really Conservative. It is still true, therefore, that Britain has had few coalition governments and that these have generally been short-lived and seldom very successful. Disraeli maintained that the British do not care for coalitions, and always revert to a single-party government whenever possible. Any differences which arise within the majority party tend to be resolved through internal party channels. In this way the unity and stability of the government are preserved, its powers are clearly defined and its position consolidated by strong party organisation and discipline.

The Cabinet and the Government

In considering the composition of the government, a clear distinction must be drawn between the Cabinet and the government.

The government is a broader term embracing all those persons, united by ties of loyalty to their party, who are jointly responsible to Parliament for the policies followed by the leaders of the majority. The government usually consists of some sixty to ninety persons, including not only the leading ministers but all other heads of departments, ministers of state, secretaries and under-secretaries of state, parliamentary secretaries, Junior Lords, law officers and officers of the Royal Household, some of whom are parliamentary whips. There is a parliamentary secretary or under-secretary for each of the principal government departments, who is the minister's political deputy. A government is thus a large body which does not meet together or decide on national policy. It is, however, an important group of men who, having agreed to serve under the Prime Minister, can be relied upon to defend the Cabinet in Parliament and to cast a substantial number of votes in its favour whenever the outcome of a division is at all in doubt.

The Cabinet itself is the pivot of the whole system of government, consisting of a small number of leading men in the government who are also the leaders of the party in power. It includes the heads of some important departments, such as the Lord Chancellor, the Chancellor of the Exchequer, the President of the Board of Trade, the First Lord of the Admiralty, the Ministers of Defence, Education, Labour, Agriculture and Health, and the Secretaries of State for Foreign Affairs, Home Affairs, the Colonies, Commonwealth Relations and Scotland. Other Cabinet ministers occupy important offices of state which carry few administrative responsibilities, like those of Lord President of the Council, Lord Privy Seal, and Chancellor of the Duchy of Lancaster. All these offices are generally considered as either necessarily or potentially of Cabinet rank. There are no fixed rules, however, and it is left to each Prime Minister to decide in the light of the political situation at the time which ministers to include in his Cabinet. The Attorney-General and the Postmaster-General have sometimes been included, while the Chancellor of the Duchy of Lancaster, the President of the Board of Trade and the First Lord of the Admiralty are sometimes omitted. Ministers not in the Cabinet are usually invited to attend its meetings if matters relating to their departments are to be discussed. The Prime Minister may in fact invite any person, including those who hold no government office, to any Cabinet meeting at which it is thought that their advice may be of value.

The number of Cabinet ministers has never been rigidly fixed, and the growing complexity of modern politics has naturally tended to result in larger Cabinets. In Pitt's time there were usually six or seven ministers in the Cabinet, in the nineteenth century more often about a dozen, and today the total is generally in the region of twenty. The British regard this as a maximum which no Cabinet should exceed, and have so far managed to keep within this limit by making some important changes in the structure of the Cabinet and its methods of work. In times of crisis the Cabinet is usually smaller. The War Cabinet in the first World War had five members. That of 1940-45 varied between five and nine, who worked in conjunction with other specialised organs concerned with conduct of military affairs. The Cabinet formed during the economic crisis of 1931 contained only ten ministers. The Prime Minister always has full discretion to vary the composition of his Cabinet in accordance with the dictates of the current political situation.

The Members of the Government

Prime Ministers had more difficulty in asserting another of their constitutional prerogatives—the right to choose the other members of the government and submit their names to the sovereign for appointment. The sovereign was obviously in a position to exert some influence on the choice of ministers. Queen Victoria in particular often expressed personal preferences or made objections to a particular candidate. But even she had to give way where her objections were political, and subsequently the sovereign has assumed a far less active rôle. If there were any disagreement between the Queen and the Prime Minister, the latter would inevitably have the last word. If the Queen refused to give way, she would have to find another Prime Minister, but she could not choose anyone else from the same party without interfering in the internal affairs of the party, which would be contrary to the established constitutional practice. Yet she could not call upon the leader of another party without going against the wishes of the people, which are usually quite clear from the results of the last general election.

The Prime Minister naturally does not form his government without consulting the other leading men in the party. In allocating the principal portfolios, he is often limited by the personal preferences of his colleagues, their standing in the party hierarchy, and the positions they have already held in the outgoing Cabinet or whilst in opposition. From the political point of view, it is important for different points of view in the party, or at least its two main wings, to be accurately represented in the government, which must therefore be a kind of coalition between the various groups. It is also desirable to have a Scot as Secretary of State for Scotland and a Welshman in charge of Welsh affairs. Younger members of the party must be included, at least in the more junior positions, in sufficient numbers to prevent the government becoming too much out of touch with its back benchers. The principal ministers and heads of departments must always be consulted on the appointment of the secretaries and under-secretaries of state, junior ministers and parliamentary secretaries who are to work under them, and it is sometimes important that a minister and his deputy should not sit in the same House, not even if they were both to be in the House of Commons.

All the same, the Prime Minister has a large amount of discretion in the choice of his colleagues. Similarly, he alone has the power to ask the sovereign to dismiss a minister or, as more frequently occurs, to secure a minister's resignation should this become necessary. This does not happen very often, as no one who has not the full confidence of the Prime Minister is ever appointed to any position in the government. On the other hand, the longevity of British governments means that changes in the political situation or other practical considerations sometimes make it necessary for a Prime Minister to reconstruct his Cabinet, although this is always managed very discreetly.

The Prime Minister thus surrounds himself with Cabinet ministers and other members of the government who are chosen primarily on the basis of their standing in the party, their parliamentary record and their experience in previous governments also being taken into account.

Ministers are not usually experts in any particular subject, since party government seldom permits the appointment of specialists. British opinion on this point is similar to that in France and other parliamentary democracies. An expert may be a first-rate executive head of a department, but he is rarely a good departmental minister. There are only a very few questions to which the minister can give close personal attention, so specialist knowledge is of little value and might even be a positive hindrance.

The qualities required in a minister are not the same as those which make a good civil servant. In the first place, the minister ought not as a rule to make a close personal study of any of the questions with which his department is concerned. Consequently he needs to be a good judge of men, so that he can rely upon the advice of his officials and delegate responsibility wherever necessary. He must be able quickly to grasp the essentials of any problem with which he is faced and to bring the light of common sense to bear upon controversies between experts, and he must always see the affairs of his own department as part of the policy of the government as a whole. He must be able to sense what is politically desirable, and what would be acceptable to public opinion. Finally, he is responsible for taking decisions, and must therefore be able to act quickly and to take a sufficiently broad view of the issues at stake. These qualities are not common. Where they exist they are sometimes accompanied by a certain lack of initiative and imagination. The British, however, do not consider the latter necessarily undesirable in a minister, especially in time of peace. Sir Robert Peel, a man utterly without imagination, is still regarded as the model Prime Minister. Nevertheless, in war-time, it has been found better to replace men like Salisbury, Asquith and Neville Chamberlain with such personalities as Disraeli, Joseph Chamberlain, Lloyd George and Winston Churchill.

Nor must it be forgotten that a minister has to be a skilled politician able to win support for his policies in the country and, even more important, to defend his policy convincingly in Parliament. Gladstone was equally gifted in both these respects. Some Labour leaders, however, of whom Ramsay MacDonald was one of the earlier examples, found that qualities which made them very successful public speakers in the country put them at a disadvantage in the House. Others, such as Disraeli and Sir Robert Peel, have been infinitely more at ease in

Parliament than in the country. Despite all developments in publicity and propaganda techniques, the kind of external show and theatrical mannerisms which are such an asset to a candidate for the Presidency in the United States still make very little impression in Great Britain. Ministers are chosen primarily on the basis of their performance in the House of Commons. The House is still considered the best judge of the qualities which go to make a good minister, and it is never carried away by eloquence or intelligence alone. Consequently, apart from the leading Cabinet ministers, the majority of the government are frequently quite unknown to the general public.

Though the qualities which go to make a good minister are revealed by a member's performance in Parliament, they can only be developed gradually as he is given experience in a variety of different government offices. Transfers from one department to another, although upsetting to the more pedestrian characters, are generally a valuable means of broadening a man's outlook when it has been too narrow. They prevent the men who should be directing the government of the country from becoming mere bureaucrats with nothing but their seniority to distinguish them.

It is the essence of parliamentary government that there should be a minister in charge of each department to ensure that the government is carried on in accordance with the wishes of the people. The composition of the British Cabinet clearly has to reflect the prevailing public opinion. The organisation of the Cabinet reveals other ways in which it is a genuine form of government by opinion.

II. THE ORGANISATION OF THE CABINET

The organisation of the Cabinet developed empirically to meet the needs of concrete political situations. For a long time the law was absolutely silent on the subject, which still is almost exclusively determined by custom and in the last resort is within the discretion of the Prime Minister.

From the legal point of view, the Cabinet is still an informal gathering of 'Her Majesty's trusted servants'. Just as there is no statute governing its composition, so there is no law that requires it to meet, defines its powers, or lays down the general conditions under which it must conduct its affairs. Until the first World War there was no Cabinet Secretariat, no record was kept of Cabinet decisions, and its procedure was left entirely to the discretion of the Prime Minister. In so far as there was any co-ordination of government activities, this was almost always achieved by *ad hoc* devices, chiefly through the personal influence of the Prime Minister. Today the position has changed somewhat, but the Prime Minister is still the keystone of the whole government edifice, whose rôle in the British political system is possibly even more important now than ever before.

The Prime Minister

The Prime Minister was originally a privy councillor chosen by the King to form a Cabinet and upon whom the sovereign used to rely to secure parliamentary support for his policies. The growing prominence of financial issues and the increasing powers of the House of Commons meant that the First Lord of the Treasury was generally the most influential member of the lower House. His position was strengthened when George I ceased to attend Cabinet meetings and left Sir Robert Walpole to take the chair and keep the sovereign informed of the proceedings. The King could only secure the support of a majority in Parliament through his chief minister, who soon found himself in a position to direct the policy of the government and keep it in line with the wishes of the parliamentary majority. As early as 1803, the younger Pitt spoke of the absolute necessity 'that there should be an avowed and real Minister, possessing the chief weight in council and the principal place in the confidence of the King. . . . That power must rest in the person generally called the First Minister.'

The title of Prime Minister was not used officially until many years later. In 1878 Disraeli signed the Treaty of Berlin as 'Prime Minister of England', and in 1905 the Prime Minister was included in the official order of precedence immediately after the Archbishop of York. The Prime Minister was not mentioned in an Act of Parliament before the Ministers of the Crown Act, 1937, which granted him a salary of £10,000 and a pension of £2,000 a year. Long before that, however, the Prime Ministership had been an office of great importance politically. Its occupants had included such distinguished figures as William Pitt, Lord Melbourne, Sir Robert Peel, Lord Palmerston,

Gladstone and Disraeli. The office could not attain formal recognition until Parliament had first overcome its mistrust of the sovereign's advisers. After the Cabinet had become an executive committee of Parliament, it had to be accepted that the leader of the majority should invariably be the chief minister. Then the House of Commons had to be made the fount of political power by means of the series of electoral reforms begun in 1832. The majority in the Commons had then to be persuaded that they ought to support those who exercised power on their behalf. Finally, the Prime Minister, who was already the acknowledged leader of the party chosen by the electorate to form a government, had to be recognised as the unquestioned leader of the Cabinet.

By these distinct but overlapping stages the Prime Minister emerged as the head of the government of Great Britain. His actual power naturally varies according to his personality and the extent to which he is supported by his party. His present position, however, does not at all correspond to what Lord Morley defined as '*primus inter pares*' and Sir William Harcourt as '*inter stellas luna minores*'. The Prime Minister can control the composition of the Cabinet, because of his power to ask for the resignations of his colleagues, to resign himself, or to ask for a dissolution. He presides at Cabinet meetings, where his influence is always dominant, though it varies somewhat according to his personality and that of his colleagues. He decides whether any question shall come before the Cabinet, and it falls to him to resolve any differences between Cabinet ministers and so to exercise his authority as its leader of the government that its unity is not endangered.

Many decisions which do not need to be referred to the Cabinet are made with the approval of the Prime Minister, either in case of urgency or simply where it is thought fit to do so. Prime Ministers have often made public declarations or taken important decisions entirely on their own initiative without consulting the Cabinet. Instances in which a Prime Minister thus acted on his own authority and responsibility include Lord John Russell's policy regarding the Catholic hierarchy in 1850, Disraeli's purchase of the Khedive's Suez Canal shares in 1875, Mr Asquith's declaration on the introduction of universal suffrage, and Lloyd George's decision to summon an Imperial War Conference. During the second

World War, Mr Winston Churchill's exceptional position frequently enabled him to take essential military decisions without constantly consulting the War Cabinet, whom he merely informed at regular intervals of what was going on.

The authority of the Prime Minister has been further enhanced by his position in the various committees and sub-committees performing the preparatory work for full Cabinet meetings. These have developed, partly in response to war-time requirements, into a regular feature of the Cabinet system. The creation of the Cabinet Office—the administrative organ of the Cabinet Secretariat—has also helped to strengthen the position of the Prime Minister. His powers as regards internal affairs include the overall control of the Civil Service through the instrumentality of the Treasury. Appointments of permanent heads and chief financial officers of government departments require his approval. The Prime Minister also decides who shall be awarded titles and honours. In Commonwealth affairs he occupies a leading position on account of his contacts with other Commonwealth Prime Ministers and his chairmanship of Commonwealth Conferences and formerly of the Committee of Imperial Defence. In the international sphere, though the Prime Minister may not assume the active control of British foreign policy, it is nevertheless always directed in accordance with his views. Moreover, as the Prime Minister has to bear the chief burden of responsibility for Cabinet decisions, he may always refuse to countenance the ideas of other ministers and penalise any who refuse to conform by dropping them from his government. This means that it is normally impossible for any Cabinet minister to take an independent line on any issue.

Nor can other ministers enter into any direct relations with the sovereign without the full knowledge and consent of the Prime Minister, who has been the recognised channel of communication between the Cabinet and the Crown ever since Walpole's time. The precise nature of this relationship depends largely on the personality of each individual Prime Minister, but is also governed by a number of constitutional conventions.

Yet it cannot be said that the Prime Minister is free to determine policy just as he thinks fit. Many constitutional conventions provide an effective safeguard against any attempt at autocratic personal rule. First and foremost are the basic principles of parliamentary government itself. Nor could any modern Prime Minister follow the example of Sir Robert Peel and exercise personal supervision over the entire range of departmental activities. He must to a large extent rely upon his colleagues in the government. When the latter have been men like Joseph Chamberlain, Gladstone or Harcourt, the Prime Minister has certainly not been the dominant figure. To inspire confidence in the country, a Prime Minister needs to have a fairly strong personality, but he must not try to take upon himself the functions which properly belong to the Cabinet as a whole.

Though the rôle of Prime Minister varies with each occupant of the office, it is nevertheless true to say that he is always in fact the dominant figure in the executive, which is itself the dominant organ in the state. Although the preponderance of the executive is primarily due to the British system of party government and the consequent significance of general elections, another contributing factor is the position of the Prime Minister in relation to Parliament. In any other country, the lower house would probably be suspicious of an executive virtually elected by plebiscite, but there is no danger of this in Britain, since the Cabinet is really the executive committee of the parliamentary majority and the Prime Minister himself is a leading member of Parliament. The Prime Minister originally owed his authority to the fact that he had the confidence of the sovereign, but he only attained that position because he had had the confidence of Parliament, where it has always been the custom for the majority party to support the policies of its leader. The Prime Minister consequently attains the supreme office because of his standing in the party, which enables him, with the assistance of the whips, to control the votes of the parliamentary majority. Furthermore, it is always in his power to cut short the life of a Parliament by asking for a dissolution, which the sovereign cannot refuse.

Even without at this stage considering the extensive power of the Cabinet and the Prime Minister under the British parliamentary system, it will be clear that the Prime Minister is substantially free to organise the Cabinet as he thinks fit.

Cabinet Meetings

Cabinet meetings are held at number 10 Downing Street and now take place on the average about twice a week, compared with once a week before 1945. The Prime Minister will summon the Cabinet more frequently should the need arise, but it has hardly ever met more than about a hundred times in any one year, and seldom for more than two hours at a time. The Cabinet is essentially concerned with broad questions of general policy. It is not expected to be familiar with all the details of every issue before the government. Its functions were described in the report of the Machinery of Government Committee of 1918 as '(a) the final determination of the policy to be submitted to Parliament; (b) the supreme control of the executive in accordance with the policy prescribed by Parliament; and (c) the continuous co-ordination and delimitation of the activities of the several Departments of State'. Consequently a large number of questions never come before the Cabinet, which considers only such matters as are referred to it by the minister concerned or by the Prime Minister. Decisions made under prerogative powers, such as appointments of officials or awards of titles and honours, are not discussed in the Cabinet unless they have special political significance. Nowadays the Cabinet is never formally consulted on the question of when to ask the sovereign to dissolve Parliament. The budget proposals are never circulated to Cabinet ministers, but merely explained orally at a Cabinet meeting immediately before the budget is due to be presented to Parliament. Urgent questions may, in case of necessity, be decided by the responsible minister in consultation with the Prime Minister without reference to the rest of the Cabinet, as is particularly likely to happen in matters of foreign policy.

Another reason why the growing complexity of government business has not necessitated much longer or more frequent Cabinet meetings is because of recent efforts to improve the organisation of the executive and its methods of work.

The Cabinet Office

Until the first World War, there was no Cabinet Secretariat, no definite agenda for Cabinet meetings, and no records of Cabinet decisions apart from the Prime Minister's report to the sovereign.

Under war-time conditions the disadvantages of these haphazard methods were only too obvious. One of the first acts of

Lloyd George after he became Prime Minister was to equip the War Cabinet with a secretariat. For this purpose he took over the existing secretariat of the Committee of Imperial Defence, out of which the present Cabinet Office has developed. The initial success of the Cabinet Secretariat and the subsequent extension of its activities undoubtedly owed much to the personality and abilities of the first Secretary to the Cabinet, Sir Maurice (Lord) Hankey, and his successors, Sir Edward (Lord) Bridges (1939-45) and Sir Norman Brook. The Cabinet Office was reorganised in 1938, and its functions expanded considerably during the second World War. It is now responsible for circulating papers and memoranda on matters coming before the Cabinet and its committees; preparing agendas for their meetings as directed by the Prime Minister; summoning those required to attend meetings of the Cabinet or its committees; and taking and keeping minutes of their proceedings. In addition to the Secretariat proper, the Central Statistical Office is also part of the Cabinet Office. It used also to include the Economic Section responsible for preparing annual economic reports, but this was incorporated in the Treasury in 1953.

It should also be remembered that unless matters which come before the Cabinet are exceptionally urgent, they will already have been the subject of consultations between the departments concerned, and memoranda thereon will have been circulated to all Cabinet ministers. The Cabinet decides each week when it will meet in the following week, and the agenda is supposed to be drawn up two days before each meeting. Despite these preparatory arrangements, however, there is nothing to stop the Prime Minister postponing any item he does not consider ripe for discussion or altering the agenda, just as he could in former times.

Cabinet Committees

The most important development in the organisation of the Cabinet which has brought about a radical change in its traditional methods of work has been the increasing use of Cabinet committees. These have developed empirically, having first been set up by Prime Ministers who wished to discuss important issues with a small group of Cabinet ministers particularly concerned with or well qualified to advise on the subject. A committee was set up in 1853 on the question of whether to send the fleet to protect Constantinople. In 1878 the same issue was considered by a small 'inner Cabinet' which had already been formed by the Prime Minister to supplement the deliberations of the full Cabinet. Between the outbreak of war in 1914 and the formation of the War Cabinet, many decisions were taken in small Cabinet committees. The committee of 'the Six' assumed a leading rôle in the MacDonald Cabinet of 1931-35. In the Neville Chamberlain Cabinet, a small group consisting of the Prime Minister, Lord Halifax, Sir John Simon and Lord Runciman used to deliberate on major issues of policy.

It was in war-time, however, that the most striking developments in the committee system have taken place to meet the special circumstances of the time. In 1916-19 only the most crucial issues went before the War Cabinet, all lesser matters being referred to Cabinet committees. Similar arrangements were in operation during the second World War. Cabinet committees are less numerous in peace-time but they are still valuable for purposes of preliminary consultation on questions which have to go before the Cabinet for decision, and for deciding other questions under powers delegated to them by the Cabinet.

There are some standing committees, each concerned with some specific branch of government business, and other committees appointed *ad hoc* to deal with a particular issue. These committees reduce the burden of work falling upon the Cabinet and lessen the demands upon its members. They often include ministers not in the Cabinet and sometimes even parliamentary secretaries. The government representatives are usually accompanied by senior officials who attend in an advisory capacity and whose presence results in valuable savings of time. The Cabinet Secretariat also provides the secretariat for Cabinet committees and is responsible for preparing and circulating their reports and papers and for co-ordinating the work of the various committees.

Yet it is still unfortunately necessary for members of the government to work under great pressure, as there are many committees and there must be some Cabinet Ministers at least on every committee that deals with major issues. The Prime Minister always has to be chairman of a number of committees, and the Chancellor of the Exchequer must either sit or have a representative on nearly all, as practically all government business has some financial implications. But these drawbacks of the committee system are more than outweighed by its advantages. A committee is sometimes able to agree on a policy which the Cabinet can then adopt without further deliberation. Even if it fails to reach an agreement, it at least helps to prepare the way for a compromise as the basis for the ultimate decision.

The time taken to obtain a Cabinet decision on any matter naturally depends on many different factors. Amongst the most important is the attitude of the Prime Minister, whose wishes are often decisive. It is very rare for a vote to be taken in the Cabinet. When it is quite impossible to avoid 'counting heads', it is done discreetly and informally. Discussion usually continues until some compromise can be agreed. This may mean holding the matter over to a later meeting. In the end, however, differences are generally resolved because of the dominant influence of the Prime Minister and his colleagues' readiness to accept his leadership, owing to their anxiety not to be dropped from the government.

Inter-departmental Co-ordination

One of the essential purposes of the Cabinet is to co-ordinate the activities of different government departments. The function of determining a consistent overall policy originally belonged to the King. The Cabinet subsequently became the channel of co-ordination and the financial powers of the First Lord of the Treasury gave him, through the Cabinet, supreme control over every branch of government business. In the nineteenth century the Cabinet and the Prime Minister had only about a dozen departments to co-ordinate, and their activities were mostly far less extensive than they are today. The subsequent increase in the functions of the state has led to the creation of many new departments and services. Moreover, most of the questions with which modern governments have to deal involve collaboration between several different departments. Co-ordination is nearly always essential to ensure that they do not follow contradictory policies or encroach upon each other's responsibilities, and to prevent duplication of work, to resolve differences between departments, and to secure concerted government action.

In some instances co-ordination has been secured through the creation of new departments to take over a number of related functions, such as the Ministry of National Insurance and the Ministry of Town and Country Planning.

Since the first World War the most serious problems which have faced all governments have been in the military and economic spheres, where special co-ordinating machinery has had to be devised. On the military side this developed out of the Committee of Imperial Defence which was established well before 1914 and proved able to work very effectively in conjunction with the War Cabinets of 1914-19. A similar system was in operation between 1939 and 1945, and was gradually improved in the light of experience. The Prime Minister himself was in supreme control, by virtue of his very extensive powers as Minister of Defence and through his position as chairman of the Chiefs of Staff Committee and the Defence Committee and head of the War Cabinet. The Ministry of Defence remains in existence, and Mr Winston Churchill resumed the office for a short period when the Conservatives were returned to power in 1951.

The arrangements for the co-ordination of economic affairs have their origin in the Haldane Report of 1918 and the rather ineffective Economic Advisory Council which existed from 1930 to 1939. During the second World War, a special steering committee was established under the chairmanship of the Lord President of the Council to relieve the Cabinet as far as possible of the responsibility for co-ordinating economic policy. The committee was assisted by the Economic Information Unit of the Cabinet, the Production Committee and the Imports Committee. In the Attlee government, the primary responsibility for co-ordinating economic policy rested in turn with the Lord President of the Council, the Minister for Economic Affairs and, finally, with the Chancellor of the Exchequer, who had the services of a special Central Economic Planning Staff.

Particular ministers or 'superministers' have at times been given special responsibility for co-ordinating particular aspects of government business. Such arrangements were advocated by Mr Attlee in his book, *The Labour Party in Perspective*, published in 1937, and he tried to put these ideas into practice in his Cabinets of 1945-51. Mr Herbert Morrison, as Lord President of the Council, was chairman of a number of committees dealing with relations with Parliament and the legislative programme;

the Foreign Secretary, Mr Ernest Bevin, had general co-ordinating functions in respect of all overseas affairs; and Sir Stafford Cripps and his successor Mr Gaitskell were generally responsible, as Chancellor of the Exchequer, for the co-ordination of economic policy.

Somewhat different arrangements were introduced by Mr Winston Churchill in 1951, when a number of peers were appointed as special co-ordinating ministers. Lord Woolton, as Lord President, was made responsible for the co-ordination of the Ministries of Agriculture and Food; Lord Leathers was charged with the co-ordination of Transport, Civil Aviation and Fuel and Power; and Lord Cherwell, the Paymaster-General, was placed in charge of research and scientific policy. This system of 'overlords' was attacked by the Labour opposition on the ground that it blurred ministerial responsibilities and, in particular, that it undermined the control of the House of Commons over the government because the 'superministers' sat in the upper House and could not reply to their critics in the Commons. This experiment came to an end when the government was reconstructed on 14th September 1953. There was then a return to the usual system whereby co-ordination is secured, not through any special machinery, but by means of discussions in the Cabinet and through the influence of the Prime Minister, inter-departmental consultations before matters are brought before the Cabinet, frequent informal contacts between civil servants in different departments, and the preparatory work of the various Cabinet committees.

The work of the Cabinet is carried on within this organisational framework, most of which has been built up empirically. The Cabinet has to consider all the important questions that come before the government—changes in policy, proposed legislation, matters concerning more than one department, and issues upon which difficulties are likely to arise in Parliament or which have attracted particular attention among the public at large. These are the usual functions of the executive under any system of parliamentary government. The distinguishing feature of Cabinet government in Britain today, however, is the extraordinary political power which the government and the Prime Minister have acquired as a result of their administrative responsibilities.

III. THE POWERS OF THE CABINET

The Cabinet and the Prime Minister today exercise the supreme powers of government which used to belong to the sovereign in the days of absolute monarchy and are now only nominally vested in the Queen. With the development of parliamentary government, a clear distinction has emerged between the monarch as a person and the Crown, which is now a complex concept embracing, if not all the powers of public authorities, certainly all the most important powers of the state which are no longer exercised by the monarch but by the ministers of the Crown.

By comparison with those of the sovereign in the past, ministers' powers are in some ways more circumscribed and in others more extensive. The Cabinet has less power in so far as it has to be constantly mindful of Parliament and public opinion, and must respect the liberties of the individual and the supremacy of the law, and sometimes also, to a lesser extent, pay heed to wishes of the sovereign. On the other hand, ministers' powers have of course increased over the centuries as a result of the enormous growth in the functions of the executive. They are also able to rely on the unwavering support of a parliamentary majority which is usually politically homogeneous, of their party 'machine' and of the nation, which has given them a mandate to carry out their programme.

The powers of the executive are therefore exercised by the Cabinet or the Prime Minister. Some kinds of business are normally decided personally by the Prime Minister alone. These include the exercise of the prerogative of mercy, awards of titles and honours, the majority of appointments and, since 1918, the dissolution of Parliament. The Prime Minister does not usually consult his colleagues on these questions, though there is nothing to stop him bringing them before the Cabinet if he so desires. In any case, the Prime Minister will not take any important decisions without consulting the five or six leading men in his government—the 'inner Cabinet' in whom he places special confidence. Government policy is the outcome of informal discussions within this small group, which help to preserve ministerial solidarity and to ensure that the party remains loyal to its leader.

General Policy

The Cabinet and the Prime Minister are first of all responsible for laying down the broad principles of the foreign and domestic policy of the United Kingdom. All the most important issues are submitted to them and must be decided by the Cabinet. The Cabinet is responsible to its party, to Parliament and to the country, but in fact it is to a very large extent free to act as it thinks fit. We shall see this more clearly when we examine the nature of their accountability to Parliament. Decisions of the Cabinet also carry weight because its electoral success generally leaves it in a very strong position politically. It is no exaggeration to say that the British government holds the destiny of the country in its own hands, although this statement does perhaps call for some qualification in so far as Britain is a democratic country where freedom of opinion is respected.

Administration

The powers of the Cabinet give it control over the administrative system generally. This is made the more effective because the ministers in charge of the most important departments are generally themselves members of the Cabinet. The Cabinet itself, however, is the supreme deliberative and co-ordinating body with general responsibility for all departmental affairs, and the activities of semi-autonomous public corporations and other independent authorities are always subject to some measure of ministerial control. It is true that senior officials can in practice exert considerable influence in their departments. The traditional duties of a civil servant are, however, to see that his minister is fully informed on the questions to be decided and, once the decision has been taken by those politically responsible, to do everything in his power to carry out their policy even if it is at variance with what he would have advised. Ministers may also seek advice from sources outside their own departments and frequently consult various advisory bodies or independent experts unconnected with the Civil Service. Sometimes a department may become generally disposed to favour a particular line of policy, as the Board of Trade is said to have remained a stronghold of free trade at least until 1932, and the Foreign Office under Sir Robert Vansittart became markedly anti-German and pro-French. In practice, however, any change in the policy of the government implies a corresponding change in the policies of the officials concerned. This may mean some changes among the senior civil servants, though these are by no means inevitable and never very numerous, since the political neutrality which is a basic principle of the Civil Service tends to make new appointments unnecessary. Civil servants are generally ready to serve with equal loyalty under each successive government, while the responsibility for everything that goes on in the department falls exclusively on the minister in charge.

The Cabinet also decides who shall be appointed to all important public offices in the service of the Crown, whether in the United Kingdom or overseas. The government still retains control over Civil Service appointments even though recruitment is now based on individual merit. Each department has an Establishments Officer, who acts as a kind of chief personnel officer, and is responsible to the minister but works under the direction of the Treasury. The Prime Minister appoints the chief officials in each department, in all about a hundred permanent secretaries and deputy secretaries. The most striking characteristics of the British administrative system are, in the first place, the clear distinction between civil servants and politicians, and, secondly, the fact that the Cabinet has complete control over government policy and can rely on the Civil Service to do all in its power to assist it in carrying out its programme.

Appointments, Titles and Honours

The government can also exert some influence through its power to make certain appointments and decide on awards of titles and honours. These are no longer distributed primarily as a means of political patronage, but rather in the light of the principle enunciated by Sir Robert Peel, who maintained that in the long run the interest of a party will be better promoted by exercising this power honestly than by the perversion of it for the purpose of satisfying individual supporters. Nevertheless, Prime Ministers are not usually in practice indifferent to the political views of those whom they recommend for appointments or for important titles.

Although there is a merit system in the Civil Service, the

Prime Minister and his colleagues can still fill the leading positions in the departments with persons of their own choice.

Appointments in the church are still a matter of some general concern, even though the church no longer plays the active part in politics that it did in the past. There are about a thousand ecclesiastical appointments in the gift of the Crown, and of these some 700 of the most important dignitaries, including the archbishops and bishops from among whom the Lords Spiritual in Parliament are drawn and the deans and canons, are appointed on the recommendation of the Prime Minister, who usually seeks the advice of the Archbishop of Canterbury.

Judges are also appointed by the Crown. The puisne judges of the High Court are chosen by the Lord Chancellor, generally with the approval of the Prime Minister, and other judges of the higher courts are nominated by the Prime Minister, usually after consultation with the Lord Chancellor. Judges are not selected on political grounds, although political considerations may on occasions have some influence, but as their appointments are decided by the government they inevitably come under the control of the Cabinet. Since the end of the Victorian era the influence of the sovereign in all these questions has diminished and that of her ministers correspondingly increased, until it is now quite exceptional for a monarch to try to bring any pressure to bear.

The same could be said of the award of titles and honours. Apart from the Royal Victorian Order and the Order of Merit, which are the personal award of the sovereign, all other titles and honours are only conferred on the recommendation of the Prime Minister, or occasionally of some other minister. This obviously does not rule out the possibility of personal intervention by the sovereign, but it does mean that the Cabinet has now acquired most of the influence which can be derived from the exercise of these prerogatives.

At one time, titles were of course commonly conferred for political reasons. This was done by Sir Robert Walpole, and his method continued to be employed throughout the eighteenth century as a means of ensuring a government majority. After the Reform Act, the source of political influence shifted and direct undisguised patronage gave way to democratic action through organised parties. Nevertheless, a party can still benefit from the power to dispose of titles in recognition of services rendered.

Honours and decorations are awarded each year on New Year's Day and on the Queen's birthday, and also on such special occasions as a coronation or a jubilee. They are conferred on the recommendation of the Prime Minister. Lists of candidates for political honours are drawn up by the party organisation and receive particularly close scrutiny from the Parliamentary Secretary to the Treasury, the chief government whip. This practice has sometimes given rise to allegations that the Cabinet has been selling titles to raise party funds and political support. Such charges were made in quite definite terms on several occasions, notably in 1894, 1906, 1914, 1917 and 1919. Although no conclusive proof was given in support of these allegations, it was felt that nominations for honours should be made subject to examination by a committee of three privy councillors, not being members of the government, who would make a report to the Prime Minister which would ultimately be submitted to the sovereign. This procedure was introduced in 1922. Nowadays much less is heard of scandals in connection with honours, and it has become the custom for the Prime Minister to invite the leader of the opposition to put forward some recommendations. It is still true, however, that so long as respect for titles and their consequent prestige show no sign of abating in Britain, the power to dispose of these honours definitely adds to the influence of the Cabinet, at least in certain sections of the community.

Finance

None of the foregoing activities is of course as important as the day-to-day conduct of the government. Here the unchallenged supremacy of the Cabinet can be seen in several different ways.

One of the fundamental bases of Cabinet supremacy is the system of public finance. In some other countries, such as France, the lower House has always been sufficiently powerful to preserve the financial initiative of Parliament and see it was not severely curtailed. In Britain, on the other hand, the government has virtually the monopoly of initiative in financial affairs. No financial business, whether it relates to revenue or to expenditure, can be introduced in Parliament except by the Crown. The Crown asks for supply, and Parliament votes it funds to be spent in accordance with the budget estimates. The national finances are essentially a matter for the government. The Cabinet is left to assess the needs of the state in the light of its own particular policies, and to decide how these requirements should be met. It is one of the oldest conventions of the constitution that the Crown cannot levy any tax without first obtaining the approval of Parliament, and Parliament must authorise all expenditure. But despite the apparently complicated budgetary procedure, the government really has supreme control over the entire process.

The government's financial programme is presented to the House of Commons by the Chancellor of the Exchequer in his budget speech. The Chancellor is the minister in charge of the national finances, subject to the overriding authority of the Cabinet and the Prime Minister, and is responsible for preparing the budget in consultation with the various government departments. Any new tax can be brought into force at once, as it may be authorised by a simple resolution until the necessary legislation can be passed. The House of Commons has power to reduce any item in the estimates, but it cannot add to any vote, and only a minister can propose any new expenditure.

The various parts of the budget are considered in committees of the whole House. The Committee of Supply examines the estimates, and the Committee of Ways and Means is concerned with the methods of raising revenue. Several Acts of Parliament have to be passed before the budget proposals can come into effect, the most important being the Finance Act and the Appropriation Act.

This procedure ensures that all expenditure is approved by the House of Commons and no funds are used for any purpose other than that for which they were voted. Nevertheless, Parliament has very little effective control over finance. There are several reasons for this.

In the first place, Parliament has never thought it necessary to limit its authorisation to levy taxes to one year at a time. The income tax is voted annually, though the statutory provisions under which it is levied remain unchanged, but all other taxes are authorised by permanent legislation which continues in force until such time as Parliament decides otherwise. There are also a number of items of expenditure not subject to annual review. The chief amongst these are the Queen's Civil List, the service of the national debt, and the salaries of judges and of the Comptroller and Auditor-General, which have all been given permanent statutory authorisation. They constitute charges on the Consolidated Fund, for which there is no need to present estimates or to secure appropriations.

Moreover, the House of Commons is only allowed twenty-six days in any one year for consideration of the estimates, which is the means by which it exercises its power to approve the budget proposals. After the twenty-fifth day no further discussion is possible, and all the items not yet approved have to be put to the vote without debate. This means that only the most important votes are actually debated, and large sums are voted on the twenty-sixth day without any preliminary examination. In addition, provided that the Cabinet has a clear majority, as is usually the case, its estimates are in fact certain to be approved.

Finally, the government has in recent years secured a remarkably broad degree of freedom from parliamentary control in regard to borrowing, which is now a matter of fundamental importance. During the first World War it was recognised that detailed parliamentary authorisations for every state loan were no longer a practical possibility. The Treasury was therefore empowered to borrow large sums subject to very slender controls. Its powers have been continued and extended by other financial legislation since 1919, including the National Loans Acts of 1939 and 1944, the Miscellaneous Financial Provisions Act, 1946, and the various nationalisation statutes. A considerable proportion of the national revenue is thus required for the service of the national debt, and the sums necessary for this purpose are paid automatically out of the Consolidated Fund. The original loans are of course sanctioned by Parliament, but it only approves the total amount to be borrowed. The Cabinet is thus left almost completely free to direct the economic, financial and social life of the country, subject only to parliamentary scrutiny of its broad general policies.

Parliamentary control of the government's financial proposals has become more and more a mere formality on account of the increase in government expenditure and the great mass of detail contained in the estimates. This explains what was meant by

Professor Ramsay Muir, when he said that the power of the purse, supposed to be the source of the authority of the House of Commons, has now become quite unreal. Under no other parliamentary regime, he maintained, had Parliament less power in regard to finance than in Great Britain. This was the view of a very forthright critic of the 'Cabinet dictatorship', and his opinions may have been somewhat exaggerated. Nevertheless, there can be no doubt that the British government does possess extraordinarily large powers over finance.

Legislation

The power of the Cabinet is further increased by one other factor—its pre-eminent position in the field of legislation. This may appear a more surprising source of power, since the making of laws used to be regarded as essentially the function of Parliament, and legislative procedure is still based upon the principle that Parliament is sovereign. In the early nineteenth century it was still comparatively unusual for the government to initiate legislation, but what was then exceptional has now become the rule. The government in Britain is not merely the executive but also the leaders of the majority party, elected to give effect to policies that the nation has approved. The government has therefore to carry out a definite programme, which demands numerous changes in the existing laws and new Acts of Parliament. The interval between general elections gives the Cabinet only a relatively short time to carry out the tasks committed to it by the people, and whenever the 'swing of the pendulum' puts a different party in power, the newly elected government is always particularly pressed for time.

The Queen's Speech at the opening of each session announces the legislation which the government intends to ask Parliament to pass. The actual bills are later communicated to the two Houses, both of which are required to give almost complete priority to the consideration of government bills. Of the time devoted to public bills—the only ones of general application— only a very small proportion is given to 'private members' bills' introduced by members of Parliament outside the government. During the second World War the Churchill Cabinet decided to reserve all the time which the Commons could give to legislation for debates on government measures. Private members have since regained the rights which were then suspended, and under the present Standing Orders a definite number of Fridays are set aside each session for private members' bills. Nevertheless, these seldom get beyond the second reading stage, and even fewer finally reach the Statute Book. Usually they either succumb to opposition from the government or else the private member does not manage to steer them over all the procedural obstacles which they are liable to encounter in the legislative process, or—what most frequently occurs—the House chooses to devote its limited time to government bills. The Cabinet can also encroach upon the small amount of time reserved for private members' bills, as the Standing Orders allow a business motion to be passed to give the government's legislative programme what amounts to complete, overriding priority.

Before a minister introduces a bill in either House of Parliament, it has usually been approved by the Cabinet, put into shape by the Parliamentary Counsel to the Treasury, and passed by the Cabinet committee on legislation. Most bills are introduced in the House of Commons, and this is necessarily the case with all relating to finance. Altogether, the government initiates 90% of all Acts of Parliament.

Delegated Legislation

The Cabinet can also legislate on its own without recourse to Parliament, in a way reminiscent of the manner in which Kings were once able to legislate by royal decree. The growth of delegated legislation is a modern phenomenon, not at all peculiar to Great Britain, which results from the impossibility of adapting the principle of the separation of powers to fit the practical requirements of government in the twentieth century. Even in countries where the legislature is dominant, statutory regulations which are binding on all citizens are much more often made by the executive than by Parliament. In Britain where the Cabinet is dominant, there have, *a fortiori*, been even more substantial inroads upon the legislative functions of Parliament.

During the last fifty years innumerable Acts of Parliament have authorised the government or some particular minister to make regulations which have the force of law. The executive has acquired powers analogous to those granted by French laws that have conferred 'full powers' on a minister for a limited period. Parliament has expressly renounced all right to intervene in a great variety of subjects. The government's statutory instruments are just as much part of the law of the land as any Act of Parliament. They sometimes have to be confirmed by Act of Parliament, but more often they need only 'lie on the table' for a certain number of days, after which they come into force automatically unless Parliament has raised any objection, and the majority of regulations come into effect when made by the minister without any further preliminaries.

These powers of the executive were denounced as the 'new despotism' in the celebrated book by Lord Hewart, then Lord Chief Justice, and in some quarters criticisms were levelled against the 'dictatorship' of the Cabinet. This led to the appointment of a committee to inquire into ministers' powers, which reported in 1932. The Committee recommended a number of measures designed to prevent possible abuses but admitted that, for good or ill, delegated legislation was bound to be employed on an increasing scale. Most of their recommendations were never put into effect. The second World War called for an extension of all the prerogatives of the executive, and of its legislative powers in particular. The Emergency Powers Act, 1939, remained in force after the cessation of hostilities. The Supplies and Services Act, 1945, was severely criticised by the Conservatives while in opposition, but in 1951 Mr Churchill's government had to admit that it must not be allowed to lapse until the government could present Parliament with some other scheme to enable the executive to continue to exercise its rule-making powers.

Delegated legislation is still a controversial subject, regarded by some as a threat to the liberty of the individual, and a number of measures have been taken to establish more effective control over the prerogatives of the executive.

The Statutory Instruments Act, 1946, laid down provisions governing the exercise of delegated legislative powers, and specified the procedure to be followed in bringing statutory instruments before Parliament where this is required by the Act under which they are made. Two categories of statutory instruments are subject to proceedings in Parliament—those that may be annulled by a resolution or 'prayer' of either House, and others that cannot come into force until formally approved by an affirmative resolution in both Houses. There is a special procedure whereby, during a period of forty days, any member of Parliament may raise objections to a statutory instrument or draft made under delegated legislative powers. The House of Commons can keep watch over the exercise of these powers through its Select Committee on Statutory Instruments or 'scrutiny committee' which examines all instruments laid before Parliament and draws the special attention of the House to any whose purport makes this desirable, and in particular to any relating to finance or affecting the liberties of the subject.

These provisions do not attack the principle of executive legislation, but rather provide safeguards against abuses of the system or against excessive bureaucratic power. Though Parliament still has the last word, the initiative in subordinate legislation belongs to the Cabinet by whose authority statutory instruments are made.

The United Kingdom is now faced with the problems of operating a welfare state and a planned economy in which a large part of the economic and social life of the country has been brought under the control or influence of the state. Many activities in which the government is engaged could not be carried on without broad powers of delegated legislation. In present circumstances, therefore, there is no likelihood of any diminution of Cabinet supremacy in the field of legislation.

The supremacy of the Cabinet is clearly fundamental. It should not be considered in isolation but rather as an organic feature of this unique system in which the government and Parliament should be viewed as a single entity. The political situation is usually such as to give the Cabinet a homogeneous majority in the House of Commons, so that it can secure the passage of whatever Acts of Parliament are needed to carry out its party's legislative programme. But it would be technically impossible for Parliament to enact all the necessary legislation except at the cost of gross inefficiency and delay. Recognising this, the party in power continues to exercise general oversight over the government but leaves a great deal to be decided by the executive by means of statutory instruments.

So far as legislation is concerned, therefore, the Cabinet is undoubtedly dominant. This is another respect in which it seems to have succeeded to the powers of the sovereign. In the past, laws used to be made by the King in his Parliaments. Today, as we have seen, there has been a transfer of power. It is the Crown which legislates in Parliament, and the Crown, from the political point of view, really means the Queen's ministers. The government derives its power from its control over legislation, together with the other prerogatives of the Cabinet and the Prime Minister.

This so-called 'dictatorship' of the Cabinet has been strengthened under the impact of the exigencies of war, the expansion of the Civil Service, the growth of government activities, and the creation of state monopolies. Critics seem to find it difficult to understand how Parliament, which for several centuries carried on a struggle against absolute monarchy, can now countenance another form of dictatorship. But this apparent change of front can be easily explained. However powerful it may be, the Cabinet is still essentially a democratic organ. It has not usurped its powers, but derives its authority from the people.

Chapter Two

GOVERNMENT BASED ON THE WILL OF THE PEOPLE

THE Cabinet has gradually been allowed to assume all the powers which Parliament, and the House of Commons in particular, had slowly acquired over the sovereign. Yet this has never been thought at all anomalous since Parliament has every reason for putting its full confidence in the Cabinet, which, from the political point of view, is simply a government drawn from the party with a majority in the House of Commons. 'The steady confidence reposed by the Parliamentary majority in the Cabinet of the day' has been described by Trevelyan as 'the secret of the English Constitution. . . . In eighteenth-century England the requisite confidence of Parliament in the Cabinet could have been obtained in no other manner than through the bond of a party loyalty held in common by the Cabinet and by the majority of the House of Commons.' The same could equally well be said of Great Britain in the twentieth century.

Cabinet government is based upon the party system and is essentially a form of government by public opinion. All governments, even dictatorships, recognise the need to take account of public opinion, but in Great Britain the government is actually founded upon the will of the people. After a long period in which the aristocracy was dominant, democracy has been slowly but surely established. The franchise was gradually extended in response to changes in the social structure and as the people became better informed of political affairs. As one Englishman has said, a well-informed and intelligent voter cannot easily be corrupted, so it has become usual to leave the elector to make up his own mind.

This development was by no means inevitable. In France, for example, the lack of mutual confidence between Parliament and the electorate has been the subject of much comment, and attention is frequently and quite justifiably drawn to the tendency of the French system to become 'ultra-representative'. But in Great Britain, though Parliament may be afraid of the verdict of the people, it will nevertheless await and respect it.

In France, the quinquennial elections tend to be the only point of contact between the government and the governed. During the life of each Parliament the people leave the formation and the fall of governments and the conduct of the nation's affairs to be decided by agreements between the parties. The British House of Commons, on the other hand, has to be constantly aware of the wishes of the country and alive to changes in public opinion. As Sir William Anson remarked, 'In the last hundred years the power which determines the existence and extinction of Cabinets has shifted, first from the Crown to the Commons, and then from the Commons to the electorate.'

The first stage in this process was the transfer of effective political power from the King to Parliament. From the time of William the Conqueror onwards, England had a system of absolute monarchy which reached its zenith under Queen Elizabeth I in the second half of the sixteenth century and lasted until 1688, when Parliament finally emerged victorious from its long struggle against the prerogatives of the Crown. Circumstances favoured the development of a parliamentary system because the Hanoverian Kings, who were to some extent regarded as usurpers, were weak and tended to withdraw from active participation in politics. Instead of trying to follow a policy of their own, they began to work in collaboration with Parliament. The monarchy ceased to arouse much enthusiasm, and although it regained prestige under Queen Victoria, by then it was too late to do away with the firmly established parliamentary system. The sovereign's withdrawal from politics and the emergence of the Cabinet and the office— though not yet the actual title—of Prime Minister brought a corresponding increase in the powers of Parliament and, from as early as 1689, of the House of Commons. Since the fifteenth century, the Commons had had full control over finance, and from that time onwards legislation had been passed by Parliament, legislation by royal ordinance ceasing altogether after 1688. Finally, the Commons secured control over the activities of the government: first, they demanded the right to know who were the King's advisers; then they obtained power to decide who these should be; documents began to be countersigned by ministers as a guarantee that the government was acting in accordance with the wishes of Parliament; the Speaker of the House of Commons began to be selected by the House; and by the end of the eighteenth century the political responsibility of the Cabinet had become quite distinct from the old criminal sanction of impeachment. The development of politically homogeneous governments and ministerial solidarity helped to strengthen the dominant position of the House of Commons. The functions which had formerly belonged to the King were taken over by Parliament, and as time went on by the House of Commons in particular. The Commons made Cabinets and kept them in being, the Cabinet deriving its authority no longer from the Crown but from the support of the majority in the lower House. The Whigs and Tories who filled both Houses of Parliament were politicians whose distinctive qualities were their breadth of outlook, their awareness of the practical necessities facing the government, and their sense of responsibility. But the power of Parliament was not democratic power. The House of Commons was controlled by the same oligarchy that had brought about the Revolution of 1688. Power lay with the aristocracy, the monarchy being allowed to remain in existence only on condition that it did not try to govern.

A new phase opened with the progressive democratisation of the political system which we considered in the section on the electoral system. With the expansion of the electorate that began with the Reform Act of 1832 and was carried further by subsequent legislation, political power passed from the Commons to the people. The legal supremacy of Parliament was not impaired and there was no abrupt change in the type of persons elected. Nevertheless, the forces of democracy gradually destroyed the bases of the old oligarchy, who were no longer able to manage elections as they had when there were fewer voters. Elections began to be contested, seats became insecure, and candidates had to secure the support of the sovereign people. Parliamentary hegemony disappeared, because the House of Commons had become a reflection of the will of the people.

The third and latest development has been the transfer of political power from the electorate to the Cabinet. Political parties have assumed a vital rôle as intermediaries between the government and the people in general elections, the outcome of which can never be a foregone conclusion under a system of government by opinion. The parties have increased in importance until it is now for a party that the elector votes. Each major party goes to the country with a potential Prime

Minister and a political programme, and the Commons and the Queen have then to accept the verdict of the nation. Parliament has surrendered to the Cabinet the substance of the powers which it had acquired over the Crown and over the exercise of which the people had gradually assumed control. The Cabinet meanwhile relies on public opinion to enable it to control Parliament.

These successive developments have not left the British parliamentary system entirely free from the imperfections inherent in any constitutional device and in the working of all man-made institutions. They have, however, made it to a very large extent a system of government by the people.

This explains the preponderance of the executive which is the result of its being a reflection of the will of the people, who are recognised as the ultimate source of power. The democratic nature of Cabinet government can be seen in three principal ways: the government is quite clearly chosen by the people; its programme is that which the electorate has granted the successful party a mandate to carry out; and the Cabinet is in practice accountable to the country rather than to the House of Commons.

I. A GOVERNMENT CHOSEN BY THE PEOPLE

We have already seen how under the British party system the Prime Minister and the Cabinet are appointed by the Queen but really chosen by the people.

The Queen has no choice in the exercise of her power to appoint ministers. When only two major parties contest an election, as is usually the case today, the sovereign has no discretion as regards the composition of the Cabinet or the appointment of a Prime Minister. Indeed, one of the fundamentals of democratic government in Great Britain is that elections are far more than the mere designation of representatives. The electorate actually votes for members of Parliament, but they are really choosing the government by deciding which party is to have a majority in the House of Commons. Every five years at least, and more frequently if the power of dissolution is employed, the people are free to choose between the candidates and policies of the opposing parties. This clearly introduces an element of semi-direct rule which makes the British regime more than merely representative democracy.

The Commons, like the Cabinet, has to respect the wishes of the people. The electoral and party systems make it quite impossible for the British House of Commons, like lower chambers in other countries, to claim to be more representative than the government. Bagehot, exaggerating somewhat, went so far as to say, 'We have in England an elective first magistrate as truly as the Americans have an elective first magistrate.' Lord Robert Cecil pointed out the principle of the plebiscite which is inherent in the system of Cabinet government. It is certainly true that general elections may be and sometimes have been tantamount to the indirect election of a particular statesman as Prime Minister.

The Cabinet is also guided by the wishes of the people. It remains sensitive to public opinion because it is always under threat of being replaced by the opposition after the next general election. It therefore examines the size and significance of its majorities to see in what circumstances it would be likely to win another election. Above all, it knows that its majority is derived from the will of the people, and that the 'quasi-dictatorial' power which is possesses is really the power of the people and must be exercised in conformity with their mandate.

II. POPULAR APPROVAL OF GOVERNMENT PROGRAMMES

Apart from its plebiscitary element, which should not be overemphasised, a British general election is also virtually a referendum. The programmes of the two opposing parties may be very vague or there may be very little difference between them. Nevertheless, when the electorate is called upon to choose a new House of Commons, it is often, if not invariably, required to pass judgment on some question vitally affecting the future of the country, or on the need for some reform, or on whether a particular policy should be continued or other measures adopted.

The idea of the mandate rests precisely upon the theory that the people have expressed a wish to be governed by a particular group of men whose policies and actions should follow the lines already indicated to the electorate. The parties take up definite positions on the questions they consider important, so choosing men normally implies choosing measures as well.

Ever since the beginning of the eighteenth century, general

elections in Great Britain have been regarded as a means of consulting the electorate. Throughout this period, dissolutions have frequently been motivated by the government's desire to put some controversial issue before the country or to obtain or renew a mandate. Every Cabinet selects the time which appears most to its advantage for such consultations, and considers the result of the election as the people's verdict on the questions on which it sought to discover their wishes.

The exact scope and implications of the theory of the mandate have never been at all clearly defined. There is no simple and straightforward answer to the question of whether the Cabinet can embark upon an entirely new policy without consulting the electorate. Precedents provide no conclusive ruling. Some British governments have considered it necessary to have a general election before inaugurating a new policy, as Mr Baldwin did when he came out in favour of protection in 1923. Others have been criticised for not taking this course. Disraeli attacked Peel for not putting the question of free trade before the country in 1841, and Lord Hartington criticised Gladstone for launching the plan for Home Rule without first having made his intentions known to the electorate. But it does not follow that the government is constitutionally bound to do nothing for which it has not received an express mandate. In actual practice, the Cabinet appears to be allowed a considerable amount of freedom, as it must have if it is to deal effectively with changing political situations.

Another debatable point is whether, after fighting a general election with a definite programme, a Cabinet is bound not to repudiate the nation's mandate. The answer in this case would appear to be in the negative. An instance frequently quoted in this connection is the Conservative government's abandonment of sanctions against Italy in 1936 and its adoption of a foreign policy directly opposed to the principles of the League of Nations and collective security for which the electorate had expressed its preference in 1935. The precedent is not conclusive, however, even in the limited sphere of foreign policy, since subsequent events clearly produced great changes in public opinion after 1935. The Conservatives lost only thirteen of the fifty-seven by-elections between 1935 and December 1938. Neville Chamberlain retained the support of the House of Commons and did not choose to dissolve Parliament, but it seems unlikely that, had he done so, the decisions taken would not have been endorsed.

Although so imprecise, the theory of the mandate has two quite definite implications.

In the first place, except in case of urgency or on trivial matters, the Cabinet is firmly—though perhaps not very straitly—bound by the nation's mandate. It has an opportunity and also an obligation to carry out the broad lines of policy outlined in its programme which has been approved by the electorate. Ministers must be very cautious about making any departure from this programme, and are able to do so only in so far as they have reason to believe that public opinion has itself changed since the last general election. It would be wrong to suppose that the Cabinet can do whatever it pleases. Unless its policies can command the support of the nation, the party will be swept from power at the next general election, the date of which can sometimes be advanced by dissolving Parliament. Party government and Cabinet government are thus inevitably reduced to a form of government by the people. The doctrine of the mandate has frequently been interpreted in this sense, and most British authorities are of the opinion that it could properly be invoked to justify the opposition of the predominantly Conservative House of Lords to Liberal measures, as occurred in the early twentieth century when the Lords rejected bills to reform the educational system and to abolish plural voting, and the proposals for financial reform put forward by the Liberal Cabinet without a mandate in 1909.

Secondly, there can be no doubt that if a government's policies have been specifically presented to and approved by the electorate it derives great authority from its victory in the combined plebiscite and referendum. Party programmes, particularly under a two-party system, are bound to be somewhat vague. The compact between the nation and the party in power therefore leaves the Cabinet room to modify its policies as circumstances may dictate, while still investing it with greater authority than is often enjoyed by executives that have to rely on the support of a heterogeneous collection of parliamentary groups.

Although the mandate is not at all rigid, it does ensure that government policy is determined democratically with regard to the wishes of the people, and also that the Cabinet retains its pre-eminence. Under the two-party system the people are able to choose their government and, in broad outline, determine its policy. Both these things are frequently impossible under other forms of parliamentary government. The rôle of Parliament is consequently smaller than in many other countries. It is by no means negligible, however, for it has not been impaired so much as transformed.

III. CABINET RESPONSIBILITY TO THE ELECTORATE

The essential feature of continental systems of parliamentary government is that the executive is politically responsible to the lower House, which makes and destroys governments and has supreme control over their activities.

In theory the same concept of political responsibility is equally valid under the British parliamentary system, and, as we shall see, the House of Commons has important powers of control over the Cabinet. Nevertheless, the Cabinet is now politically responsible to the electorate rather than to Parliament. This has come about as the result of a number of factors whereby in most cases the Cabinet is quite clearly, albeit indirectly, chosen by the people.

The majority in the House of Commons have usually been elected with a view to a Cabinet being formed from their ranks which they should then support until the next election. Loyalty to the party makes the majority remain faithful to the government, thus accepting the inevitable and abiding by the mandate granted by the electorate. The Cabinet leads the party into battle at the next election, when they present a united front to the nation and are held jointly responsible for the policies they have pursued and for any violations of their mandate. During the lifetime of a Parliament, members of the majority party might conceivably try to urge the government to take some course of action which would command popular support and therefore be electorally advantageous. But the whole apparatus of party discipline would make it quite inconceivable for any member to withdraw his support from the government without making a complete break with his party.

The underlying principle is that, while the government is exposed to criticism from the opposition, the majority should at the same time assist it in its task and give it the support which is its due. This same idea is reflected in parliamentary procedure and in the committee system.

Votes of censure are possible, but could not occur often as the government normally has no difficulty in securing a majority.

There are only three kinds of situation in which a Cabinet might be defeated in the House of Commons.

In the first place, divisions might appear within a party which had won an election but had only a small majority. Such differences are not at all unusual, but, unless there is a really deep split within the party, they are very seldom allowed to become apparent except on secondary questions. The party can generally be kept together in important divisions in Parliament because of the authority wielded by the Prime Minister and the party organisation. A member who disagrees with his party can abstain from voting and in an exceptional case he might desert the party and vote with the opposition, but if he does this often he runs the risk of losing the backing of his party in the next election.

Secondly, there may be a fundamental split which destroys the majority. This happened when Peel was deserted by the Protectionists in 1846; to Lord John Russell in 1851; to Palmerston in 1858; to Gladstone over the budget in 1885 and over Home Rule in 1886; and to the Liberal Cabinet in 1895. But members are certain to know what the Cabinet regards as vital issues, and in recent years it has become increasingly rare for governments to leave their supporters free to decide any matter for themselves. The strengthening of party discipline has tended to promote party cohesion, and a divided majority will now rally together if the Prime Minister announces that a particular division will be treated as a vote of confidence.

The third type of situation is less complicated, but it has only arisen at periods when, contrary to the normal position in Britain, there were three or more rival parties in Parliament none of which had a majority in the House of Commons. Such circumstances gave rise to the alliance of Whigs and Peelites against the Conservative government of Lord Derby in 1852; the alliance of Liberals and Irish Nationalists against Lord Salisbury's Conservative government in 1886 and again in 1892; and the unusual situation between the two World Wars when there were three main parties—Liberal, Labour and

Conservative. At such times, Great Britain has had to resign herself, like other countries, to either coalition government or else a minority government dependent on support from the opposition, with all the risks of government instability inherent in such arrangements. But, as we have seen, under the two-party system such situations have always been quite exceptional and never of long duration.

There are nevertheless a number of circumstances in which a Cabinet might be defeated in the House of Commons. What is more important, however, is that the government does not necessarily have to resign even if it is defeated in Parliament. There are two reasons for this.

1. In the first place, the Cabinet can weigh up the importance of any vote cast against it in the Commons. If it does not consider the issue vital, it would not be at all arbitrary for it to remain in office, maintaining that its relationship to Parliament remained unchanged.

A Cabinet could not, of course, carry on if it had lost the confidence of Parliament or received an express vote of no confidence. The Commons have power to paralyse the government of the country by refusing to pass the legislation required in order to maintain the public services, levy taxes and incur expenditure. They can also petition the Queen to dismiss her ministers or threaten them with impeachment. But although they have these powers in theory they do not exercise them in practice, and in any case they would avail little if the government refused to resign. The problem is simplified by the party system, which makes the confidence of Parliament in the government merely a matter of the confidence of a party in its leaders. This will not be automatically destroyed by a single adverse vote. Not since 1895 has a Cabinet which originally had a majority been overthrown in the House of Commons. When majority Cabinets have resigned, they have done so because of internal dissensions and merely used defeat in the Commons as a pretext. On the other hand, it would not be good political strategy for a Cabinet to accept adverse votes with complacency and treat them as a matter of course. This would encourage defection amongst its members until its majority tended to disintegrate. All the same, there is no reason why the Cabinet should ever lose sight of their proper rôle, which is to lead the majority and not submit docilely to their often vacillating or vaguely expressed opinions.

The essential point is that no one questions the right of the government to decide what course it should take after a defeat in Parliament. In the past these have often been simply accepted. Peel was defeated on an amendment to the address in 1834, but continued in office and did not resign until several months later, over a financial resolution; Lord Melbourne's Whig government was defeated in the House of Commons fifty-eight times between 1835 and March 1840. In 1853 Lord Aberdeen's coalition was defeated three times in a single week, but did not resign. In 1924 the Labour Prime Minister, Ramsay MacDonald, whose government admittedly did not have a majority, explicitly declared that he would resign only if defeated on a fundamental issue. Between January and August 1924 he actually accepted ten adverse votes. Mr Attlee stated in the House of Commons after being defeated in March 1950 on questions relating to coal and solid fuels, that as this was not really a vote against his policy there was no question of resignation.

A number of considerations influence what course the Cabinet takes after an adverse vote when there are any alternatives open. It is bound to take into account the circumstances in which it was defeated and the political significance of the vote. The importance of the occasion on which it suffered a reverse counts for much. On certain questions, such as the budget and the address, the support of the Commons is practically indispensable. Another important factor is the nature of the issue under discussion, and whether it is a point on which the Cabinet considers itself particularly vulnerable. Finally, the defeated Cabinet will form an estimate of its own strength. When it tries to assess how much its prestige has suffered, a Cabinet riddled with internal divisions and feeling that its end is near, may decide that it ought to attach considerable importance to an adverse vote in the Commons.

2. Even in such cases, the Cabinet still does not necessarily have to resign. Instead, it can always ask the Queen to dissolve Parliament.

This alternative is a survival from the days when the King had the power to summon and dismiss his Parliaments. This prerogative is now quite different from what it was in the days of absolute monarchy, owing to the gradual transition to Cabinet government and democratisation of the political system.

Under the British parliamentary system, a dissolution is simply the normal and frequently used means of appealing to the country on any matter on which it has not previously been consulted, and which the Prime Minister considers sufficiently important to be put before the electorate.

If there were no power of dissolution, the nation would only be able to express its views at fixed intervals, as provided for by the electoral law. In the intervals between elections to the lower House, the last word would rest with the representatives of the nation in Parliament, who alone could give expression to the will of the people. In Great Britain, however, it is the people who have the last word. The power of dissolution means that, in addition to the general elections held at statutory intervals, the people can be given other opportunities to make their views known whenever the government thinks this is necessary. When we come to examine the monarchy, we shall see how the sovereign has practically no discretion as to the use of her power to dissolve Parliament. The principal aspects of the power of dissolution must be mentioned at this point, however, because it is one of the fundamental sources of the power of the Cabinet which derives its authority from the result of an appeal to the people.

Under a parliamentary system, a dissolution can in theory serve two purposes, and in Britain it does in fact fulfil both these functions. First, it acts as a check against an excessively powerful legislature by providing the executive with a means of ascertaining directly the wishes of the electorate and seeing whether their views are being accurately expressed by their representatives in Parliament. This helps to compensate for the defects of the system of parliamentary representation and acts as a substitute for a referendum.

When the power of dissolution exists and is exercised, it is undoubtedly a valuable disciplinary weapon. Though this may have been questioned by a number of somewhat superficial critics, it is nevertheless true, even under a system of Cabinet government where the executive normally has a majority in the House of Commons. Governments derive considerable influence from their power to appeal to the country when this appears politically desirable and likely to be to their own advantage.

In Britain, for example, a Cabinet which decides not to resign after being defeated on an important issue in the House of Commons can appeal to the people against the opposition. Lord Melbourne did so in 1841, Lord Palmerston in 1857, Lord Derby in 1859, Disraeli in 1868, Gladstone in 1886 and Ramsay MacDonald in 1924. The Cabinet does not have to resign unless its defeat is confirmed by the electorate; otherwise it can remain in office and will be the stronger for having secured a fresh mandate.

Moreover, there still has to be a dissolution even if the government decides to resign after a defeat in the House of Commons. The new Cabinet will be bound to ask for this, as occurred in 1847, 1852, 1885, 1895, 1906 and 1922 after a defeated government had resigned, and after the radical reconstruction of the Cabinet in 1931. It is therefore true to say that, although theoretically responsible to the House of Commons, the Cabinet is responsible primarily to the people. A new Cabinet would have no authority to govern the country unless it had the support of the people, so it is bound to ask the electorate to decide whether the opposition ought to have defeated the government. This ensures that the government is not paralysed or prevented from acting effectively without good cause.

A minority government or one with an unduly small majority can also use the power of dissolution to try to win additional support. This is now generally recognised as a legitimate ground for dissolution except immediately after a general election, when it could serve no useful purpose. Here admittedly additional risks arise which are not otherwise involved in a dissolution. The opposition is able to contend that the government's weakness is itself a reason for not allowing it to remain in power, so that it would really be wiser to vote for its opponents. Nevertheless, the weapon of dissolution is still available to the government and, if skilfully employed, can help it to strengthen its position.

The power of dissolution is not used so frequently today as it was, for example, in the nineteenth century. As a result, it has sometimes been argued that its importance in the British parliamentary system has been overestimated. Yet this is to overlook the important deterrent effects which such a power can have even when not actually employed. The Prime Minister can keep his party together without difficulty simply by threatening to dissolve Parliament, as it is common knowledge that the fate of any waverers will be in doubt if there is a sudden general election, while a dissolution is generally fatal for any third party. This discourages dissension within the parties, particularly as members are aware that their loyalty to their party determines what party backing they receive the next time they stand for election.

The overhanging threat of a dissolution thus helps to sustain the majority in the belief that its task is to support the government until the next general election. This does in fact happen, save in quite exceptional circumstances. Usually the Cabinet remains in office throughout the lifetime of a Parliament. The Commons recognise that the government is politically responsible primarily to the electorate. British governments enjoy a stability greatly envied by other countries. Between 1801 and 1951 Britain has had only forty-four different Cabinets, which makes the average life of each government nearly three and a half years, although some were admittedly reconstructed during this time.

Yet the Cabinet seldom allows Parliament to last for the whole of its statutory term. Its life is usually cut short by dissolution. In the nineteenth century only one Parliament lasted its full term, then seven years. Since 1911, apart from the two World Wars, when its life was specially extended, no Parliament has endured for the maximum of five years laid down by the Parliament Act. This is because of the idea that the old Parliament has exhausted its mandate, which brings us to the second purpose of a dissolution—to fulfil the function of a referendum.

A general election often begins to be anticipated as Parliament nears the end of its term, even though the Cabinet has not yet decided to dissolve. This was the case in 1847, 1865, 1874, 1892 and 1929. More often, however, governments have timed a dissolution for the moment they considered the most opportune to appeal to the country and seek a mandate for a particular policy.

Though it may be exhausted by the burdens of office and

labouring under heavy difficulties and will come under heavy attack from the opposition in the next general election, the Cabinet does at least have the undisputed right to decide when that election shall be held. This is one of the prerogatives of the Crown which gives the government a considerable advantage over its opponents, as the timing can greatly affect the outcome of an election. The doctrine of the mandate in particular could not function without the power of dissolution. It would be impossible to raise or revive at regular intervals prescribed by an electoral law all the issues on which the nation is invited to voice its opinions and to express its confidence in one of the two parties.

The Cabinet therefore decides when to appeal to the country in the light of the questions which it wishes or feels obliged to put before the electorate. If new issues have arisen since the last general election, if there have been new developments in some matter on which the people were previously consulted, or if it proposes to change the general line of its policy, the Cabinet can try to secure the necessary mandate from the electorate to whom it looks as the source of its authority. Even if no particular political issue has arisen, the Cabinet can still seek electoral approval of the general lines of its policy whenever it thinks fit, without waiting for Parliament to run its full term.

It is a debatable point whether it is always wise to take advantage of a strong movement of public opinion or popular emotion to appeal to the country on a leading controversial issue. Peel strongly criticised Lord Melbourne for adopting this course in 1841, and since then a number of governments have somewhat magnanimously renounced the opportunity of reaping the benefits of a wave of popularity, as did Lord Beaconsfield after his diplomatic triumph at the Congress of Berlin in 1878; Mr Baldwin in 1926 when the Liberals were divided and the Labour Party out of favour for their association with the General Strike; and Mr Neville Chamberlain in 1938, when he decided not to hold a plebiscite on his foreign policy after Munich, though in this case the outcome was not quite so much a foregone conclusion.

Usually, governments have entertained no such scruples. Tactical considerations have tended to make them adept at exploiting the advantages to be gained from appealing to the country after they have scored some special political triumph. Well-known instances of elections held at a moment particularly favourable for rallying popular support are Lord Salisbury's dissolution after the victories in South Africa in 1900, that of the coalition government after the armistice in 1918, and Mr Baldwin's in 1935 when he secured the approval of the country for a policy founded upon the League of Nations and collective security.

The power of dissolution is a democratic device, since it tends to increase the number of occasions on which the people can make their voice heard. At the same time, it provides the Cabinet with an important means of influencing events. It is generally agreed that a Cabinet would hardly ever be absolutely bound to dissolve Parliament, though it would probably have to do so after a major change in the size of the electorate, as after the Reform Act of 1832. Normally, however, the Cabinet is free to dissolve or not as it thinks fit, according to the dictates of expediency and tactical considerations. The government must be ready with a programme likely to appeal to the electorate, or the dissolution cannot possibly serve its purpose. If defeated, a government always has the alternative of resigning and leaving to its successor the task of dissolving Parliament and taking the offensive in the election. Whatever happens, the Cabinet must choose the right moment at which to dissolve if it is to recoup the maximum support from its appeal to the country, and it must therefore watch the trend of public opinion as indicated, for example, in the results of by-elections.

In whatever way we try to account for the preponderance of the Cabinet in Great Britain, we come back to the fact that it rests upon the support of the nation. Cabinet government has now become government by the people. That is why the House of Lords has, amongst other things, lost the power to overthrow the government; why the Cabinet normally retains the support of the House of Commons until such time as it decides to seek the verdict of the electorate on its policies; and why, as one Anglo-Saxon politician has said, members of Parliament today have no more control over the executive than the electorate has over members of Parliament in the intervals between elections. Parliament is not in a position to question the authority of the executive, which is generally quite securely based upon the mandate it obtained at the last general election and the compact which it manages to maintain between the government and the people. This happens even when there is a sizable minority in the country. However large this may be, it recognises the right of the majority to form the government and acquiesces in its political decisions, while reserving its inalienable right of public criticism. The Cabinet realises that, since it derives its political authority from the people, it ought constantly to be trying to assess how much support it can command by keeping watch on the numbers and significance of its electoral successes and on the state of public opinion as revealed through its own party and, even more, through the opposition. It knows that it must always be ready to fight a general election should the need arise, and that it will not be able to defeat its opponents unless it has been acting in accordance with the will of the people. It also knows that with elections by simple majority, a comparatively small swing of votes will be enough to turn it out of office. Consequently it knows or ought to know how it should govern the country and just how far it can go in any particular direction.

The British Parliament was first a feudal and later an aristocratic institution. It has now become democratic, but without developing the features which have frequently led to government by assembly. The British knew what it was to have an absolute monarch as executive and for several centuries strove to do away with that system, but they still remain devoted to the monarchy. Today, the people themselves uphold the supremacy of the executive, but this is now a responsible executive to whom the nation has entrusted the prerogatives that Parliament earlier acquired from the King. The people are also perfectly free to withdraw this authority at any time and thus have ample power to justify the conclusion that they are indeed truly sovereign.

The unquestioned authority of a small group of ministers has thus been made compatible with government by public opinion. The executive is dominant but not all-powerful. We must therefore turn to consider what safeguards for individual liberty are provided under the British political system.

PART THREE

The Limitation of Power

THE BRITISH CONSTITUTION AND THE LIBERTIES OF THE SUBJECT

GREAT power is not necessarily unlimited power. Despite the supremacy of the Cabinet and the dominant position of the Prime Minister, Great Britain nevertheless has a balanced system of government that works by discussion and compromise. It may be open to question how much emphasis on liberty is appropriate under present-day conditions, but there can be no doubt that respect for individual liberty is one of the basic features of political life in Great Britain and inherent in her institutions. Montesquieu showed remarkable insight into the future when he wrote:

> 'If . . . some foreign power should threaten the State or put its prosperity or its glory in danger, the little interests of party would then yield to the more strong and binding, and there would be a perfect coalition in favour of the executive power. . . . This nation is passionately fond of liberty, because this liberty is real; and it is possible for it, in its defence, to sacrifice its wealth, its ease, its interest, and to support the burden of the heaviest taxes, even such as a despotic prince durst not lay upon his subjects.'

History has shown how very true this is. In peace or in war, the British have always been prepared to make the greatest sacrifices in order to preserve their liberties, which they regard as absolutely fundamental. 'Britons never will be slaves', they proudly proclaim in 'Rule, Britannia', and this dread of slavery would unite the whole nation in resisting domination by any one man, party or ideology, as well as against subservience to any foreign power.

The reasons for this continuing respect for the liberties of the individual are both more difficult to explain and more fundamental than in any other country, because in Britain this depends much more on custom than on positive law.

When we speak of the British constitution we are really talking about a whole collection of very diverse elements—a 'living organism' that is continually being changed by the actions and reactions of individuals and groups in response to changing circumstances. This is a continuous process which can be seen in the course of history and is still going on before our very eyes. The rules which make up the constitution do not form any distinct body of law. They may be altered not only by the legislature but by the very organs whose behaviour they are intended to govern. Yet it would be quite wrong to suppose that they are at liberty to modify these rules just as they please. On the contrary, as one writer has said, the key to the development of the British constitution is to be found in the interrelationship between the Crown and the people, which is a process of discussion and mutual agreement in which Parliament and public opinion play an important part.

Respect for the constitution is founded upon the Rule of Law, which is also the basis of the entire judicial system of Great Britain. This is a concept which cannot be defined with precision, but is at the root of the whole idea of individual liberties. It implies much more than compliance with the law on the part of the individual subject. It also imposes limitations on the power of the government and the administrative authorities, and embodies both the concept of the state as a law-making body and the liberal idea that the state may only exercise its power within certain limits prescribed by law. The Rule of Law is a comprehensive term which could be used to expound an abstract theory as well as in analysing how the government actually operates. If we examine the functioning of the machinery of government we shall see that the whole political system is genuinely inspired by the Rule of Law. This embraces many principles which, although somewhat imprecise, are nevertheless criteria of, or means of attaining, a system of government based on respect for the liberties of the individual. It postulates free elections and government in accordance with the will of the people, with the corollary that a government can be removed from power if it loses the support of the country. It also implies the equality of all citizens before the law, the recognition of certain civil liberties as absolutely fundamental, and a general atmosphere of individual freedom, more easily perceived than analysed, which is quite incompatible with any kind of arbitrary rule and requires some measure of collaboration between the government and the opposition.

Many states have sought to attain these objectives by defining them in precise terms in a written constitution. In Britain these same principles, which have always been implicit in the Rule of Law, also form a constitution, but one which is very different in many respects from what is usually meant by the term, particularly as regards the various elements of which it is composed.

In the first place, one striking feature of the British constitution, especially so far as individual liberty is concerned, is the absence of any basic law on the structure and functioning of the machinery of government. The rules which make up the constitution are in no way more fundamental than any other part of English law. Moreover, it is actually considered an advantage that they are not rigidly fixed, because they can be the more easily modified in the light of changing circumstances.

The most remarkable feature of the British constitution, however, is that, like the law of the land of which it forms part, it is composed of many quite different kinds of rules. These may be divided, according to their origin, into four distinct categories of greatly varying importance.

One such element is legislation, upon which there is no need to dwell at length. The legislature has often intervened to settle controversial constitutional problems or to introduce reforms, and some basic constitutional documents have resulted.

We have already mentioned some important acts that constitute major landmarks in the struggle against absolute monarchy, to which the sovereign either agreed or was compelled to give his assent. They are still held in very great respect. This, however, springs from respect for tradition and devotion to the ideals by which they were inspired and has little to do with their actual provisions, which are clearly no longer really relevant to the problems of government in the twentieth century. Today, the real significance of most of these major acts, from Magna Charta onwards, is symbolical. They have become associated in men's minds with ideals of individual liberty far surpassing anything that they were originally intended to achieve, and it is for this reason that they are regarded as sacred texts. Their actual provisions are not of paramount importance. Nor are they, in the eyes of the law, any different from any other statutes. Parliament could repeal Magna Charta in just the same way as it can determine the organisation of the television broadcasting service or amend a Finance Act. Besides these fundamental texts there are also other Acts of Parliament which relate to such constitutional questions as the succession to the throne, the position of judges, the electoral system, the government of Northern Ireland, and the organisation of central and local government.

The second element in the constitution is case law. This is obviously not so important in Britain as in countries where the courts have power to decide whether legislation is compatible with the constitution. But judicial decisions have given rise to many rules of Common Law relevant to the political system, and it is by reference to the principles of Common Law that the courts decide how Acts of Parliament are to be interpreted. In the definition and safeguarding of the liberties of the subject the courts have played a particularly important part.

The Law and Custom of Parliament forms a third element of considerable importance in the British constitution. This includes many rules regarding the machinery of government that have not been laid down in any statute and are not enforceable by the courts. Thus the House of Lords itself is normally the authority which decides whether anyone is entitled to sit in the House. Each House of Parliament regulates its own procedure, that of the Commons often in fact determining the principles on which the whole parliamentary system operates. The party system within Parliament, the institution of parliamentary questions and the rules determining what is a breach of the privileges of the House of Commons all form part of the law and custom of Parliament. This is derived from a variety of sources: precedents preserved in the records kept by the clerks of the House; resolutions of the House; Speaker's rulings; and sometimes customary practices, such as those regarding the relations between the government and the opposition, which have grown up without ever being mentioned in any ruling or resolution.

This brings us to constitutional conventions, undoubtedly the most characteristic element in the British constitution. They are not essentially different from customs and precedents which may be built up on constitutional questions. But, since the rules which make up the British constitution are not at all rigid and have never been formulated in specific terms, constitutional conventions are extremely important. It is no exaggeration to say that it is on conventions of this kind that the functioning of the whole parliamentary system depends. The most outstanding examples are those relating to Cabinet government itself, which enable the Cabinet to exercise the powers of the Crown so long as it has the confidence of the House of Commons. Other conventions make the Cabinet responsible to the House of Commons and require it to resign or ask for a dissolution if it loses the confidence of the Commons. Constitutional conventions make it impossible for the sovereign to refuse her assent to a bill which has been passed by Parliament, for a Cabinet to be overthrown by the House of Lords, or for a peer to become Prime Minister. The position of the opposition in Parliament, the powers of the Prime Minister, and many other firmly established rules rest upon constitutional conventions. These rules have grown out of precedents which have become generally recognised as authoritative, and have developed chiefly where there is no case law or statutes or where the law is inadequate on its own. They have been described as the flesh which clothes the framework of the law and so permits the constitution to function effectively by making it possible to apply the law in the way that seems most appropriate in the light of the constitutional theories prevailing at the time.

Some conventions have grown up which are inconsistent with the law and yet Parliament has not always seen fit to amend it. Compliance with the law, in the strict sense of the word, is enforceable by sanctions applied by the courts. There are no legal sanctions, however, to ensure observance of constitutional conventions. A convention cannot override positive law, but it can be used to amplify it, to put a new interpretation upon it or to nullify its effects. Powers which still exist in law may be neutralised in practice through the establishment of conventions, as has happened to the powers of the sovereign. A pre-existing convention can acquire legal recognition if mentioned in an Act of Parliament, as occurred when the Prime Minister was referred to in Acts of 1917 and 1937. A convention which has become fairly well established is sometimes actually converted into a law by being incorporated in an Act of Parliament, thus becoming more clearly defined than when it depended on the interpretation of precedents weighed one against another. Before the Parliament Act of 1911, for example, a convention already existed whereby there were certain limits beyond which the House of Lords could not go in resisting the will of the Commons in case of any conflict between the two Houses.

Professor Dicey, who as early as 1885 stressed the importance of constitutional conventions, always maintained that they derived their force in part from public opinion, but most of all from the fact that if a government were to violate them it would either be forced to resign or else could not avoid violating some express provision of the law.

This is because a large body of legislation presupposes that the executive is responsible to the people or to their representatives—the convention which is really the essential basis of government by opinion. Another important factor is the people's instinctive sense of what is constitutional, bred of long-standing acceptance of the parliamentary system and its rules, that the British undoubtedly possess in a very marked degree. Any violation of accepted rules, even if never set down in writing, or merely a failure to comply with them in spirit as well as in letter, would be enough to arouse general public disapproval.

Though the constitution itself is important, what is most vital is the constitutional conscience of the people. They are completely at one in wanting to maintain a spirit of fair play in politics and to ensure respect for principles and practices which it is politically impossible to alter as long as the general opinion of the country is opposed to any change, even though there are no legal difficulties in the way of their modification.

The democratisation of the system of government has been reflected in a number of Acts of Parliament which have helped to make democracy a living reality. This does not, however, mean that there is no distinction between law and conventions, even though the latter may be equally binding in practice. Once constitutional conventions are clearly formulated, as many, though not all, now are, the Cabinet finds itself compelled to respect them by strong and direct pressure of public opinion expressed through the political parties and in the House of Commons. No legal text, however precise, could be more firmly binding on those in power than these constitutional conventions.

The British constitution thus consists of an elaborate collection of rules, in which respect for tradition has been successfully reconciled with the impossibility of standing still. One thing, however, which all its diverse components have in common is their fundamental respect for the liberties of the individual. In

Britain the whole environment is favourable to individual freedom. In the course of time, and particularly since serious religious controversy has died out, the British have learnt to be tolerant. A certain amount of narrow-mindedness which may be ascribed to Puritanism can still be detected. Nevertheless, it would be true to say that, even if they do not always do so in a spirit of great humility, the British will invariably respect any opinion not opposed to liberty itself, and even those which are will be allowed as much freedom of expression as possible. There is really no great danger in this, because any kind of totalitarianism is so completely contrary to all British political thinking that there is no likelihood of such ideas gaining any substantial following. Under the British system of Cabinet government, the opposition is always ready to acknowledge the power of the majority, and the government refuses to be deterred by criticism from the opposition, which it endeavours to turn to its own advantage. Each side recognises that in the end the people will decide between them when they cast their votes at the next general election, when victory will go to the party whose policy has the support of public opinion.

The fruits of this fundamental political liberalism can be seen in the development of self-governing institutions in Great Britain. It has also been one of the factors behind their establishment in the Commonwealth and their introduction in different forms in the rapidly developing colonial empire.

It was not without some misgivings that the British people have acquiesced in the recent growth in the powers of the central government, with restrictions on economic freedom, planning and socialistic reforms. Some regrets continue to be expressed at these developments. The increase in the power of the Cabinet has led upholders of the liberal tradition to invoke spectres of dictatorship and to dwell on the dangers of totalitarianism. A foreign observer, however, is more struck by the happy success with which the liberties of the subject are still upheld in Great Britain.

Here again, the geographical advantages of Great Britain must not be overlooked. They have protected her against contagion from political passions originating elsewhere, and from becoming involved in totalitarian political movements. History has also favoured the establishment and development of a regime which manages to combine monarchy with democracy, a strong executive with respect for the will of the people, and freedom with efficiency; to preserve institutions which are anachronisms, yet adapt them to suit changed circumstances; and to reconcile the authority of the state with the liberties of the subject. Yet it must be admitted that, apart from fortuitous historical factors, the political wisdom of the British people themselves has also played an important part. Mutual agreement and compromise are the basis of the British system of government. No arrangements arrived at in this way could possibly endure unless the nation as a whole had a deep conviction, acquired by experience and in some cases after much suffering, that nothing fruitful can be achieved by intolerance and oppression. Their respect for individual liberty contains elements of both mysticism and realism. One wonders how far religious influences and the effects of the Reformation have restrained or, as seems more likely, contributed to its development; how much it is due to the Anglo-Saxon temperament; and to what extent it is the outcome of the social structure or of economic conditions.

These are not questions which a political scientist is competent to answer, but they raise matters that have been of fundamental importance in creating an environment in which no institution can exist that would be detrimental to the liberty of the subject. Only by such considerations can we explain how the government can have such great power without this leading to dictatorship by the Cabinet or by the Prime Minister.

The limitation of power means something radically different in Britain from what it does in the United States, where government is based upon the separation of powers and a system of checks and balances. The British constitution has grown up empirically, and it is difficult to know exactly where to draw the line in deciding what to class as constitutional questions. It is left to individual judgment whether to include the organisation of the army, the position of the Church of England, the established churches or the churches generally, the principle of trial by jury, or *habeas corpus*, all of which are really relevant. Apart from the Instrument of Government drawn up by the army under Cromwell, the British have never attempted to direct and control the development of their political system by laying down a definite logically conceived plan reflecting the theories of a particular age or group. They seem likely to go on simply establishing, modifying and adapting institutions as the need may arise. In this continuous process of evolution and constant adaptation, the main elements in the constitutional framework—the Crown, the Cabinet, Parliament, political parties, the courts, local authorities and the established church —have all played some part and still continue to make their influence felt in many different and varying ways. Many factors conducive to individual liberty are quite incapable of analysis. We shall try, however, to show as clearly as possible exactly how the functioning of British institutions and the many different influences at work in the country help to protect the people against the abuse of power.

Chapter One

THE RÔLE OF THE ELECTORATE
AND PUBLIC OPINION

GOVERNMENTS come to power as the result of general elections, when the nation expresses its support for the majority in the House of Commons and gives the Cabinet a mandate to govern the country.

On the other hand, general elections also provide a very effective guarantee against executive dictatorship. Whatever the people have done, they must be free to undo. The Prime Minister and his colleagues only acquire power for a limited term, so they are never allowed to forget the vulnerability of their position.

In the first place, no Cabinet is ever invested with supreme power for an unlimited period. The Prime Minister and his government derive their power from the will of the people as expressed through the party system at a general election. The longest that they can hope to remain unchallenged in office is a little under five years. This would undoubtedly be a long term for any government under a parliamentary system, but it is comparatively rare for British governments to last so long. Their average life, as we have seen, is a little under three and a half years. That is still long enough to enable a government to carry out its programme and present an impressive and consistent record of achievements. Yet it always knows that, when Parliament reaches the end of its term, if not before, its policies and actions, its successes and failures, will all be exposed to the full light of public criticism in an election campaign. The party system ensures that Cabinet policies are subjected to close and searching scrutiny by the electorate.

The Prime Minister must therefore exercise his weapon of dissolution with great caution. We have already remarked on the importance of this power. It is a two-edged weapon, a costly and cumbersome expedient which paralyses the legislative process, the action of the government and virtually the whole life of the country for several months at a time. Moreover, in using it to try to undermine the opposition, a Cabinet may bring about its own downfall if it cuts short the life of a Parliament when it has no positive record of achievement or convincing programme of action on which to appeal to the country, or if its popularity has been declining or has failed to increase proportionately to that of the other party, or simply if the election is badly timed. The minority is tolerated and treated with respect because from time to time it has a chance to become the majority and thus replace a Cabinet which has lost the confidence of the country. The Cabinet cannot influence the outcome of elections. Both law and custom guarantee that voting is free and secret and so give the people a genuine power of control over the government.

Apart from its limited term, the position of the Cabinet is insecure on account of the system of election by simple majority.

If the British had not already been temperamentally disposed towards toleration and compromise, they would have been forced to develop these qualities because of the hazards which invariably result from elections by a plurality of votes and the consequent sharp swings of the pendulum between the parties. We have seen how the outcome of an election is really determined by the behaviour of a comparatively small number of floating voters who, by shifting their allegiance from one side to the other, can completely alter the respective strengths of the parties in the House of Commons. These floating voters in the last resort decide whether the Cabinet must give way to the opposition. Moreover, past experience has shown how a majority which seems perfectly secure can quickly be changed into a minority, and how the two parties hold office alternately in response to regular swings of the pendulum that seem very difficult to upset. This again tends to make the Cabinet more cautious in its behaviour.

The swing of the pendulum is a factor of great political importance. In a country like France, which is normally governed by a coalition based on an alliance between a number of different parties in Parliament, some parties—particularly those of the centre—are practically certain to be able to join any government if they so desire, and some politicians in those parties are fairly regularly if not invariably called upon to assume office in the ministry. These political leaders will not be completely indifferent to the problems facing the country, but the government will not normally act in a very determined fashion. The parties and the men have been forced together by circumstances, and the ever-present problem of keeping a majority together is too important for one-party governments to be frequent or long-lasting. Thus multi-party systems often result in paradoxical situations where the divisions between the parties in Parliament allow tiny groups that have fared very badly in the elections to emerge as the arbiters of the political situation.

In Great Britain, on the other hand, Cabinet government normally operates under a two-party system. The minority party is completely excluded from office, even though it may have obtained a substantial share of the popular vote—possibly more than its victorious opponents. The implications of an electoral defeat are thus perfectly clear. Its consequences are particularly harsh for the defeated party, which will have to spend several—perhaps almost five—years on the opposition benches before it has another chance to return to power.

This discourages any precipitate action. It tends to make each party treat the other side with respect, because its future supporters may be among those who voted for its opponents. The converse is also equally true. As it needs to be able to retain or to win the support of the greatest possible number of floating voters from all social classes at the next election, the Cabinet tends to follow a policy of compromise. It may also be reconstructed during the life of a Parliament. Although the apparent stability of the government often obscures the significance of these changes, they may indicate that some genuine change in policy has been decided upon in the light of new developments in public opinion. There is thus a constant check against any attempt by the majority to abuse its power. Governments are the more conscious of these restraints, the more uncertain their political prospects. The Cabinet also has to be ready to meet the challenge of the opposition, not perhaps at any moment, but at least whenever the political situation forces it to ask for a dissolution, which may be long before Parliament has run its full term. This again helps to make the government act in accordance with the will of the people.

The rôle of public opinion is thus absolutely fundamental. Its importance is all the greater because the liberal political regime will not tolerate more than a bare minimum of restrictions on freedom of thought, expression or action. There are a number of channels, including political parties, the press and interest groups, through which public opinion seeks to express itself in an organised fashion. Parliament, however, is the traditional channel through which it has made itself felt most effectively. We must therefore turn to consider the extent to which Parliament acts as a check on the power of the Cabinet.

Chapter Two

PARLIAMENT

PARLIAMENT in Great Britain still, strictly speaking, means the Queen, the Lords and the Commons meeting and agreeing together. Today, however, the term is increasingly widely used as in other countries to refer to the two chambers of the legislature.

Parliament, in the strict classical sense of the term, is legally sovereign and has unqualified juridical supremacy. The will of Parliament is not open to question by any other body, save possibly by the people when called upon to elect a new House of Commons. 'Parliament . . . has . . . the power to make or unmake any law whatever; and . . . no person or body is recognised by the law of England as having a right to override or set aside the legislation of Parliament.' In theory it is still quite true, as Genevois de Lolme put it, that 'Parliament can do everything but make a woman a man and a man a woman', and an Englishman would be inclined to add that there is no legal obstacle to prevent it doing even this. At all events, as there is no rigid constitution, there is nothing to stop the most revolutionary changes from being brought about by a simple Act of Parliament.

The Cabinet not only, as we have seen, dominates the whole political life of the country. It also stands in a very close relationship to Parliament, and nowadays to the House of Commons in particular. We must therefore examine the respective rôles of the two Houses, and try to see just how much influence Parliament can exert under the British system of Cabinet government.

I. THE HOUSE OF COMMONS

The history of Parliament or of the House of Commons, which has gradually emerged as the dominant organ in this composite institution, is really no less than the entire political history of Great Britain. Here we shall not attempt to do more than give a brief account of how the present parliamentary system has evolved through the steady growth in the influence of the Commons.

Parliament, as we have seen, originally came into being as a means whereby the King sought the collaboration and support of the freemen. Yet even in the Middle Ages it became clear that the political institutions of England would not develop in the same way as those of France. The latter were then based upon a very firmly established feudal system. This made the King try to assert his authority over his very powerful vassals by seeking the support of the bourgeoisie, who partially surrendered their liberty in return for the security which he offered. By this means absolute monarchy was established. The bourgeoisie later tried to do away with this absolutism, and it was this which produced the French Revolution.

England started with an extremely strong monarchy in the period immediately following the Norman Conquest. Feudalism existed, but the King soon succeeded in weakening his vassals, mainly by dividing up their lands. In order to strengthen themselves against the King, the feudal lords united themselves with the knights of the shire and the burgesses from the boroughs in Parliament, the power of which gradually increased until it became impossible for the King to resist its demands. When Parliament had become so powerful, parliamentary government was able to develop without any need for a revolution comparable to that of 1789. Gradual modifications in the structure of Parliament sufficed to give expression to the decline of the aristocracy, the dominant position of the House of Commons, the consolidation of the party system, and the supreme power wielded by Cabinets drawn from the majority party.

Parliament was originally an assembly of 'those who pray, those who fight and those who work'. The House of Commons became a distinct political organ as the outcome of two successive developments already described. First, the clergy abandoned their claim to be represented in Parliament because, not wishing to sit and act jointly with the laity, they chose to make a separate agreement with the King to determine what taxes they should pay. At a later stage, what remained of Parliament split up into two Houses—the Lords consisting of the bishops and the barons, and the Commons made up of representatives of local communities—knights of the shire and burgesses from the boroughs. No precise date can be given for the split, but the two Houses met separately in the middle of the fourteenth century, and a Speaker was elected in 1377.

At the same time, the House of Commons, at first relatively insignificant, was assuming an increasingly important rôle. It was acknowledged to be the equal of the other House when it was recognised that they should deliberate separately and that the Lords could not meet if there was no House of Commons in existence owing to prorogation or dissolution. Peers still take precedence over members of the House of Commons, but the political influence of the Commons has been on the increase ever since the sixteenth century.

The Commons made their influence felt through the 'power of the purse', an important factor in bringing the monarchy to accept a parliamentary system. The lower House was elected by those who bore the brunt of the burden of taxation, and from 1395 onwards supply was voted by the Commons 'with the advice and consent of the Lords Spiritual and Temporal'. By 1407 they had the right to vote taxes in the first instance and exclusive control over the expenditure of the public revenue.

The legislative powers of Parliament developed out of the right to present petitions to the King, which the Commons soon secured on the same terms as the Lords. Legislation used to be enacted by the King in the form of ordinances, but in the fifteenth century Henry V undertook to make these in accordance with the wishes of Parliament as expressed in its petitions. During the reign of Henry VI towards the end of the fifteenth century, Parliament was no longer content to petition the King to make ordinances but itself assumed the legislative initiative by presenting him with texts already drawn up in the form of bills. When the two Houses had agreed upon a text, they had still to obtain the consent of the sovereign, and for many years it was possible that this might be refused, as it frequently was under Elizabeth I and William III. Since 1707, however, the royal consent has become a formality. Parliament's conquest of the legislative power became completed when, after 1668, the King lost his power to legislate by ordinance.

Finally, the power of Parliament and the influence of the Commons were further enhanced by the recognition of the authority, first of the two Houses and later of the Commons alone, to control the activities of the government. With an irresponsible monarchy, it would have needed a revolution to give Parliament control over the executive. Under the incipient parliamentary system, however, the same end was achieved, as we have already seen, by Parliament gaining control over the King's advisers. First, it secured the right to be told who these were; then it gradually managed to ensure that persons of its own choice were appointed; and subsequently the King undertook to submit his ordinances for ratification by his advisers so that they became publicly responsible for the decisions of the Crown. Cabinet responsibility developed out of the procedure for impeachment, the earliest instances of which are found in the fourteenth century. This has now been imitated in many other countries but is no longer employed in Great Britain. It made it possible for a minister to be tried by the House of Lords on charges brought against him by the Commons, since the Lords had inherited the judicial powers recognised in Magna Charta as belonging to Parliament. Impeachment dropped out of use in the Tudor period, but it was revived under the Stuarts and employed by the Commons in an attempt to secure redress against the executive. The process whereby the Cabinet became politically responsible fell into several clearly distinct stages. First, ministers began to be impeached on serious charges of a political nature instead of solely for criminal offences. Next, Parliament stopped the King pardoning anyone found guilty on impeachment. Then, in the eighteenth century, several Cabinets resigned on account of opposition in the Commons, although it was not yet generally accepted that a government must resign in such circumstances. Finally, in 1782, Lord North and his government chose to resign after an adverse vote in the Commons rather than risk impeachment. Ministerial responsibility, originally individual and penal, thus became collective and purely political. The last occasion on which impeachment was used to bring a minister to trial was in the case of Lord Melville in 1805. As the King had to act on the advice of his ministers, it was better from the political point of view to remove them from power than to subject them to penal sanctions. In the nineteenth century, electoral reform produced a democratic political system and gave rise to the constitutional convention whereby the Lords, no longer predominant in the Cabinet, were deprived of the power to overthrow a government.

The Commons thus increased in importance until it became

the House we know today. The basis of its power is the
sovereignty of Parliament. We must therefore see how the
juridical supremacy of Parliament has been reconciled with the
de facto political supremacy of the Cabinet. For this purpose,
we shall examine in turn the composition of the House of
Commons, its organisation and its powers.

The Composition of the House of Commons

The composition of the House of Commons explains why the
lower House is in theory supreme and in practice tends to
collaborate with the Cabinet without questioning its *de facto*
supremacy.

The sovereignty of Parliament or, for all practical purposes,
of the House of Commons is largely due to its popular origins
and representative character.

We saw in the chapter on the electoral system how the
modern House of Commons bears no resemblance to the
assembly of more or less arbitrarily chosen representatives of
local communities out of which it has developed. We need not
dwell again on the existence of universal suffrage, the abolition
of the last survivals of plural voting, and the absence of restrictions on candidatures, the combined effect of which has been
to make the House of Commons quite as genuinely representative as any other assembly elected by majority vote.

The system of election by simple majority means that
different opinions are not always represented in the House
anything like proportionately to their respective strengths in
the country. But this injustice is generally accepted as a lesser
evil than the disadvantages associated with proportional representation. The important point is that the injustice is recognised, and is partly counteracted by the fact that any party
which benefits from it is always conscious that after the next
election it may itself have less than its fair share of seats. This
provides a stronger check against abuse of power by the
majority than exists in many other states where much intrigue
goes on behind the façade of proportional representation.

As far as the different social classes are concerned, practically
every section of the community is now certain of some representation in the House of Commons. The extension of the
franchise led to demands for members of the newly enfranchised

classes to sit in the Commons. This became possible once large private fortunes ceased to be important in securing election, while the rise of the Labour Party has naturally produced a marked change in the social background of members of Parliament.

In the course of the last century there has thus been a marked change in the proportions of members of Parliament drawn from various different walks of life. Members of titled families used to be in the majority. In the inter-war period they were estimated to account for at least two-fifths of the Conservatives, a quarter of the Liberals and an insignificant proportion of Labour members; the overall percentage was probably much higher—about 40% of the whole House. The subsequent eclipse of the Liberal Party and the increase in the number of Labour members has since reduced the aggregate percentage by more than half.

Persons of no definite occupation used to be fairly numerous, but this category of member has almost completely disappeared. Even on the Conservative side it would now include barely 3% of the total. In 1867 landowners were preponderant in both parties, whereas today, even among the Conservatives, they are far outnumbered by businessmen and professional people. More than half the successful candidates in each election since 1945 have come from the liberal professions or managerial and administrative positions or have held commissions in the armed forces. Almost another third have been wage-earners or manual workers.

The average level of education of members of Parliament is actually higher than formerly, despite Trevelyan's illuminating comment on the level of parliamentary debates, that in the seventeenth century members quoted the Bible, in the eighteenth and nineteenth centuries the classics, and in the twentieth century nothing at all—an observation applicable to many elected assemblies at the present time. The standard of education has risen considerably. Even among Labour members, the proportion with a university education has grown from 17% in the inter-war period to 33%, though admittedly only half of these were at Oxford or Cambridge. Labour still has the highest proportion of members who have only had an elementary school education. They accounted for 24% of Labour members elected in 1950, compared with less than 5% of the

Conservatives, but that was nevertheless a considerable decline from 72% in the inter-war period and 53% in 1945. Meanwhile the proportion of Labour members educated at the leading public schools (Eton, Harrow, Winchester and Rugby) is now nearly 30% compared with about 10% between the wars. Conservative members still mostly come from the higher strata of society: 64% of those elected in 1950 were educated at public schools and 24% at Eton alone; 59% were university graduates, of whom 27% had been at Oxford and 21% at Cambridge.

This brief analysis not only illustrates the differences between the Labour and Conservative Parties but also gives some very general indication of the change in the type of person elected. Conservative members still come from the more prosperous classes and the upper rungs of the social ladder. In the nineteenth century this was true of nearly all members, but since the Labour Party replaced the Liberals as the second major party a considerable number of middle-class members and persons in relatively humble circumstances have sat in Parliament. Nevertheless, Labour supporters are not exclusively trade unionists or drawn from the less prosperous sections of the community. Even in Great Britain there is now a relatively democratic educational system, especially at the university level, and the general rise in the standard of education has been much more marked and rapid in the Parliamentary Labour Party than in the country as a whole.

In these circumstances, it seems wrong to maintain, as was widely asserted only a few years ago, that the social background of members of Parliament is still, using the term in its broadest sense, aristocratic.

Yet it is clear that the composition of the House of Commons is by no means a completely accurate reflection of the social structure of the country. Even on the Labour side, for example, there are very few manual workers, only 92 of the 617 Labour candidates in 1950 coming into this category. It is less surprising to find that only 7 of the 621 Conservative candidates could be included in this class.[1] Women are also definitely under-represented in the House of Commons. In 1950 there were only 126 women candidates, of whom 21 (14 Labour, 6 Conserva-

---

[1] In 1955 the 623 Conservative candidates included 19 manual workers, of whom 1 was elected, and the 620 Labour candidates 175 manual workers, of whom 97 were elected.

tives and 1 Liberal) were elected.[1] The liberal professions, businessmen and the more privileged and educated sections of the community occupy a far larger place in the House of Commons than would be justified by their numbers in the population as a whole. Yet this is surely true of most of what are regarded as classic examples of democracy. In Great Britain the over-representation of these groups is also a reflection of the relatively conservative social structure, the absence of any very deep divisions of opinion or real class struggle, the respect still accorded to those in the higher positions in the generally accepted social hierarchy, and the distinctive character of British socialism.

The unique social structure of Great Britain is on the whole fairly accurately reflected in the composition of the House of Commons, which, socially at least, is a truly representative assembly. This representative character is the basis of its juridical supremacy.

At the same time, the House of Commons cannot claim to be *more* representative of the British nation than the Cabinet, in whom the people, albeit indirectly, have specifically expressed their confidence. The Cabinet could have no existence apart from the House of Commons, as Bagehot realised when he spoke of 'this fusion of the legislative and executive functions' as 'the latent essence and effectual secret of the English constitution'. The fortunes of the Cabinet and the majority party in the Commons are so inseparably linked that they should really be considered as one. The opposition, on the other hand, is merely the official organ for criticising the government with the hope of replacing it after the next election, and the electorate would not wish it to assume any other rôle. The system of elections by simple majority means that, except when the two-party system is temporarily in abeyance, the House of Commons normally tends to co-operate with the government.

The Organisation of the House of Commons

The above considerations help to explain the organisation of the House of Commons. The victory of Parliament over the Crown made the Commons, from a legal point of view, an

---

[1] In 1955 only 75 of the 1,409 candidates were women (32 Conservative and 43 Labour); of these, 24 (10 Conservative and 14 Labour) were elected.

independent sovereign assembly. In practice, however, it normally refrains from using its independence to attack the government, and in this it is actually acting in accordance with the will of the people. This same combination of ideas that we have discussed above will also help to explain the organisation of the House.

The arrangements governing its sittings, the privileges of the House and its members, and the office of the Speaker all reveal the independence characteristic of a sovereign body.

The Commons enjoy the freedom of assembly which is a necessary condition of parliamentary sovereignty. Parliament today might somewhat loosely be described as a permanent institution, continuing in existence from one generation to another, although periodically suspended for brief intervals. Eight centuries ago it was entirely within the discretion of the King to summon Parliament whenever he thought fit, but today the sovereign has to act in accordance with the will of the people and must therefore convoke regular sessions. It would really be more accurate to say that Parliament is a temporary institution brought into existence by a general election and terminated either by completing its statutory term or, more usually, by a dissolution. The law merely requires that fresh elections be held within three years after the dissolution of Parliament. In practice, however, the same royal proclamation which dissolves the old Parliament also summons the new one.

This, like other conventions of the British constitution, has only very gradually become an established rule. The earliest Parliaments only lasted for a few days or weeks. A statute of Edward III required Parliament to meet at least once a year, but this was almost invariably disregarded. Later, in the reign of Richard II, the King found himself obliged to have resort to Parliament and kept it in existence for a long period during which it was prorogued from time to time and recalled for further sessions. Thence arose the idea that a Parliament does not cease to exist unless prorogued or dissolved. One Parliament in the reign of Charles II lasted for no less than eighteen years. In 1694 its life was restricted to a maximum of three years. The limit was raised to seven years after the accession of George I by the Septennial Act of 1715. For the next two centuries this remained the maximum term for which Parliament might continue in existence if not previously dissolved. This period was reduced to five years by the Parliament Act of 1911.

The supremacy of Parliament means that it has the power to prolong its own existence, even though this is not expressly provided for in the Parliament Act. The life of the Parliament elected in 1910 was prolonged by Acts passed in 1916 and 1918, and during the last war the term of the Parliament elected in 1935 was similarly extended from year to year until it was finally dissolved in 1945. The supremacy of Parliament is also reflected in the provision of the Representation of the People Act, 1867, whereby its powers ceased to terminate automatically on the death of the sovereign.

Meetings of Parliament are of course grouped into sessions, in the course of which either House may adjourn as it thinks fit, independently of the Crown or of the other House. A new session is opened every year by the Queen, when the Speech from the Throne is read either by the Queen in person or else by the Lord Chancellor. But after the Commons have heard the Speech from the Throne they always begin a new session by giving a reading to a bill, following a procedure which is now a pure formality, to reassert their freedom to decide whether or not to accept the programme outlined in the Queen's Speech. At the beginning of the first session of a new Parliament, when the Speaker's appointment has been submitted to the Queen for approval, he then asks the sovereign to reaffirm the ancient and undoubted privileges of the House, and this request is duly granted. The length of each session is in practice a matter for the Cabinet, whose decisions are accepted by the House.

The rights and privileges of the House of Commons are not merely full of historical significance but also visible evidence that it is still not subject to any kind of formal restraint. In the first place, members have complete freedom from arrest while Parliament is sitting and for forty days before and after each session, except in cases of treason, felony or breach of the peace. Their freedom of speech, claimed since very early times and finally recognised in the Bill of Rights, means that no proceedings may be taken against any member on account of any speech or statement made by him in Parliament, and not since 1629 has legal action been taken against any member for voicing seditious opinions in Parliament. The Commons, through the Speaker, have the right of access to the Queen. They can

regulate the composition of their House subject to the provisions of the electoral law. They have the right to determine
their own procedure and to exclude strangers. Debates are
normally open to the public, but strangers may be asked to
withdraw from the Chamber if this is thought necessary, as in
fact occurred in 1908-09 in order to prevent suffragette disturbances and in 1920 to avoid the risk of demonstrations over the
Irish question. The House can also refuse to allow the publication of its debates, and has exercised this right on several occasions, notably in 1738 and 1762. Reports began to be published
by Hansard in 1803 and were made official in 1909, but in theory
they still appear only on sufferance and not by positive right.

Members of Parliament are entitled to a salary, originally
fixed at £400 in 1911, rising to £600 in 1937 and to £1,000 in
1946, in addition to which since July 1954 they have received
an allowance of £2 for every day the House sits. The House has
the right to refuse the resignations of its members. Those who
wish to resign therefore have recourse to the Act of 1705,
designed to protect the independence of the Commons by
providing that any member who accepts an office of profit under
the Crown automatically vacates his seat. It is still the practice
for any member who wishes to resign to ask to be appointed to
a purely nominal office—Steward of the Manor of Northstead
or Steward of the Chiltern Hundreds—which he surrenders
again as soon as he has been installed. Finally, the House of
Commons has the right to impose sanctions for breach of
privilege of the House, which may take the form of warnings,
reprimands, imprisonment or possibly a fine, though the latter
has never been imposed since 1666.

None of these prerogatives, some of which are substantially
similar to those of other parliamentary assemblies, is as vital as
the rôle of the Speaker. This merits special attention. The independence and supremacy of the Commons are personified in
this distinguished figure, clad in wig and gown, who moves in
procession with the mace, which is the symbol of the authority
of the House and therefore also of the Speaker himself.

Though the Speaker's is one of the oldest and most respected
offices in the state, it is very different from what it was when
Thomas Hungerford was appointed as the first Speaker in 1377.
Today, the Speaker still has the same dual function of upholding
the privileges of the House of Commons and presiding over and

controlling its debates to prevent them getting out of order and to see they result in valid decisions. The first of these functions was originally the more important, but over the last five centuries the emphasis has gradually shifted to the second.

Initially, the independence of the Speaker declined until it was soon practically non-existent. In the fourteenth century the Speaker was expected to defend the rights of the Commons against any external threat. When the King became particularly anxious to obtain the support of the Commons, he therefore found it a great help to have a Speaker who was fully in his confidence. Under the Tudors, Speakers were actually nominated by the Crown, and it became customary for them to receive an annual allowance of £100 from the sovereign and to be appointed to some high office in the state; in 1593 Sir Edward Coke was simultaneously Speaker and Solicitor-General, and under Queen Anne, Harley was both Speaker and a Secretary of State. The Speaker thus became a 'King's man' upon whom the Crown relied to control the House and keep it on the right lines at the time when the sovereign was trying to use his patronage to dominate the Commons. The Speaker steered the debates in whatever direction the King desired, and would see that matters which the King did not wish to have discussed were on no account raised. He informed the Commons of the wishes of the sovereign, and communicated to him the advice of his faithful Commons. During the reign of James I the Commons protested that the King had no right to intervene through the Speaker in this way. If they had important issues to debate, they sometimes even went so far as to deliberate without the Speaker being present.

As the Commons grew more influential, the powers of the Crown over the Speaker gradually declined. The House became increasingly self-assertive, and the Speaker found himself obliged to act as its spokesman in defending its rights. During the conflict between Charles I and the House of Commons it became established that the Speaker's first loyalty was to the House. The election of a Speaker by the House began to assume far greater significance than the royal consent to his appointment, which became a mere formality. His name is still submitted to the sovereign for approval, but the last occasion on which this was refused was by Charles II in the case of Sir Edward Seymour in 1679.

After the Crown lost control over the Speaker, the office was for many years exposed to risks of partiality of another kind through becoming involved in party politics. Onslow, who was Speaker for thirty-four years at the beginning of the eighteenth century, set a good example of impartiality by resigning his office as Treasurer of the Navy in order to show that he was independent of the government. But his successors for the next hundred years did not adhere to his conception of the office. Not until the nineteenth century did it become the generally accepted principle, never questioned since 1870, that a Speaker, once elected, takes no further part in party politics.

Several factors combine to guarantee the political neutrality which is basic to the modern concept of the Speaker's office. When a Speaker is elected at the beginning of a new Parliament, the traditional procedure is for the Clerk of the House, who sits at the Table, to rise and point to two different members in turn, each of whom may nominate a candidate. No member of the government is ever called upon by the Clerk. If, as has usually been the case, the election is uncontested, the new Speaker is nominated by one member from each side of the House. Should two candidates be nominated, however, a vote has to be taken. This was necessary in 1951, when, after a heated debate, the House finally chose the Conservative ex-Minister, Mr W. S. Morrison, in preference to Major Milner of the Labour Party. But the House does not usually divide on party lines over the election of a Speaker. Generally there has been only one candidate, who has been appointed by unanimous agreement. The non-partisan character of the office is strengthened by the tradition that no other candidate should stand against him in a general election.[1] Mr Gully in 1895, Mr Fitzroy in 1935 and Colonel Clifton Brown in 1945 were opposed in their constituencies, but these have been very rare exceptions. Finally, it is now customary to go on re-electing the Speaker as long as he wishes to remain in office, even if the party responsible for electing him in the first place is no longer in the majority. In the nineteenth century the previous Speaker was invariably re-elected after the opposite party had won an election, with the result that between 1801 and 1934 there were only twelve different Speakers. In 1945, when

[1] In 1955, when, for the first time since 1929, there were no uncontested elections, the Speaker was opposed but re-elected by a large majority.

Labour had a majority of over 200, it did not oppose the re-election of Colonel Clifton Brown, who had been the Conservative nominee in 1943.

The same concept of the Speaker as a figure above party is reflected in the functions of his office. Since 1855 the Chairman of the Committee of Ways and Means, and since 1902 the Deputy Chairman, have been empowered to act on behalf of the Speaker. His functions include representing the Commons in their relations with outside persons or bodies. The Speaker is the intermediary through whom the Commons can communicate with the Queen, and to whom documents and messages intended for the House are addressed. It is his duty to defend the privileges of the House and to execute its orders and decisions. His most important functions, however, are concerned with his control over debates, for which purpose he acts as an impartial arbiter, armed with substantial powers.

When the House is sitting, the Speaker sits in his Chair with the mace before him on the Table and has complete control over the debates. Anyone entering or leaving the Chamber must bow to the Speaker, and members must always address their remarks to the Chair, a practice which helps to prevent their becoming unduly vehement or abusive. The Speaker decides who shall address the House by calling on one of the members who rise uncovered on both sides of the House to ask for permission to speak. He sees that the debate does not wander from the question under discussion, rules out all dilatory motions, and is responsible for interpreting and ensuring compliance with all the rules and precedents which go to make up the procedure of the House. He ensures that the debate is always free, loyal and courteous. Although the House itself is in theory responsible for maintaining order, there are many detailed rules by virtue of which the Speaker in practice has the power to intervene. He usually has little difficulty in restoring order, even though he has no bell with which to command attention, and the most severe penalty that he can impose is to exclude a member from the Chamber for the rest of the sitting. Apart from a few tempestuous sittings, of which there were some surprising examples in the spring of 1951, the House is, comparatively speaking, extremely calm and respectful. It responds to a call of 'order, order' from the Speaker more readily than many other assemblies would react to the most moving appeals from their presiding officers. There is a polite convention which helps in restoring order whereby any members who are on their feet must sit down whenever the Speaker rises. The Speaker may then call upon a member to apologise or withdraw any remark which was out of order. The member will do so forthwith and the debate can then proceed peaceably once again.

On the very rare occasions when a member does not respond to his call to order, the Speaker has the power, on his own initiative, to exclude him from the Chamber for the rest of the sitting. Alternatively, he can employ the stronger weapon of 'naming' the erring member, in which case he will rise in his place and declare, 'I am obliged to name the honourable Member for such and such a constituency who has held the authority of the Chair in disrespect.' The House can then vote, on the motion of a government spokesman, to exclude the member for either five or twenty sitting days. Very few members, however, have so repeatedly indulged in disorderly behaviour as to run the risk of a general rebuke of this nature.

As the Speaker presides over debates, it falls to him to determine points of order, upon which there can be no appeal against the ruling of the Chair. He also puts questions to the vote, sees that there are no irregularities in the voting, decides whether the 'ayes' or the 'noes' have it, and announces the decision of the House. If necessary, he can require a division to be taken. He also decides whether to accept or refuse motions to apply the closure, and whether to admit or rule out amendments. When the Parliament Act of 1911 almost completely deprived the House of Lords of its powers in regard to money bills, the Speaker was made responsible for examining every bill and certifying which were money bills. The Speaker also appoints the chairmen of standing committees, whom he chooses from the Chairman's Panel, a list of not less than ten members drawn up by the Committee of Selection. He decides how bills are to be allocated between the various standing committees, and in this respect has a comparatively free hand. It is for the Speaker to decide who is the leader of the opposition should this ever be in any doubt. In addition to the foregoing, the Speaker has many other functions, all of which help to reinforce his unchallenged authority.

His authority is recognised both by law and by custom. He lives in apartments within the Palace of Westminster and receives a salary of £5,000 a year. When he retires, he is normally created a viscount and granted a pension. Since 1689 he has taken precedence over all other members of the House of Commons. He used to rank immediately after the Lords, but now, by an order in council of 1919, he has become the seventh person in the kingdom after the royal family. The independence and authority of the Commons are personified in its Speaker.

Yet the Speaker must exercise his functions with strict impartiality if he is to retain the confidence and respect of the whole House. He never uses his vote as an ordinary member of Parliament. He has a casting vote as Speaker in case of an equality of votes, but always uses this so as to maintain the *status quo*, uphold established precedents and previous decisions of the House, and avoid making himself personally responsible for bringing about any change. What he really does, therefore, is to put a temporary stop to the debate on an issue that will probably be revived at a later date. As Colonel Clifton Brown remarked, the Speaker is neither a government man nor an opposition man but a House of Commons man. The essence of his impartiality lies in the way he maintains an atmosphere of fair play by ensuring that the opposition have an opportunity to express their views and criticisms, yet at the same time seeing that there is no parliamentary obstruction to hinder the Cabinet in its task of governing the country.

Thus the organisation of the House of Commons does not in any way tend to bring it into conflict with the executive. The government is fully accountable to the Commons, but does not find itself hampered in its work by the committee system or by the procedure of the House.

THE COMMITTEE SYSTEM

The House of Commons, like other legislatures, has been obliged to do some of its work through committees. Its committee system, however, is quite peculiar to Great Britain, and bears no resemblance to such systems as those of the American Congress or the French Parliament.

The British have never had the kind of committee which is a permanent specialised organ responsible for controlling a particular branch of government activities and administration, and which usually develops into a powerful and outspoken body and tends to assume some of the functions of the assembly itself in regard to legislation and criticism of the government. It would indeed be true to say that there is no other country where committees play as small a part in the work of Parliament as they do in Great Britain. Britain now has an elaborate committee system, but the basic principle is still that the House itself, sitting as a committee of the whole House, should undertake the preparatory work for its sessions. This rule was strictly observed for two centuries, and even in modern times it has not been seriously undermined. Other committees were originally set up solely in order to divide up the work of the committee of the whole House. They were conceived as smaller replicas of the House itself and were expected to give general expressions of opinion of the same order as the decisions of the House on the legislative or financial business referred to them for report. Committee members are not specialists and are sometimes appointed in a purely temporary capacity. Some committees of inquiry have also been set up to undertake tasks which a large assembly was unsuited to perform, such as conducting investigations or examining credentials, where no issue of outstanding political importance has been involved.

The importance of the committee of the whole House increased during the seventeenth century. This can easily be explained by reference to the historical circumstances of the time. Committees had been used by the House since early in the sixteenth century and were first mentioned in its Journals in 1571. Originally, however, a committee did not imply a group of persons but a single individual, usually a privy councillor, appointed to consider and report on a particular bill. Committees in the normal sense of the word were established at a later date. These were small at first, but increased in size until they included somewhere between thirty and forty members appointed by the Speaker, over whose choice the privy councillors exercised a dominating influence. The more important of these select committees gradually developed into permanent institutions which the Commons employed for the simple reason that they had not been able to devise any other method of preparing the business of the House.

Yet the House was always distrustful of committees because they could be influenced by the King through his power indirectly to control the appointment of their members. The committee of the whole House emerged when James I gave up trying to control the House as the Tudors had done before him. The Commons included fewer privy councillors than formerly, and ordinary members wanted to discuss publicly and not under the eye of the Speaker, at that time an officer of the Crown, questions which until then had only been considered in the secret counsels of a few leading ministers. The first mention of a bill having been considered in a committee of the whole House, the Speaker having left the Chair, was in 1607. Standing committees also emerged at about this time, when five were appointed at the beginning of one Parliament and remained in existence throughout the session. One, the Committee of Grievances, played an important part in the conflict between the Commons and Charles I. The idea of specialist committees was afterwards abandoned. Once the government was fully accountable to the Commons, it had no need to set up special committees to become the rivals of ministers. After the Restoration it generally worked through a committee of the whole House, and this has been its normal practice ever since.

This system is admittedly not without its drawbacks. As Gladstone declared as far back as 1881, 'There is no legislative assembly in the world that works itself so pitilessly, so relentlessly, as the British House of Commons.' Today it is naturally much more overburdened with work, and it has proved impossible to adhere rigidly to the tradition principle which ruled out any division of labour. Yet the House has never shown the least desire to divest itself of any of its all-embracing political responsibilities or to set up specialist standing committees which might restrict the freedom of action of the Cabinet. Some smaller committees have been established, but for the sole purpose of assisting the House as a whole. The committee system remains centred upon the committee of the whole House. Law-making and the control of the executive are still, not merely in law but in fact, functions of the whole House sitting together.

A committee of the whole House is really no more or less than the House itself, meeting more informally and deliberating under a more flexible procedure. The outward sign of this greater informality can be seen in the initial procedure whereby the Speaker leaves the Chair and his place is taken by the Chairman of the Committee of Ways and Means, while the mace is placed underneath the Table upon which it usually lies.

This recalls how the House used to assert its independence from the Speaker when he was the agent of the Crown.

What makes procedure in committee more flexible is primarily that members may speak more than once on the same question. This is essential if bills and financial measures are to be examined in detail. Each committee of the whole House is regarded as a separate institution specially created for the particular purpose indicated in its title. Thus there are, on the one hand, the committees on public bills, and committees for other business, mostly relating to finance, of which the Committee of Ways and Means, the Committee of Supply and committees on Money Resolutions are the main examples.

Committees sit by order of the House. The chairman reports to the Speaker at the end of each sitting, when he returns to the Chair and the mace is replaced upon the Table. If a committee has completed its assigned task, its chairman says, 'The committee have come to certain resolutions'; if not, he says, 'The committee have made progress in the matters referred to them, and ask leave to sit again.' The House then fixes the day on which it will receive the committee's report, or on which it is to meet again. Eventually, on the appointed day, the House will adopt the committee's resolutions.

There are also some smaller committees, more like parliamentary committees in other countries, which are employed to undertake certain specialised tasks, or simply to permit some division of the work of the House.

Joint committees of Lords and Commons, under the chairmanship of a peer, may be set up by agreement between the two Houses to discuss some question of mutual interest, generally matters to which relatively little political significance is attached such as the proposal to build an underground railway in London in 1864. A Joint committee has also on occasions been appointed to undertake an inquiry, such as those on the problem of closer unity in the territory of East Africa in 1931 and on Indian Constitutional Reform in 1933. The competence of such committees is generally limited by the decisions of the two Houses, who must agree on what they are empowered to do.

Select committees have a far longer history. They are employed on specialised tasks which the House itself is unsuited to perform, such as the examination of bills which will later be considered in a committee of the whole House. They are chiefly used to carry out inquiries. They seldom have more than fifteen members, who are appointed by the House. The House may also grant a committee special powers should it consider this necessary to enable them to carry out an investigation, including power to examine witnesses and call for papers. A select committee reports to the House, which may debate its report.

Apart from temporary select committees of this kind, a number of perennial select committees on various topics are reappointed every year and remain in existence throughout the session. The best known of these are the Public Accounts Committee, the Committee of Selection, the Standing Orders Committee, the Estimates Committee, the Committee of Privileges, and the Committee on Public Petitions.

So far as the main work of Parliament is concerned, however, the most important committees are the standing committees. These have been set up to undertake certain functions on behalf of the whole House and are normally entrusted with the task of examining and making amendments to all public bills. The Scottish Standing Committee is somewhat exceptional, in that it includes all the seventy-one members for Scottish constituencies, together with ten to fifteen others, and considers all bills that relate exclusively to Scotland. This is a gesture to Scottish nationalist aspirations. Otherwise, a standing committee is simply a miniature of the House itself.

Until 1945 the number of standing committees was limited to five, but the House is now authorised to exceed this figure. The non-specialist character of these committees is shown by the fact that they are distinguished simply by the letters of the alphabet, A, B, C, D, etc. Each committee has a permanent nucleus of 20 members, to whom others up to a maximum of 39 may be added for the consideration of any particular bill. Committee members are appointed by the Committee of Selection, which has the difficult task of ensuring that the various parties and different currents of opinion are represented in proportion to their strength in the House. Chairmen of standing committees are appointed by the Speaker from a Chairman's Panel consisting of not less than ten persons nominated by the Committee of Selection.

Since the standing committee system was adopted in 1907, every bill has automatically been referred to a standing committee unless the Standing Orders of the House (S.O. 38) specifically require that it be considered by a committee of the whole House or by a select committee. The Speaker allocates each bill to a particular committee, and is also empowered to transfer bills from one committee to another. Reports of standing committees are subsequently debated in the House.

The growing volume of legislation has forced the House to make more extensive use of committees, and it seems possible that this process may have to be carried still further in the future. The increasingly technical character of much modern legislation is another important factor which might be held to justify the establishment of specialist committees such as have become a normal part of the machinery of government in most other countries. But there are strong forces of tradition in favour of the House retaining all its principal powers in its own hands. Nor have the British been favourably impressed with the way the committee system functions in other countries. The Cabinet prefers to defend its programme on the floor of the House, where Cabinet ministers can be present and the government can summon up its majority to defeat any undesirable amendment. Nor have the Commons themselves any wish to surrender part of their all-embracing responsibilities to any subsidiary organ. The existing committee system, despite its imperfections, in practice justifies itself by allowing the House to exercise a reasonable amount of control over the executive without paralysing the activity of the government.

PARLIAMENTARY PROCEDURE

The procedure of the House of Commons is directed towards maintaining a similar equilibrium by leaving the House free to express its views without restraint and yet avoiding the twin dangers of Cabinet dictatorship and parliamentary obstruction.

This is particularly true of the legislative procedure. As we have already seen, the government has almost completely monopolised the right to initiate legislation. The bulk of the time of the House is devoted to government business. Ministers have access to special sources of assistance and expert advice, and thus find no difficulty in surmounting all the hazards of the elaborate procedure through which a bill has to pass before it reaches the Statute Book. Private members, on the other hand, have seldom either the means or the opportunity to secure a majority for any measure they may wish to put forward.

The government is generally anxious to carry through its legislative programme with the least possible delay, and to this end sets up special machinery of which that established by the Attlee Cabinet between 1945 and 1951 may be considered typical. A Cabinet committee on future legislation drew up a provisional list of bills that ought to be passed, on the basis of requests from the various departments, and this was submitted to the Cabinet for approval. A definite programme of legislation was then announced in the Speech from the Throne at the beginning of each session, and an inter-departmental Legislation Committee supervised the drafting of the necessary bills.

Bills are drafted in the Office of the Parliamentary Counsel, a subordinate department attached to the Treasury, set up in 1869 and staffed by non-practising lawyers. Each bill is drafted by one of the Parliamentary Counsel on the basis of directions received from the government. The Legislation Committee then approves the bill and decides in which House it should be introduced.

No government bill can become an Act until it has passed the traditional three readings in each House and received the royal assent. From the political point of view the most important part of this process is clearly its passage through the House of Commons, where the government and the opposition each marshal all their forces to its defence or attack. Only in exceptional circumstances, however, do the two sides meet on anything like an equal footing. Usually, the government can be certain of a majority, so that in the end its bills will be passed in the form it desires. The opposition cannot hope to do more than publicly criticise the proposals and put forward a number of amendments, which the House may accept if the Cabinet does not see fit to resist them. Within these fairly narrow limits the debates are conducted with the courtesy traditional in the British Parliament and, at least at the committee stage and afterwards, usually tend to be serious in tone and concerned with technical rather than purely partisan issues. The government has to present its critics with a closely reasoned case and is sometimes kept on the defence for a period of several months. But although there is always the possibility of unexpected developments in the course of a bill's passage through Parliament, the whips have sufficient power to ensure that the final voting will accurately reflect the strengths of the various parties in the House.

Bills are normally presented as written documents, and their first reading is a brief formality. On the appointed day the Clerk of the House simply reads the short title of the bill, whereupon the Speaker then calls upon the minister concerned, who announces the date fixed for the second reading.

The text of the bill is then printed. Before it comes up for a second reading there are usually some discussions in which plans are laid for the later stages of the bill, bearing in mind any likely amendments. The second reading is undoubtedly the most important stage, for it is then that the basic principle and general lines of a bill will be debated. The opposition can vote against this, or alternatively can move to postpone it for six months, which is also tantamount to rejection. The debate which follows may last for one or two days, but the Cabinet does not allow it to drag on indefinitely. For the House to refuse a bill a second reading is considered a defeat for the government comparable to a vote of censure. Peel resigned after a second reading defeat in 1846 and Gladstone in 1873, but it is just as rare for the Cabinet's proposals to be rejected at this stage as at any other time. Nevertheless, it is by no means unknown for the government to decide to withdraw a bill altogether if it has met with very strong opposition on the second reading.

After receiving a second reading, bills are examined in committee. If they impose any tax or relate to the Consolidated Fund or confirm Provisional Orders, they are required by the Standing Orders to be referred to a committee of the whole House. All other bills are allocated by the Speaker to one of the standing committees unless the House specifically decides otherwise. Once a bill has been given a second reading, the general principles are regarded as accepted. The next stage takes the form of a detailed examination, clause by clause, in the course of which amendments are proposed and resisted. When the committee stage is completed, the chairman of the committee moves in the House that its report be accepted, either with or without further amendments.

There is almost always another debate on the report stage, unless the bill has been considered in a committee of the whole House and has not been amended. The third reading follows, usually on the same day. By this time the opposition has generally acquiesced in the victory of the government, and there is only a brief discussion. Occasionally, however, there are important debates in which the government is hard pressed, as the Labour Cabinet was over the nationalisation of iron and steel. After the third reading, the bill is sent to the House of Lords in the form in which it has been passed by the Commons, with possibly some further amendments on points of detail.

It is not possible here to go into all the details of the legislative procedure. There is clearly scope for the government to encounter strong opposition in the course of the debates. The opposition can hold up a bill at the committee stage, when the procedure is more flexible, and the government may quite easily be defeated on a point of detail in a standing committee as these have comparatively few members and not all attend regularly. A minority of six members on the committee which considered the Cinematograph Industry Bill was able to force the committee to hold twenty-three meetings between April and July 1927, in the course of which they forced the committee to divide nearly three hundred times. Nevertheless, ministers, with the help of their expert advisers and of the Parliamentary Counsel, generally manage to overcome or outflank all the obstacles in their path. The risk of parliamentary obstruction is reduced to a minimum by the rules of procedure, and the Speaker or the chairman of the committee sees that these are not allowed to fall into disrespect.

There are also a number of special devices which help the government to carry through its legislative programme by preventing the use of dilatory tactics which would unduly prolong the debates.

Among these is the closure, which may be moved at any time, even in the middle of a speech, provided the Speaker and at least a hundred other members are agreeable. The House (or, *mutatis mutandis*, the committee) votes on the question 'That the question be now put.' If this is carried, the debate comes to an end and the House may proceed to a division on the main question.

Secondly, in order to keep the number of amendments within reasonable bounds, the Speaker and the Chairman of the committee of the whole House have been given drastic powers of deciding which amendments shall be debated. This prerogative was conferred upon them by Standing Order 31 in 1919, and is known as the Kangaroo because Speakers and Chairmen have used their powers to exclude amendments which in their opinion do not merit discussion, even though they may be perfectly in order. The Speaker may state his reasons for excluding an amendment, but he is free to use his powers exactly as he thinks fit, and there can be no doubt that this discretion has been used to very good effect.

Finally, the guillotine, or closure by compartments, can be applied by means of an allocation of time order. The debate is then restricted by laying down a timetable allocating a certain number of days to each stage of the bill. The Cabinet will introduce a motion to apply the guillotine to any bill which it thinks may have difficulty in passing the House. These motions sometimes give rise to lengthy debates, but, once they have been adopted, the House adheres strictly to the timetable and the question is put to the vote automatically at the end of each appointed stage. This makes it quite impossible for the opposition to hold up the passage of a bill, and thus greatly strengthens the hand of the government. It has been suggested that instead of using the guillotine the government and the opposition should agree on what would be a reasonable amount of time to allocate to the various stages. This has not proved acceptable, however, and the growing pressure of legislative business has led to more extensive use of the guillotine. Since 1947 it has been possible for this to be applied to debates in committee, provided that the motion is passed by the House itself. Once an allocation of time order has been passed, a business committee will then divide the bill up into portions corresponding to the stages in the timetable adopted by the House.

By such devices as these, the Cabinet is able in times of emergency, if some vital reform is at stake, or if other circumstances so require, to enact legislation with a minimum of delay without having to refuse a public debate on its proposals. In this way, the traditional procedure of the House has been adapted to meet the exigencies of modern government, and the supremacy of the Commons has been made compatible with the system of Cabinet government.

The Powers of the House of Commons

After considering the development of its organisation and procedure, we must now conclude our study of the House of

Commons by examining its powers and seeing how far it is still in fact an effective check on the power of the executive.

The answer to this question is bound to be very different in the British context from what it would be for any other country, or even for other parliamentary regimes.

The House of Commons on its own can do nothing. Nevertheless, as the Queen and the House of Lords are alike powerless to resist the will of the Commons, they have become the dominant power in a Parliament whose powers are quite unlimited. Parliament set up a new state church in the reign of Henry VIII; it altered the order of succession to the throne in 1701; it united England and Scotland in 1707 and England and Ireland in 1800, and in the twentieth century it has dissolved the union with Ireland, with the exception of the northern counties; in 1911 and 1949 it reduced the powers of the House of Lords and made it merely a revising chamber; it could completely alter the character of the upper House or abolish it altogether, just as it could also abolish the monarchy whenever it chose; it could enact retrospective legislation, suspend individual liberties, or confer absolute power upon a single party or individual. The British Parliament could do any of these things and still be able to show that what it had done was strictly in accordance with the established law of the constitution.

From the political point of view, however, the ascendancy of the Cabinet has been matched by a decline in the influence of the House of Commons and thus of Parliament itself. The authority of the Cabinet is founded upon its mandate from the nation, and it is many years since Parliament enacted any important reform against the wishes of the government. Although the government can do nothing without parliamentary approval, the Commons are usually ready to carry out its wishes. This is really another aspect of the constant mutual interdependence of the Cabinet and the House of Commons which is the key to the functioning of the British political system. There has never been any true separation of powers. The party system has helped to maintain close collaboration between the executive and the legislature, and if this were ever to break down it would mean the end of Cabinet government. It manifests itself in each of the three principal spheres of parliamentary activity: legislation, finance, and the control of the executive.

LEGISLATION

The influence of the government over legislation has already been described. The vast majority of bills reaching the Statute Book are government measures. The Cabinet can count on a majority for its bills, both on the floor of the House and in committee, since they will be measures to give effect to the programme of the majority party. Nevertheless, bills introduced by the opposition or by some influential private member are occasionally passed by the House. Sometimes, too, the Cabinet has been virtually compelled by pressure from the Commons to adopt a private member's bill as its own and endeavour to secure its passage through Parliament. The government may also decide, rather than run the risk of a split in its own party, to make drastic changes in its proposals or even to withdraw completely a bill that has met with particularly shattering criticism from some opposition speaker. This does not happen very often, but is still by no means impossible.

The committee stage provides an opportunity for serious debate in which the government is often led to accept amendments that seem likely to improve the bill from a technical or a political point of view and likely to facilitate its execution. No Cabinet, no matter how secure its majority, can afford to neglect reasoned criticism. By paying heed to its critics it can strengthen its own position. On the other hand, a Cabinet with a small majority is obliged to pay attention to criticism. The Standing Orders and procedure of the House make it possible to prevent obstruction, but it is still within the power of the opposition repeatedly to press matters to a vote and thus force the majority to give frequent proof that it is still united. Labour governments have to hold their majorities together over a longer period than Conservative ministries, as the latter do not have to contend with an adverse majority in the House of Lords. Even where Parliament has delegated to ministers part of what used to be its most important function, the supremacy of the Commons over legislation is still in principle unimpaired. Statutory instruments have to be laid before Parliament, and there is a specified period during which either House may move that they be annulled. Since 1944, a Select Committee on Statutory Rules and Orders or, as they are now called, Statutory Instruments has been set up to examine delegated legislation and draw the attention of the House to the use which ministers have made of their far-reaching powers.

In view of all these considerations, it is impossible to contend that there is any immediate danger of Cabinet dictatorship.

FINANCE

The Cabinet does undoubtedly have a great deal of power in regard to finance, as has already been shown. Finance was always allowed to remain a matter for the government, even after Parliament emerged victorious from its great struggle against the King and secured the powers on which is founded the supremacy of Parliament and, ultimately, the sovereignty of the people. Today, however, Parliament is no longer in conflict with the monarchy, which has lost all its former powers. Under the present system of party government it can be assumed that there will be no divergence of views between the Cabinet and the lower House. The power of the Commons to control finance has therefore ceased to be an important issue.

The formal provisions for parliamentary control of finance rest on the principle that no tax may be levied or expenditure incurred without the consent of Parliament. All financial business must be introduced in the House of Commons, which alone has the sovereign right to decide whether to grant the necessary authorisations. All government proposals are subjected to detailed scrutiny by a committee of the whole House. No new expenditure is ever authorised until any departure from previous estimates, if not already sanctioned, has at least been fully disclosed.

On the other hand, there is another rule whereby only the Crown, which in effect means the Cabinet, can introduce any kind of financial business, whether it relates to revenue or to expenditure. Supply is likewise voted to the Crown. Thus no private member can ever propose any increase in expenditure or any additional taxation. His normal right to propose amendments to government proposals is exceptionally limited, since he can only move a reduction in the sums requested. The Commons do not determine financial policy, but merely pass the financial legislation necessary to give effect to the policy of the government. This is mainly the responsibility of the Chancellor of the Exchequer, assisted by the Treasury, the

Central Economic Planning Staff, the Inland Revenue and the Department of Customs and Excise. Income tax has to be voted annually, but many other taxes go on being levied year after year under permanent legislation and so escape annual review. Parliament can only consider them if the Chancellor of the Exchequer asks the Committee of Ways and Means to authorise some change in the rate of tax or in the method of its assessment. On the expenditure side, many annual outlays are permanent charges on the Consolidated Fund which the state is quite unavoidably obliged to incur. They are simply authorised by annual resolutions passed by the House without debate on the day that the Chancellor of the Exchequer presents his budget, shortly after 1st April when the new financial year begins. Other resolutions are passed at the same time so as to allow any change in taxation announced in the budget speech to be put into force straight away, under the Provisional Collection of Taxes Act 1913, until such time as it can be embodied in the Finance Act which will not become law until several months later. The estimates are examined by the whole House in Committee of Supply, which begins its sittings in February each year. Some are also discussed by the Select Committee on Estimates. Only a few of the estimates are actually debated, however, as the Standing Orders only allow a maximum of twenty-six Supply Days a year.

Provisions for raising revenue are considered by the whole House in Committee of Ways and Means, where the proceedings are usually brief. Taxation is finally authorised in the Finance Act. The House concludes its financial business for the year towards the end of July or the beginning of August, when it passes the Appropriation Act formally granting the supply requested in the estimates.

It is generally agreed that these arrangements leave the Commons little effective control over finance. The majority are certain to support the government's financial proposals at every stage, just as they do any other aspect of its programme. Since 1688, the Commons have never once refused to grant the funds requested by the Cabinet, which now amount to about £5,000 millions a year, the budget for 1952-53 having been £4,661 millions.[1] The limited time allowed for financial debates, together with the guillotine, rules out any detailed examination

[1] £4,758 millions for 1956-57.

of the more technical aspects of the budget proposals, for which a committee of the whole House would in any case be quite unsuitable. The Select Committee on Estimates was set up in response to demands for more searching scrutiny of the estimates, but it has so far only had a limited success. In any case, a large proportion of public expenditure is now covered by Treasury borrowing, and the House has frequently shown itself very ready to grant the government wide powers to raise loans in times of national emergency or to meet any urgent needs for funds. This was done, for example, in the National Loans Acts of 1939 and 1944 and in the Miscellaneous Financial Provisions Act of 1946, which gave the government what many considered to be excessively broad discretion in the administration of the national finances.

Nevertheless, the government does not have a completely free hand. It cannot behave in a completely arbitrary fashion for, just as with any other aspect of its programme, the proposals which it presents to Parliament must take account of the political situation and the state of public opinion. The House of Commons realises that, though it may criticise the government's proposals, it will have to accept them all *en bloc* in the end. Instead of trying to pit its judgment against the experts responsible for the details, it very wisely concentrates on the political aspects of the government proposals, which are singled out by the opposition from among the mass of figures before the House. Here again we can see the fundamentally democratic nature of the regime, whereby the functions of the Commons in regard to finance are in fact one aspect of their control over the general policy of the government.

CONTROL OF THE EXECUTIVE

The most important power of the lower House under any system of democratic parliamentary government is generally considered to be its control over the executive through the system of Cabinet responsibility. In Britain the government is responsible exclusively to the House of Commons. As we have already shown, the House exercises its power with restraint, or rather, to be more precise, a general election usually gives the Cabinet a sufficiently large and cohesive majority for it to be practically sure of remaining in office until the next election. Party discipline and the ever-present possibility of a dissolution ensure that the majority does not disintegrate. Even if defeated in Parliament, the government is not necessarily bound to resign. It will not do so unless the Prime Minister considers the question at issue to be of major importance, and even then he still has the alternative of appealing to the country for a fresh mandate for his policy. Finally, votes of censure have become practically obsolete.

Almost every vote taken in the House is governed by a strict system of party discipline. Only on a small number of questions of no political significance will the government 'take off the whips' and allow members to vote according to their own personal convictions. Party discipline has been greatly strengthened by the fact that all important votes take the form of a division. Under this method of voting, members not only have to vote in person but must leave their places and actually divide themselves into two groups for all to see—the 'ayes' and the 'noes', or supporters and opponents of the government. When the House proceeds to a division, bells are rung and the words 'Division, division' are called out in all the corridors. Any member wishing to vote for the government leaves his place and goes out of the Chamber through the door behind the Speaker's Chair, turns to his left and passes through the 'ayes' lobby. Opposition members leave the Chamber by the door opposite the Speaker's Chair and turn left into the 'noes' lobby. The government and opposition each appoint two tellers, who count the members as they pass through their respective lobbies and give their names to the division clerks. Members then return to the Chamber, the 'ayes' by the door facing the Speaker and the 'noes' by the door behind the Speaker's Chair.

This method of voting clearly gives ample opportunities for taking the other side by surprise. The whips are past masters of the art of picking the right moment to call for a division when the other side are widely dispersed, summoning up reserves of potential voters at the last moment from obscure corners of the Palace of Westminster, and making a rapid search for absent members at their homes or clubs or at the theatre should a division seem likely. The whips will arrange pairs, now the normal device whereby any member who wishes to absent himself from a particular sitting comes to an agreement with a member of the opposite party who undertakes not to attend on that day. Nevertheless, the outcome of a division is really a foregone conclusion. It is practically unheard of for a member to vote against his party, as this would be considered an act of disloyalty to his own side. A member of the majority who went into the opposition lobby would run the risk of disciplinary sanctions from his own party and would have to be able to convince his constituents that he had some good reason for deserting the government they had given him a mandate to support. A few lapses will be tolerated, provided that they do not occur often or on important issues, but in fact they are never sufficiently numerous to endanger the government majority, save in an exceptionally delicate political situation. It is thus true to say, as Sir Ivor Jennings has remarked, that under normal circumstances when the government has a majority, it is not the House which controls the government but the government that controls the House.

Nevertheless, few would dream of questioning the importance of the House of Commons *vis-à-vis* the government. Although its rôle is very different from that of the lower house in France or elsewhere, its functions are no less important and are very effectively fulfilled. The House can make its influence felt in three principal ways.

In the first place, the House of Commons is, indirectly at least, the channel through which men rise to government office. The Cabinet is of course much more than merely a committee of Parliament. In the strictly literal sense it is nothing more, but on the other hand the Prime Minister decides on the composition of his Cabinet without consulting the Commons, and no organic relationship exists between the House and the Cabinet which is under no obligation to keep the Commons informed of its decisions. Moreover, no committee of the House would ever have been granted the right to dissolve Parliament. The Cabinet in its origins was clearly much more closely related to the Privy Council than to Parliament. Nevertheless, it would be wrong to describe the House of Commons as a mere piece of electoral machinery which exists simply to register the wishes of the electorate by putting a particular government in power. In fact, the House determines the composition of the Cabinet by acting as a kind of filter through which potential Cabinet ministers are brought to light. Very few have attained Cabinet rank through other channels. Joseph Chamberlain, who served his political apprenticeship in local government, was a notable exception. As a general rule, no politician can hope to rise to ministerial office in Britain except through a parliamentary career, generally in the House of Commons.

It is assumed that the people will not be able to judge whether a man would make a good minister, but that over a period of time this will gradually become apparent to the House. A potential minister must first of all convince his own party of his abilities, by giving proof of his general competence and by his timely interventions in debate and his skill as a debater. If he displays these qualities, his standing in the party will slowly rise until he reaches the front bench and so comes into the running for high ministerial office. Advancement will only be gained by those who show themselves likely to be an asset to their party, whether in the majority or in opposition. Although the younger Pitt was Prime Minister at the age of twenty-four, no one has attained that office in the twentieth century without having already sat for many years in the House of Commons. A. J. Balfour was member of Parliament for 28 years before becoming Prime Minister, Campbell-Bannerman for 38 years, Asquith for 22 years, Lloyd George for 26 years, Bonar Law for 23 years, Baldwin for 15 years, Ramsay Mac-Donald for 18 years, Neville Chamberlain for 19 years, Winston Churchill for 40 years, Clement Attlee for 22 years and Sir Anthony Eden for 32 years. All these except Ramsay Mac-Donald had previously held office in other Cabinets and had often occupied important ministerial positions. The leader of the majority party needs to be, and in practice always is, an experienced parliamentarian. Usually his colleagues have had considerable parliamentary experience before ever entering the government. The time is now past when a young man who had sat in Parliament for six years, spoken twice in important debates, and could show a reasonably good record of attendance at the House, could be appointed to an important office simply because he was the son of the Duke of Devonshire. Nowadays, only unusual developments within the party or exceptional personal qualifications can exempt anyone from having to serve a long political apprenticeship.

The Cabinet is consequently more than a government formed by the party with a majority in the House of Commons. It is a government actually composed of House of Commons men. One of the reasons why they are able to command the confidence of the Commons is possibly because it is through the House that they have themselves risen to power.

A second way in which the Commons make their influence felt is by providing the Cabinet with a valuable guide to the state of public opinion. The House and its committees are in session seven hours a day for nine months of the year. Although the Cabinet also has access to other sources of information, it inevitably tends to look primarily to the Commons to keep it abreast with current opinion on major political issues. Even when his party is in opposition, a private member with the requisite personality and ability has plenty of opportunities to bring pressure to bear upon ministers, either in the course of debates or through the many, usually extremely cordial, personal contacts which take place while the House is sitting.

It is of paramount importance for the Prime Minister and the Cabinet that their party should not lose its majority at the next election. They therefore value any opposition to or criticism of their policy as shedding light on the state of public opinion, so that they can size up the political situation and 'see which way the wind is blowing' before deciding whether it would be better to stand firm or to give way to the opposition and thus deprive it of a weapon which it would be sure to use against them in any future election campaign.

The Commons thus have a vital part to play in the system of government by opinion. Even a small minority in the House can sometimes rally a large section of public opinion against the government. Whenever this seems likely, self-interest and democratic principles alike indicate that it is time for the government to change its policy. The National Government was thus led to make considerable changes in the Incitement to Disaffection Bill in 1934, even though it had such an overwhelming majority that the bill could easily have been pushed through in its original form. The Hoare-Laval Agreement for settling the conflict between Italy and Abyssinia in 1935 met with very strong opposition when it became known in the country, with the result that it was violently attacked in the Commons and even some of the majority went so far as to put down a hostile motion. This led to the resignation of the Foreign Secretary and forced the Cabinet to reverse its policy as the only possible means of holding its majority together. A similar and even more

celebrated episode was the way that the Chamberlain government fell in 1940 when the Cabinet still had a majority of
eighty-one but over fifty Conservatives had voted with the
Liberal and Labour opposition. It was quite clear, as Mr
Churchill remarked, that both the debate and the vote were
in fact, if not in form, a strong expression of lack of confidence
in Mr Chamberlain and his administration. Chamberlain
actually resigned a few days later, and Churchill replaced him
as Prime Minister.

These are outstanding instances of how public opinion has
made itself felt through the House of Commons. This can also
happen without such spectacular changes of men and measures.
Less drastic methods often suffice to make the Cabinet accept
amendments to government bills, or modify its policies, or agree
to suggestions put forward by representatives of some other
school of thought.

Another equally important function of the House of Commons, closely related to the last, is to serve as a unique kind of
forum for public debate and a focal point for criticism and
discussion. Legislation, general policy, and government
decisions on particular issues can be regularly examined in full
view of the whole country, in a spirit of fair play combined with
constant vigilance. Frequent changes of government are not
essential to democracy, but if stable governments are to remain
democratic, they must always allow free and unfettered
discussion of their policies, be ready to listen to criticism, and
never disregard their critics unless they can refute their
arguments.

We have already seen how much importance is attached to
debates on the floor of the House. The Commons are aware that
the government will always be able to rally a majority for its
policies, but they nevertheless consider themselves entitled to
regular and frequent explanatory statements from ministers,
and insist upon their right to criticise their decisions to their
face. The reason why press conferences have never developed
into an important institution in Great Britain is because any
major disclosures are reserved for statements in Parliament, and
ministers are themselves agreed that the House is entitled to
explanations of their actions and policies. The House of
Commons serves as an open forum where the government
reveals its main objectives and decisions to the country, and

where the opposition points out the weaknesses in the government's case and suggests alternative solutions. In this way the nation is kept constantly informed of the government's plans and achievements. The people are thus able—indirectly at least—to express their opinions on the issues at stake. At all events, they can form definite views of their own to which they will be able to give overt expression at the next general election.

The opposition has thus come to be regarded as no less vital than the government to the working of the British political system. It is really an integral part of the machinery of government. The phrase 'His Majesty's Opposition' was originally used in an ironical sense when coined by Hobhouse, later Lord Broughton, in 1826, and taken up by Canning and Tierney. Today, however, it accurately describes the contemporary situation in which the sovereign needs an opposition just as much as a government. An opposition is universally acknowledged to be an essential element in a system of government by the majority party. The success or failure of attempts to reproduce the British parliamentary system in other lands has largely depended on how far they have adopted the same concept of the opposition.

The power of the opposition lies in the fact that both parties, as indeed the nation itself, accept the principle that the majority should govern only on condition that it does not try to suppress its opponents. The opposition is a focal point and a mouthpiece for popular grievances and discontent. Although bound to be defeated in the House of Commons, its actions are also designed to appeal to the country at large. The Cabinet is always constrained to pay attention to what it says by the fear that it may gain a majority at the next election. Moreover, since the opposition is responsible and well organised, it provides a possible alternative government for the future. Even if it has comparatively few members in the House of Commons, it may still command a wide measure of support in the country. The way that the government agrees to find time for a debate on any motion of censure put down by the opposition is striking evidence of its devotion to the liberal idea that, in a democracy, government activities must never be veiled in secrecy but always exposed to the full light of objective criticism.

Cabinets have discovered that by respecting the rights of the opposition they are also helping to further their own interests. In the first place, the way in which they treat their opponents determines what treatment they will receive when the rôles are reversed. Secondly, if the opposition manages to persuade the country that the government is afraid of criticism, this will make people think that there are genuine weaknesses in its policy. Besides, direct charges levelled against the government give it an opportunity to refute the allegations and so help to check any adverse current of opinion. A Prime Minister once said that the reason why he had lost a general election was that he had never had a chance to convince the country of the merits of his policy because it had never been under attack.

Another leading characteristic of the opposition in Great Britain is its readiness to co-operate with the government. Parliamentary obstruction is rare. It would amount to an affront to the Speaker, whose authority is respected by all sides, and it is generally regarded as a negation of the basic principle of democracy. It is interesting to see how, on the few occasions when obstruction has occurred, its organisers contended that the government had abused its powers and was itself acting un-constitutionally. The function of the opposition is primarily to criticise, but on certain matters it collaborates with the majority.

One of these is the conversations 'behind the Speaker's chair' in which both sides agree on the general arrangements for parliamentary debates. The Prime Minister and the leader of the opposition, or the whips of the two parties, arrive at an understanding as to the topics to be debated, and the amount of time to be given to each. They will also arrange for a debate on any motion of censure. There is a great deal of give and take between the parties. The Cabinet often agrees to allow time for the opposition to attack a certain aspect of its policy, and the opposition in return undertakes not to hold up the passage of a particular bill.

There are also a number of widely varying circumstances in which the opposition may agree not to oppose the policy of the government. This happens frequently in regard to foreign policy, particularly in war-time or during other periods of international tension, as occurred between the outbreak of war in 1914 and the formation of the first coalition government in the following year. Similar restraint has been shown over other issues, such as the offer of dominion status to India in 1929 and the financial crisis of 1931. Many reforms, including Catholic Emancipation in 1829 and the Reform Act of 1867, have been accomplished through the joint action of parties who both considered the measure necessary in the national interest.

Nor is it by any means exceptional for the opposition to carry its ideas of fair play so far as to defend the Cabinet against what it considers an untimely manœuvre or attack. When there is no difference of principle between them, the minority has sometimes helped the government to avoid a futile debate or to resist premature demands for an inquiry. Thus it was through the support of the Conservatives in the House of Commons that the Attlee government was able to carry bills imposing conscription in 1947 and again in 1950, even though seventy Labour members refused to vote for it.

One important reason for this co-operative attitude on the part of the opposition is the close relationship which continues to exist between its leaders, who were formerly colleagues in the same government. The opposition is an organised unit. When a party is defeated in a general election, it at once forms a Shadow Cabinet of former ministers and possibly a few other members of Parliament, who sit on the opposition front bench immediately facing the government. The opposition whips keep in close touch with the government whips. Most important of all, there is a definite leader of the opposition, usually a former Prime Minister. This position was formally recognised by the Ministers of the Crown Act, 1937, though it had actually been in existence for many years before. The Act provided a salary of £2,000 a year for the leader of the opposition. Should the government resign, the Queen is bound to call upon the leader of the opposition to form a new government. The Speaker has the power to determine who this is should it be at all doubtful, as might well happen if there were more than one opposition party. The leader of the opposition is a prominent national figure who appears on important public occasions in company with the Prime Minister, with whom he is in constant communication on day-to-day political affairs.

The House of Commons provides a forum for discussions of a general character in which the opposition has valuable opportunities for exercising control over government policy. Such general debates occur on several occasions. One of these is the debate on the humble address in reply to the Queen's Speech at the opening of each session. Another is the debate on the budget proposals which provides several opportunities for a thorough examination of the broad political aspects of some major financial issue. There are also a certain number of days when the opposition has the right to choose the topic for discussion. This debate then takes place on a motion moved by an opposition member in his capacity as a private member of Parliament. He may simply move the adjournment of the House in order to raise some general issue or, alternatively, a motion of censure may be moved by the leader of the opposition. These opposition motions may give rise to a lengthy debate. The rules of parliamentary procedure are respected and the government usually emerges victorious from the final division, but not without having had to defend itself against keen opposition. Debates have always been conducted in an amazingly courteous and sometimes elaborately formal manner. Their most striking feature, however, is their remarkably serious tone. Eloquence is never appreciated for its own sake, and anyone who adopts a declamatory style will simply make himself ridiculous. The character, procedure and traditions of the House have not been at all conducive to polished oratory and discourage anyone from speaking unless he really has something definite to say. The Chamber is comparatively small, and there is no tribune. A member called upon by the Speaker to address the House rises and speaks from his place, having first uncovered himself if he has been wearing a hat. No member is allowed to move from his place or to read a written speech. Any reference to speeches or documents not available to the House, remarks addressed to any other member personally, statements tending to reflect unfavourably on any person, and any kind of 'unparliamentary' language are all out of order. The rule that no one may speak more than once on the same question eliminates replies to speeches, prevents debates from dragging on inconclusively, and ensures that the atmosphere does not become too heated. The Speaker always remains strictly impartial, and his authority is never questioned.

In normal circumstances, no member of the opposition, however great his personal abilities, has any hope of affecting the outcome of a division by anything he says. The most that he can do is to shake the confidence of those on the opposite benches and so induce the government to adopt a more conciliatory attitude. The only way he can do this is by saying what he thinks quite clearly and producing sound arguments firmly grounded on concrete evidence. Common sense and an empirical approach may be effective, but there is absolutely no hope of achieving anything by fervent oratory.

Parliamentary questions provide another, even more informal way in which the House of Commons can exercise control over the government and the Civil Service. Questions are regarded as an important part of the work of the House and might even be described as the key to the whole system of parliamentary control of the executive. Question Time, when questions may be put to ministers for oral answer, occupies three-quarters of an hour, starting not later than 3 o'clock, at the beginning of the day's business on every day except Friday. Questions are handed in previously in writing to the Clerks at the Table, and thereafter printed and circulated with each question numbered and put down for answer on a particular day. When a question appears on the Order Paper for the day, the Speaker calls upon the member in whose name it stands, who thereupon rises and states the number of his question and the minister to whom it is directed. He then resumes his place and the minister rises and delivers his reply, unless the answer is very long, in which case he will ask permission to circulate it in the *Official Report*. The House then passes to the next question on the Order Paper. If any still remain unanswered at 3.45, the replies are given in the *Official Report*. A further five minutes are allowed for 'private notice questions', put directly to the minister concerned and not submitted through the Table.

The question is a simple and uncomplicated device, but its use has developed in a remarkable fashion. Every day, an average of somewhere between 60 and 200 questions are asked. The total number for the session 1945-46 was nearly 30,000. The government sometimes arranges for a question to be asked if it wants to make a statement of an informal character on a particular issue. The essential function of the parliamentary question, however, is to provide private members with a means whereby they can, in their individual capacity, exercise some effective control over the government, secure explanations of government action and policy, and attract public attention to significant aspects of current developments with a minimum of delay. Questions are in fact the chief way in which the private member can make his influence felt. The rules of procedure impose certain limits on the type of questions that may be put down, but members have found no difficulty in making use of them for a variety of different purposes. They are employed to draw attention to abuses, to extract promises, and sometimes to provide an opportunity to embarrass the government by asking a supplementary question, which the Speaker will normally allow to be put. A member who is not satisfied with the reply to his question can raise the matter again in one of the debates on the adjournment that take place at the end of each day's sitting.

The effectiveness of parliamentary questions in helping to ensure efficiency in the Civil Service is shown by the way in which departments go in constant dread of questions in the House. They are also important politically, because they indicate the issues which the country considers particularly important at any given moment. This is something which the Cabinet is always anxious to discover and obliged to take into account, and questions in Parliament serve to focus attention on the points on which the country will judge the whole record of the government.

The House of Commons thus stands in a unique position, by no means deprived of all political significance. Despite the ascendancy of the Cabinet, there is no question of Cabinet dictatorship. As Sir Ivor Jennings has remarked, dictators who have to appeal to the country in free elections at frequent intervals are the servants of the people and not their masters. The House of Commons compels the government to be extremely responsive to public opinion at all times, and the opposition is constantly reminding it of the vulnerability of its position and the weakness of its policies. There are thus very strong and exceedingly democratic forces within Parliament to restrain the government from using its great powers in any arbitrary fashion.

Conversely, the decline of the upper House, which in Great Britain no longer has any substantial political influence, can be attributed to the fact that it is so very far from being a democratic assembly.

II. THE HOUSE OF LORDS

Advocates of bicameralism have often quoted English experience in support of their case. It would, however, provide almost as many arguments against as in favour of a second chamber. The division of Parliament into two Houses was purely accidental, and both the structure and the diminishing functions of the House of Lords would be incapable of imitation anywhere else. The decline of the House of Lords began relatively early, well before there was any strong general trend of opinion against second chambers as being undemocratic. Today it can be said the House of Lords, more than any other British institution, remains in existence primarily owing to tradition and not because it serves any effective purpose.

The House of Lords evolved out of the Magnum Concilium of prelates and barons. It emerged as a distinct assembly when Parliament became bicameral in the fourteenth century, and its importance increased in the course of the struggle between Parliament and the Crown. It succeeded in maintaining this position for a time, but has since been gradually deprived of its former powers.

Until the middle of the nineteenth century the House of Lords remained an extremely powerful institution. Its pre-eminence was a reflection of the continuing importance of the aristocracy, from amongst whom the King had originally chosen his principal advisers in the days when even the middle classes, let alone the ordinary people, had had little say in public affairs. The country remained firmly attached to the monarchy and the descendants of the great feudal lords of England. The landed aristocracy who had later received hereditary peerages from the Crown continued to occupy a leading position corresponding to that assigned by Montesquieu to 'persons distinguished by birth, riches or honours' whom he thought should never be 'confounded with the people'.

Peers have always taken precedence over the Commons, as they still do today. Requests from the sovereign used to be sent in the first place to the Lords, and it was they who presented petitions to the Crown. The Commons gradually obtained equal political rights, and are now more powerful than the Lords in regard to both finance and legislation. Despite the changing fortunes of the aristocracy, the House of Lords continued to be

of major importance so long as the political system was fundamentally an oligarchy, owing to its influence within the Cabinet,
on the fate of Cabinets, and over the House of Commons itself.
Peers used to occupy the leading positions in the Cabinet.
Originally only the leading officers of state and courtiers were
summoned to the King's Cabinet councils. The forerunner of
the modern Prime Minister was the royal favourite, and it was
many years before the King ceased to look to the House of
Lords when he wanted ministers who could secure him the
support of Parliament. Peers are spared the necessity of securing
re-election, so they represent a stable element in the constitution
and until the middle of the nineteenth century the Prime
Minister and the majority of the Cabinet used to be chosen
from the utterly undemocratic upper House.

Not only were the Lords well represented in the government,
but they could exercise decisive influence whenever the fate of a
Cabinet was in the balance. Impeachment, the process out of
which the idea of political responsibility developed, was a
procedure whereby ministers were brought to trial before the
House of Lords, which had supreme power both to determine
the facts of the case and to impose penalties. A minister could
only be impeached on a charge preferred against him by the
House of Commons, but in this, as in other matters, the lower
House in practice left the initiative to the Lords and merely
acted on its suggestions. After the Cabinet became politically
responsible to the Commons, the Lords refrained from trying
to overthrow the government but still retained a number of
indirect means of exerting their influence over the lower House.

For many years the peers controlled elections of members of
the other House, for whom voting took place in public and went
on for several weeks. At one stage in the eighteenth century, no
fewer than 427 of the 658 members of the House of Commons
owed their seats to the patronage of 218 great landowners. Lord
Lonsdale controlled nine seats, and Lord Hertford and Lord
Fitzwilliam each controlled eight. Dickens's *Pickwick Papers*
depicts Mr Pickwick's astonishment at the way elections were
conducted at Eatanswill. The great landowners, who were often
peers, were largely responsible for the corrupt practices. Consequently, as has often been pointed out, the composition of the
two Houses remained remarkably similar right down to the
beginning of the twentieth century. The Commons were virtually

a reflection of the upper House. Yet Parliament was not entirely out of touch with the general life of the country, as the leading politicians were by and large representative of the leading social class. The same influences remained dominant in both Houses for an amazingly long period. A unity of outlook and a spirit of mutual understanding developed between their members, who were connected with the same families, shared the same interests as landowners, financiers or industrialists, and frequented the same clubs.

The social revolution which found its expression in the reform of the electoral system, resulted in the gradual decline of the House of Lords. This has been one of the outstanding developments in the British political system during the last hundred years. As it became increasingly imperative for the government always to act in accordance with the will of the people, the rôle of the Crown and the aristocracy has progressively diminished.

The Reform Act of 1832 marked the beginning of the decline of the House of Lords and the first weakening of its control over the composition of the House of Commons. The Lords apparently realised this at the time. The Tory majority in the upper House fiercely resisted the Reform Bill, and did not give way until Lord Grey's Whig government threatened to swamp the House with a large batch of new peers. The Lords thereby succeeded in preserving the traditional structure of their House, but at the same time lost all chance of being able to stay the rising tide of democracy.

The centre of British political life shifted to the House of Commons, which has become the only House that can exercise any effective control over the activities of the government. The Cabinet has likewise come to reflect the views of the lower House, on whose support it depends in order to remain in power. The number of peers in the Cabinet has steadily diminished until they account for no more than three or four in a Cabinet of getting on for twenty members. Since Lord Salisbury retired in 1902, no peer has ever been Prime Minister, as it is in the lower House that the Cabinet must defend itself and no minister can take any part in the proceedings of a House of which he is not a member. The development of political parties and the democratisation of the electoral system, besides allowing the electorate to decide who should form the government, have also dealt a fatal blow to the power of the aristocratic upper House.

The House of Lords began to present a problem as soon as the House of Commons ceased to be drawn from the same social class as the peers and the hereditary second Chamber found itself confronted with a lower House elected by popular vote. The House of Lords has not disappeared completely, owing to the British respect for tradition and the influence of the Conservative Party. It remains a force with which governments—or at least Labour governments—still have to contend. Yet if we examine the present position of the House of Lords under modern democratic conditions, we shall see what great social and political changes have taken place in the British parliamentary system since it originally came into being.

Today, the House of Lords may be regarded as an anachronism, though an extremely dignified anachronism. Its organisation reveals the greatest possible respect for its venerable traditions.

The Lords' Chamber in the Palace of Westminster, where the Commons met between 1941 and 1950, is more like a deconsecrated chapel than the meeting-place of a legislative assembly. At the far end is the throne used by the sovereign on state occasions. In front of the throne and on a lower level, is the Woolsack where the Lord Chancellor sits, and on both sides, facing each other, are the benches upholstered in red leather for the peers. All round the Chamber are galleries to which the public are admitted.

The privileges of the House are substantially similar to those of the House of Commons, though the Lords have some other special privileges in addition, notably that of access to the Crown. We have already mentioned some instances of how the Lords take precedence over the Commons. The appointment of the Speaker of the House of Commons is formally approved in the upper House. It is there that bills passed by Parliament receive the royal assent and Parliament is opened in state at the beginning of each session, when the Speech from the Throne is read before the assembled peers, arrayed in their scarlet robes, and the members of the House of Commons, who have been summoned there by Black Rod. Ordinary sittings of the

House of Lords are very different from these state occasions. The Lord Chancellor presides, and there are usually only a comparatively small number of other members present. The average attendance is somewhere between fifty and a hundred, and it is very rare for more than two hundred members to put in an appearance except for a few exceptionally important debates. Amongst these have been that on the Irish Home Rule Bill which the Lords rejected by 302 votes to 64 in 1913, and on the Labour government's Parliament Bill which was defeated by 218 votes to 36 in 1948. Only 30 members need vote for the House to record a valid decision and three are a sufficient quorum for a sitting to begin.

The composition of the House of Lords reveals more clearly than anything else how little it has really altered from the old feudal council. An analysis of the members of the House shows how the traditional elements are still overwhelmingly preponderant. Not all peerages are hereditary, but there are fewer than 60 members out of about 860 whose titles are not hereditary. These include the 16 Scottish representative peers who, since 1707, have been elected at the beginning of each new Parliament by the Scottish peers, who now number 37. There are also the survivors of the 28 Irish representative peers who used to be elected for life by the Irish peers, no new elections having been held to replace those who have died since 1920. Besides these, there are 26 Lords Spiritual—the Archbishops of Canterbury and York, the Bishops of London, Durham and Winchester, and the 21 most senior bishops— altogether far fewer than the number of prelates who used to sit in Parliament in the Middle Ages and before the Reformation. Finally, nine Lords of Appeal in Ordinary, distinguished lawyers with life peerages, were introduced into the House in 1876. They discharge its judicial functions and are the only peers who receive a salary. Every other peer has some hereditary title—duke, marquis, earl, viscount or baron. The barons are by far the most numerous, and there are only very small numbers of dukes and marquises. Baronets, though their titles are hereditary, are not entitled to sit in the House of Lords. Nor are knights, whose titles are conferred only for life.

The peerage is of feudal origin. After the King's vassals obtained the right to sit in Parliament, it became recognised that the chief barons or their heirs were entitled to a summons every time a new Parliament met. By the fourteenth century the King had begun to confer hereditary peerages, and the sovereign still has power to create unlimited numbers of peers by letters patent. The Lords have naturally been opposed to an excessive number of new peerages, but the sovereign and, more recently, the Cabinet have never allowed the prerogative of the Crown to be limited by numerical restrictions on the creation of new peers.

The peerage has thus been completely transformed. In the first place, the substantial increase in numbers has led to a corresponding decline in prestige. In the course of the nineteenth century the number of peers rose from 300 to 600, principally because of new creations by Queen Victoria. By 1910 there were 622 peers, and in 1954 the total had reached 863. Between 1922 and 1936 alone, 137 new titles were conferred. Some governments, including those of Campbell-Bannerman, Asquith and Lloyd George, made a practice of creating peers expressly in order to strengthen their influence over the House of Lords, and they were not always entirely uninfluenced by the financial support that prospective peers had given to their party funds. Another factor which has led to extensive changes in the peerage is that many old titles have become extinct because they can only be inherited by males. Only a very small proportion of the present House of Lords belongs to the old nobility. In 1936, only 47 of the 681 peers had titles dating back as far as 1689, and only 16 of these peerages were created before the accession of Henry VIII. At the same time, there were 265 peers with new titles created since 1906. Thus a new 'aristocracy of success' has grown up alongside the old aristocracy. The present Dukes of Wellington and Marlborough, and the heirs of Lord Stanhope and Lord Londonderry, have been joined by such new peers as Lord Reading, Lord Snell, Lord Leverhulme, Lord Rothermere, Lord Northcliffe, Lord Tedder, Lord Montgomery of Alamein and Lord Alexander. Peerages have been conferred on diplomats, politicians, men of letters, scholars and artists, including such eminent figures as Tennyson, Bryce, Keynes, Baldwin, Snowden and Beveridge. The House of Lords is not therefore entirely out of touch with certain aspects at least of the life of the country at the present time. It includes not only landed nobility but also a large number of company directors. As

Halévy has said, 'While business men were becoming peers, peers were becoming business men.'

Despite these changes in the peerage, the general political complexion of the House of Lords remains unaltered. Its members may differ in their social background and past careers, but for the most part they still belong to the same social class. The vast majority are Conservatives. Of those who show any interest in politics, over 700 can be classed as Conservatives or having Conservative sympathies. In the days when Whigs and Tories held office alternately, the strength of the parties in the upper House depended on how long either party managed to remain in power. In the second half of the nineteenth century, however, most of the old Whig families tended to go over to the Conservatives and the Liberal Party more or less gave up all hope of attaining comparable representation in the House of Lords. Until 1924, the Labour Party opposed peerages as a matter of principle, and in later years only a very small number of Labour peers have been created. As peers receive no salary, Labour supporters are seldom attracted by the prospect of a seat in the upper House unless they have ample private means and value honours for their own sake. Those who come into this category generally do not differ substantially in their political views from the average Liberal or Conservative peer. The result is that the House of Lords is politically a Conservative stronghold. An inquiry made in 1936 showed that 543 peers supported the Conservative government (517 Conservatives, 12 Liberal Nationals, 6 National Labour and 8 Nationals), while only 72 could be classed as opposition supporters (56 Liberals and 16 Labour). Admittedly, 126 peers refused to state their views, but there is no reason to suppose that they were socialists. Even if all these were included on the opposition side, that would still have left the Conservatives an overwhelming majority. In 1945 the Labour Party had a majority of over 200 in the Commons, but the Attlee government would still have had to create 750 new peers in order to have a majority in the other House. Peers are heirs of noble families or gentlemen of ample means who hold their seats by virtue of their titles alone. They are accountable to no one for their politics or the way they vote. They are not merely independent of public opinion but entirely cut off from the prevailing currents of thought on political issues outside purely Conservative circles. The House

of Lords invariably assumes a position strictly in line with that
of the Conservative Party and its leader in the House of
Commons.

The prophetic observations of Bagehot in 1867 deserve to be
quoted in this connection: 'The danger of the House of Commons is, perhaps, that it will be reformed too rashly; the danger
of the House of Lords certainly is, that it may never be reformed. . . . It is quite safe against rough destruction, but it is
not safe against inward decay. It may lose its veto as the Crown
has lost its veto. If most of its members neglect their duties, if all
its members continue to be of one class . . .; if its doors are shut
against genius that cannot found a family, and ability which
has not five thousand a year, its power will be less year by year,
and at last be gone.' All the subsequent history of the House of
Lords is really summed up in these words, written before the
developments they describe had come to pass.

The need to reform the House of Lords has long been recognised. The first bill with this object in view was introduced in
1719. The Lords' opposition to the Home Rule Bill of 1886
gave rise to a Liberal campaign 'to mend or to end' the upper
House, and the issue was revived in the great struggle between
Lords and Commons which was finally resolved by the Parliament Act of 1911. Since then, various possible lines of reform have been examined many times: by the Bryce Committee of 1919; on Lord Curzon's proposals of 1922; by a
Conservative Party Committee presided over by Lord Cave in
1927; in Lord Salisbury's bill of 1931; and on the proposals of
Labour Party in 1947. The Labour Party has several times
threatened to abolish the second Chamber, notably in 1922,
1932, 1933, 1935, 1945 and 1947, but it seems unlikely that
it was really prepared to do away with it completely. This
was probably only a threat used to bring pressure to bear on
the Lords and dissuade them from trying to resist the will of the
people. The reform of the House of Lords raises many difficulties. The Labour Party is anxious that the Lords should not
be able to hold up the legislative programme of any future
Labour government, and is afraid that the powers of the upper
House may be enhanced if there is any change in its composition. The Conservatives, on the other hand, do not want to
deprive themselves of a means of thwarting any future socialist
measures.

The desire to reform the House of Lords certainly appears genuine enough and numerous different proposals continue to be put forward and discussed. But while the House of Lords continues in its present unreformed state it creates a disequilibrium between the lower House representative of the people and the upper House which represents the Conservative Party. This would be hard to justify on any rational grounds.

The survival of the House of Lords is not due solely to the British respect for tradition and the established social order, or to their love of the pomp and splendour of bygone days, or to the idea that the aristocracy stands in a specially close relationship to the Crown. The main reason is to be found in the flexibility of the British constitution and the way that the position of the House of Lords has been so modified that it can no longer impede the working of more democratic institutions. With its present composition, it cannot possibly claim to represent the nation, but it now plays only a relatively small part in the political life of the country and no longer has any power permanently to thwart the will of the people.

The House of Lords still has a number of judicial attributes, although it has not been called upon to discharge its historic function in a case of impeachment since the trials of Warren Hastings in 1787 and Lord Melville in 1805. It is still in theory the supreme court of appeal for Great Britain and Northern Ireland, but since 1876 its appellate functions have been discharged by the Lords of Appeal in Ordinary sitting alone with the Lord Chancellor, who really form a special court within the House itself. In any case, comparatively few appeals ever reach the House of Lords, and the House is very rarely called upon to exercise its other judicial function of trying peers charged with treason or felony.

In the political sphere, the Lords have no power to overthrow the government which does not need to have the confidence of the upper House. Contact between the executive and the House of Lords is maintained through the small group of peers who are always included in the Cabinet. These are often former members of the House of Commons, as the offices of Lord Chancellor, Lord Privy Seal and Lord President are no longer the preserves of the old nobility, and neither the Lord President nor the Lord Privy Seal is necessarily a peer.

Finally, the House of Lords has certain functions in regard

to legislation and finance. It is a legislative assembly in which bills may be introduced, either by peers, who in practice seldom exercise their right, or by the government, which sometimes does so in the hope that a bill already discussed in the Lords will pass more quickly through the House of Commons. But the most notable changes in its legislative rôle concern its powers in regard to bills already passed by the Commons.

The powers of the House of Lords in regard to finance were very small even before 1911. The Commons granted supply to the Crown and imposed taxes on the people, while the Lords merely gave their assent to the proposals of the lower House and were without power to discuss or amend financial bills. They could still in theory have rejected the budget as a whole, but after 1861 they never tried to oppose a budget, which is perhaps a reason why British financial policy was generally conducted on conventional orthodox lines. On all other bills, the Lords in theory had exactly the same powers as the Commons, and no act of Parliament could be passed without their consent. By the middle of the nineteenth century, however, it was recognised that, to quote Bagehot, 'the House of Lords must yield whenever the opinion of the Commons is also the opinion of the nation, and when it is clear that the nation has made up its mind'. If the Lords tried to oppose the clearly expressed will of the people, the Cabinet could always ask the Crown to create a sufficient number of new peers to reverse the majority. This, however, could only be done after holding a general election. As the Conservatives became increasingly predominant, it therefore grew progressively more difficult to use this prerogative to swamp the upper House. In 1712 the creation of twelve new peers sufficed to overcome the Lords' opposition to the Treaty of Utrecht, and the threat to create a large batch of new peers finally brought the Lords to agree to the Reform Bill of 1832.

After the Liberal victory in the general election of 1906, the Campbell-Bannerman and Asquith governments became involved in very serious conflict with the upper House. We cannot go into all the details here, but the culmination was the Lords' refusal to approve Lloyd George's 'People's Budget' of 1909, which imposed important new taxes until it had been submitted to the judgment of the country. Finally, after two general elections, the government threatened to create 500 new peers. This would have been enough to enable the most drastic reforms to be carried, so the Lords thereupon agreed to pass the Parliament Act, 1911, by which their powers were considerably curtailed.

The House of Lords was almost completely deprived of its powers in regard to 'money bills', that is bills certified by the Speaker of the House of Commons as falling within certain categories specified in the Act. A money bill now receives the royal assent within one month of being passed by the House of Commons, whether or not it has been passed by the Lords.

On all other bills, the Lords were left with a suspensive veto. Any bill passed three times by the Commons within a period of two years could thereafter receive the royal assent.

The passing of the Parliament Act proved sufficient to dissuade the Lords from trying to thwart the will of the people. A Conservative government can still rely on their unwavering support, but Liberal and Labour bills have not met with systematic opposition. No bill has been radically altered in the House of Lords unless its amendments have been thought likely to be acceptable to the government. The Lords have never rejected a bill except when they have had reason to suppose that the government would not be prepared to appeal to the country, or else when the Conservative Party has been ready to run the risk of a general election. In other words, since 1911 the House of Lords has had neither the power, nor in most cases the inclination, to pit its strength in a struggle against the nation such as it was rash enough to enter upon in 1909-10 when 'Lords versus people' became the Liberal slogan in the general elections of 1910. The Parliament Act has only had to be applied to two measures—the Government of Ireland Act, 1914, and the Established Church (Wales) Act, 1914, which was not put into execution until some years later—and to two other bills of no substantial importance.

Nevertheless, this purely suspensive veto was enough to enable the House of Lords to resist some of the more revolutionary measures of the Labour Party, which found it inconvenient to have to wait two years to secure the legislation necessary for the execution of its reforms. The delay gave the Conservatives an opportunity to stir up public opinion against the government and possibly to force it to dissolve Parliament. During the last two years of a Parliament a Labour Cabinet could carry through only such bills as could obtain the support of the House of Lords.

The Attlee government were anxious for the whole of their programme of legislation to reach the Statute Book, and considered that the powers of the House of Lords were still excessive. After some negotiation with the Conservatives, they decided to resort to the Parliament Act, 1911, in order to amend that Act itself. The bill which became the Parliament Act, 1949, was therefore passed by the Commons in three successive sessions. It reduced the veto of the House of Lords to one year, thus enabling the Commons to overcome the opposition of the upper House by passing a bill twice in successive sessions. These provisions were declared applicable to bills already introduced, and so permitted the Act nationalising iron and steel to be passed before the general election of 1950.

Since 1911, the British upper House has become in law what it already was in fact—no more than a reflecting chamber. Since 1949, the time allowed for reflection has been short enough not to be any serious inconvenience to a Labour government, unless there is some urgent measure which it wants to enact with the least possible delay. Moreover, it seems as if the House of Lords will continue to follow the same prudent tactics as it has adopted in the past whenever it has felt certain that the wishes of the people had been quite clearly expressed. Thus bicameralism in Great Britain, its traditional home, is now no more than a façade.

What then is the purpose of the upper House? Its debates are generally agreed to be of a high standard and provide a forum for valuable speeches on issues of national importance, notably in regard to foreign policy, by distinguished men whose views are thus brought to the notice of the Cabinet. In addition, there is the technical advantage of being able to introduce some bills in the Lords, which means that they take up considerably less time than they would otherwise require in the Commons. The suspensive veto makes the House of Lords important as a channel for the expression of public opinion and as a check against arbitrary action on the part of the government. In this respect its influence would always be brought to bear on the same side. A Conservative government would never have any occasion to resort to the provisions of the Parliament Act, whereas a Labour government in the final year before an election has still no means of overriding Conservative opposition. It would be difficult to find any valid logical argument for retaining the House of Lords. In this connection, however, logic is not the important factor. Public opinion in Britain clearly believes that some respect ought to be paid to the conservative elements in the constitution. If the nation were really convinced that the House of Lords ought to be reformed, it would no doubt be able to exert sufficient pressure to bring this about. As Sir Maurice Amos has said, 'It is not the fashion in English politics, to take bulls by their horns, particularly when they appear to be harmless.'

Chapter Three

THE MONARCHY

THE monarchy is undoubtedly the most unique of all the political institutions of Great Britain. It is both the oldest and the most mystical element in the constitution.

It is the oldest political institution in Europe apart from the Papacy. The throne has not always descended in the direct line, but Queen Elizabeth II is a true descendant of King Egbert, who created a united kingdom of England in 829. Except for a brief interlude under Cromwell, there has been no break in the succession of Kings and Queens.

The continuity of the monarchy is clearly one of the most important reasons for the absence of violent upheavals in British political history and for the stability of the social structure and political institutions of Great Britain. It has been not merely a consequence but a cause of the British reluctance to become involved in revolutionary movements and major upheavals. Yet, despite its long history, the monarchy has itself undergone great changes. British sovereigns have shown sufficient good sense to forget the pretensions of their predecessors, and to accept a democratic form of government and allow themselves to be guided by the will of the people. Much can be learnt from the history of Great Britain in the two and a half centuries since 1688 about the art of preserving a monarchy.

The establishment of Cabinet government shielded the sovereign against criticism, rebellion, revolution and risk of deposition. Later, in the nineteenth and twentieth centuries, the monarchy was made compatible with democratic government. The sovereign is now above party and takes care that the powers of the Crown are always exercised in conformity with the will of the people. Thus the monarchy has not merely survived as a dignified institution but has also succeeded in retaining some real authority in the state.

There lies the mystical element in the British monarchy. The powers, prerogatives and sovereign rights which used to belong to the King himself have passed to the Crown, which now denotes an abstract legal entity quite distinct from the person of the sovereign. The loss of these powers has helped to raise the personal prestige of the King or Queen. In one sense, the sovereign has abdicated and left the Cabinet to govern the country. In another sense, however, she continues to reign in great splendour. The Queen is still the head of the state and the country is, strictly speaking, governed by the Queen, who acts on the advice of her ministers. Someone must be answerable to the people for the day-to-day conduct of the nation's affairs, but the Cabinet now shoulders this responsibility, leaving the monarch completely immune from attack. The King or Queen is now a symbolic figure who represents the British people as a whole and emphasises the common citizenship that unites the entire nation in common loyalty to their country.

The English have not always shown this respect and devotion to their Kings and Queens. Henry III was imprisoned; Edward II, Richard II, Henry VI and Edward V were deposed and put to death; Richard III was killed after losing his crown at the Battle of Bosworth Field; Charles I was executed; and James II escaped to France after throwing the Great Seal of England into the River Thames. Under the Hanoverians the monarchy was regarded without enthusiasm and sometimes with contempt. The first forty years of Queen Victoria's reign saw many demonstrations of hostility to the monarchy: the Prince of Wales, the future Edward VII, was jeered at in the streets, and Joseph Chamberlain and Sir Charles Dilke both professed republican sympathies. Since 1878, however, there has been no significant republican movement in Great Britain and no serious criticism of the monarchy, except during the brief crisis over the abdication in 1936. The coronation of Queen Elizabeth II on 2nd June 1953 provided striking evidence of the high regard in which the young Queen and the royal family are now held by the entire nation.

Many different factors have probably contributed to this change of attitude towards the monarchy. Amongst these should be included the extraordinary veneration in which Queen Victoria was held at the end of her reign; the character of Edward VII with his good-natured disposition and readiness to share in the pleasures of his people; George V's courage and devotion to duty in all the difficulties and crises which preceded the final victory in the first World War; and the fortitude displayed by George VI and his Queen during the Battle of

Britain, when they calmly and unquestioningly shared in the trials and hardships of their people. But two other factors appear to have been particularly important in strengthening popular respect for the highest and oldest office in the state during the period since the proclamation of Queen Victoria as Empress of India which produced a strikingly unanimous demonstration of national enthusiasm for the monarchy. One factor has been the active concern displayed by the last few sovereigns for the welfare of their people in all its different aspects. The social prestige of the monarchy has also tended to rise as the aristocracy has declined and been partially replaced by a plutocracy. The other important factor is the political neutrality of the monarchy, which has done much to give it a new moral authority. The sovereign is neither for nor against any party, but acts in accordance with a special code of fair play which in effect requires her to respect and be guided by the will of the people. The sovereign has thus become secure against attack from any quarter.

Consequently, while the importance of the monarchy in Great Britain is easily realised, it is not so easily susceptible to scientific analysis. It is obviously a phenomenon of quite a different order from the political supremacy of the Cabinet with which it does not in any way conflict. The monarchy is important from three different points of view—as a physical person, as a symbol, and as a power in the state.

I. THE PERSONAL POSITION OF THE SOVEREIGN

One very important aspect of the monarchy is the way in which the unity and continuity of the nation are personified in a sovereign descended from a long line of Kings and Queens. This gives a very definite content to the notion of patriotism, obedience to the law and devotion to the service of the community, all of which are commonly regarded as different aspects of loyalty to a King or Queen who occupies a position of unquestioned supremacy far above all political controversies. Such loyalty does not in any way impair individual liberty or rule out opposition to the government.

The importance of the sovereign as an individual man or woman is reflected in some of the leading principles of the British constitution. First, there are rules governing the succession to the throne, laid down in the Act of Settlement of 1701 and reaffirmed in subsequent Succession to the Crown Acts and in the Acts of Union with Scotland and Ireland. The Crown is inherited by the heirs of the House of Hanover, who assumed the name of Windsor during the first World War. In accordance with the ordinary common law of inheritance, the oldest male or, if there is no male heir, the oldest female succeeds to the throne. Women are not excluded from the succession, and Elizabeth II is actually the seventh queen regnant of England.

The throne is never left vacant on the death of the sovereign, as his successor is immediately proclaimed King or Queen. This is done in a Council of Accession consisting of the members of the Privy Council, the Mayor and Aldermen of the City of London, and certain other 'gentlemen of quality', including the High Commissioners of the other Commonwealth countries in London.

The new reign officially begins from the moment of the death of the previous monarch, but the coronation ceremony in Westminster Abbey, which has changed very little since 1689, takes place some time after the sovereign's accession.

No Roman Catholic can succeed to the British throne. The King or Queen must be a member of the Church of England, and used to have to make a solemn declaration renouncing the doctrine of transubstantiation. Since 1910, however, the sovereign has simply had to declare that he or she is a 'faithful Protestant' and will 'according to the true intent of the enactments which secure the Protestant succession to the throne . . . uphold the said enactments to the best of (his) (her) powers according to law'.

The Queen now has a different title in each of the countries of the Commonwealth. In the United Kingdom she is 'Elizabeth the second, by the grace of God, Queen of the United Kingdom of Great Britain and Northern Ireland and of her other realms and territories, head of the Commonwealth, Defender of the Faith'. The rules governing the succession to the throne cannot be altered except by agreement between all the Commonwealth countries as laid down in the preamble to the Statute of Westminster of 1931.

For a long time the idea that the power of the Crown resides in a physical person was carried to such an extreme that when a King died all his acts became null and void. Parliament was automatically dissolved, appointments of judges and other officials lapsed, and charters granted to the Commons were withdrawn. Gradually, however, steps were taken to eliminate these traditional consequences of the demise of the Crown, the last of which were done away with in 1901.

Until recently, there was nothing in the law to say what should happen if the sovereign were incapable of discharging his functions. In the past, particularly in 1788 and 1810, a procedure of questionable validity was employed to establish a regency. The Regency Act of 1937 now provides that the person next in the order of succession to the throne is to be appointed regent if the sovereign is under eighteen years of age or has been duly recognised as incapable of exercising the duties of office. In 1953 the Regency Act was amended to make it possible for the Duke of Edinburgh to act as regent should the need arise.

If the sovereign is ill or absent from the country for any length of time, a Council of State is appointed by letters patent of the sovereign. This consists of various members of the royal family and certain other persons whom the sovereign authorises to act in her place, subject to such conditions as she may prescribe. It is never empowered to dissolve Parliament or to confer titles. A Council of State was appointed during the illness of the King in 1928 and again in September 1951.

If a King abdicates, Parliament has to pass a special Act laying down the new order of succession to the throne, which must be approved by all the other Commonwealth countries. The Abdication Act of 1936 excluded the King from the line of succession and authorised him to marry without the consent of the sovereign, while the Crown devolved upon his successor, George VI.

The importance of the sovereign as a physical person is also reflected in the legal status of the monarch. The Statute of Treason of 1351 made death the penalty for high treason, rebellion, murdering, wounding or imprisoning the sovereign, or merely conspiring to murder, wound or imprison him. The old maxim that the King can do no wrong means that no one may institute any civil or criminal proceedings against the Crown. This was originally intended to protect the King personally, but now has the effect of protecting the government, except in so far as recent legislation has somewhat curtailed its legal immunity. Otherwise, anyone seeking redress against the

Crown has to proceed by petition of right, in which case 'the amount to which the suppliant is entitled shall be paid to him out of such funds or moneys as Her Majesty shall be graciously pleased to direct to be applied for that purpose'.

Finally, the sovereign has personal property and revenues separate from those of the Crown. This distinction has not always existed, but since 1688 Parliament has granted each sovereign on his accession an annual allowance with which 'to make provision for the honour and dignity of the Crown', and left him completely free to spend this money as he thinks fit. In return for this Civil List, the King placed his hereditary revenues from various Crown lands at the disposal of his faithful Commons. Since the accession of George V, the Civil List has been exempt from taxation. It is now fixed at £475,000 a year for Queen Elizabeth II, plus an allowance of £40,000 a year for the Duke of Edinburgh. Most other members of the royal family also receive pensions under the provisions of the Civil List Act of 1937. Since the House of Windsor has other private sources of income, these allowances seem to be quite adequate. They represent the price which the British people, with their taste for pageantry, are prepared to pay for the pomp and ceremonies traditionally associated with royalty. The people have been quick to recognise the personal qualities and charm of their sovereigns, and this has increased the significance of the monarchy as the focal point of patriotic sentiments. The importance of individual Kings and Queens in this respect is also a survival from the days when there was no distinction between the person who occupied the throne and the Crown as a political institution. This dichotomy appeared with the development of Cabinet government, which has meant that the sovereign no longer, except in a purely nominal sense, retains any executive power.

II. THE CROWN AS A SYMBOL OF EXECUTIVE POWER

The sovereign is thus a constitutional figurehead symbolising the executive power. In theory, the Queen still has a wide range of powers and prerogatives, which have never been formally abolished. In fact, however, they have all either fallen into disuse, or have to be exercised in accordance with established political conventions which do not leave her any real discretion, or else—as has usually happened—the royal prerogatives are really exercised by the Cabinet or the Prime Minister although action is still formally taken in the name of the sovereign. In Britain, as in other parliamentary regimes, the head of the state is not politically responsible for her actions and consequently has no power to determine any political issue on her own initiative. In so far as she has any independent powers of decision, she must exercise them without the least suspicion of political bias. This will become clear from a brief examination of each of the principal royal prerogatives.

As regards legislation, all Acts of Parliament must be approved by the sovereign, and no bill can become law until it has formally received the royal assent. But it is over two and a half centuries since a sovereign has refused to assent to a bill that had been passed by both Houses of Parliament, and it would be quite impossible for this to happen today. For the Queen to refuse her assent would be tantamount to dismissing the Cabinet which, if its bill had been passed, would be bound to have had a majority in Parliament. This would be virtually a *coup d'état* in favour of the opposition, and as such definitely unconstitutional.

Under some forms of parliamentary government, the head of state acquires real political influence through his power to appoint the Prime Minister and the other members of the government. This can only happen, however, when he has some real choice as to whom to appoint. In Britain, as we have seen, Cabinet ministers and other members of the government are really chosen by the Prime Minister. The sovereign might conceivably have some discretion in the appointment of the Prime Minister himself. British authorities are wont to cite numerous instances where the sovereign did have some real freedom of choice in this respect. Queen Victoria, in particular, managed to exert considerable influence on several occasions. In 1839 she sent for the Tory leader, Sir Robert Peel, but contrived to make it virtually impossible for him to form a government. In 1852, when there was no obvious candidate to succeed Lord Derby, she selected Lord Aberdeen. In 1886, when she had hoped that Lord Salisbury would have been able to remain in office, she was forced to send for Gladstone, but approached him in such a way as to give the impression of being definitely prejudiced against him. In 1894 her own personal preferences led her to send for Lord Rosebery rather than Sir William Harcourt or possibly Lord Spencer, who were both considered possible alternatives for the premiership.

None of these, however, are very recent precedents, and there is now far less likelihood that the party system would allow the Queen any real freedom of choice. In normal circumstances when there are two main parties each with its acknowledged leader, the choice of the Prime Minister rests ultimately with the people when they vote in a general election and the sovereign has absolutely no discretion as to whom to appoint. If the government were to resign, she would be obliged to send for the leader of the opposition, which is now a recognised public office, so there is not even any possibility of her holding preliminary consultations with other party leaders.

If there were more than two main parties, it might of course happen that no one party had a majority in the House of Commons. In this case, the King or Queen might be faced with a real choice and, like the President of the French Republic today, have to decide between a coalition or a minority government dependent on the support of one of the other parties. After the general election of 1923, the Conservatives were still the largest party, but were defeated on an amendment to the address and Mr Baldwin thereupon resigned. The King had then to choose between the Liberal leader, Mr Asquith, and the leader of the Labour Party, Mr Ramsay MacDonald, and he sent for MacDonald whose party only had about a third of the total seats but seemed assured of Liberal support. A more complicated situation arose in 1931, when Ramsay MacDonald's Labour government resigned because it was not prepared to introduce the deflationary measures that the Liberals insisted were the only way to deal with the financial crisis. The Prime Minister advised the King to consult the leaders of the other two parties, Sir Herbert Samuel and Mr Baldwin, and the latter might very well have been appointed Prime Minister. Nevertheless, the King asked Ramsay MacDonald to remain in office and form a National government with the Liberals and Conservatives. The King's action on this occasion does not appear to have been in any way unconstitutional, though the opposite view has sometimes been maintained. In any case, such a situation has not arisen very often, and now that the two-party system is firmly restored, the sovereign has practically no discretion as to whom she shall ask to form a government.

The Queen is likewise no more than a figurehead when she exercises her traditional prerogatives of dismissing ministers and dissolving Parliament. These two functions are closely inter-linked. The ministers are her ministers and she has the power to relieve them of their offices, but the resignation of a govern-ment always has to be followed by a dissolution in order to give their successors an opportunity of securing the majority in Parliament without which no government would be able to survive. Conversely, the Queen only dissolves Parliament on the advice of the Prime Minister, who is politically responsible for the decision. If she insisted on dissolving Parliament against his wishes, she would have to get rid of the existing government and find new ministers to take their place. In that case, it would be what is known as a royal dissolution, due to a disagreement between the sovereign and Parliament, as distinct from a dis-solution during the life of a ministry resulting from a conflict between the Cabinet and the House of Commons. Royal dis-solutions were the regular practice at the beginning of the eighteenth century, but the last two occasions on which they occurred were as long ago as 1783 and 1834. In 1783 George III dismissed Fox's ministry and sent for Pitt, who succeeded in gaining a majority in the ensuing general election. In 1834 William IV forced Lord Melbourne to resign and asked Peel to form a new government, but the verdict of the country went in favour of the Liberals. In that case, however, Lord Melbourne had already offered to resign and the King had adequate reason to suppose that the Liberal majority in the House of Commons was no longer truly representative of the state of opinion in the country.

In any case, these precedents are not really relevant to the very different circumstances of political life today. Throughout the nineteenth century there continued to be some controversy as to whether a royal dissolution would still be possible. Both Gladstone and, even more, Disraeli defended this royal pre-rogative. Today, however, a royal dissolution is generally considered out of the question, since the Cabinet is responsible in all things to the House of Commons and the sovereign is not allowed to show any sign of political bias. It has been argued that the Queen could still insist on a dissolution if she had good reason to think that the majority in Parliament did not accurately reflect the wishes of the country. This view does not command any wide measure of support, for the sovereign is hardly in the best position to assess the state of public opinion, and if she decided to dissolve on her own initiative she would appear to be trying to promote the interests of one party against another. Consequently the sovereign is no longer in a position to dissolve Parliament except on the advice of the Prime Minister.

There is still the question of whether the Queen could refuse a request for a dissolution. This was also a controversial issue in the nineteenth century. It was sometimes held that she might refuse a dissolution if it appeared contrary to the national interest or if the electorate had already had an opportunity to voice their wishes. This was the view expressed by Peel in 1846, by Lord John Russell in 1866, by Disraeli in 1868 and by Lord Salisbury in 1886. As late as 1923, Mr Asquith still maintained that the King would have been entitled to refuse a dissolution to Ramsay MacDonald. All the same, there has been no instance in the last hundred years of the sovereign refusing a dissolution. Today, it would be impossible for the Queen to do so without undermining the political neutrality of the monarchy. She is bound to dissolve Parliament if asked to do so by a Cabinet with a majority in the House of Commons. If she tried to refuse, a new government would have to be formed, and this would not be able to survive unless granted the dissolution denied to the outgoing ministry. In 1923, Mr Asquith argued that the King was not under the same obligation to grant a dissolution to a minority government, but the King himself thought otherwise and agreed to MacDonald's request. There was really no alternative, as any other government that might have been formed would have had even fewer seats and could not have remained in office unless allowed to appeal to the country.

So far as her principal prerogatives are concerned, the sovereign is thus little more than a constitutional mechanism through whom power is exercised. The political neutrality of the monarchy has been preserved partly because the sovereign has been almost completely deprived of any power of independent judgment.

An examination of some of the other royal prerogatives shows even more clearly how the sovereign has, in substance if not in form, been deprived of the power formerly vested in the Crown. The Privy Council still meets in her presence, but she is there simply as the symbol of the authority of the state, and the Privy Council itself merely gives effect to ministerial decisions without further deliberation. Many important officials, judges, senior officers in the armed forces and the highest dignitaries in the church are officially appointed by the Queen, but it is really her ministers who select the candidates. A King or Queen may of course express some personal preference or object to certain names that are put forward, as Queen Victoria did on numerous occasions, and the Cabinet may try to go some way towards satisfying the wishes of the sovereign, which naturally vary with different Kings and Queens. Nevertheless, the sovereign could certainly not place a permanent veto on the appointment of anyone recommended by the Cabinet.

The Queen has a little more discretion in the exercise of her powers of awarding honours, though here again she is normally expected to act on the advice of her ministers. Before 1911 the power to create peers was an important royal prerogative, but it has ceased to have any real political significance now that the upper House has become so solidly Conservative that it would no longer be possible to give any other party a majority by adding to the peerage. This prerogative has thus become no more than one aspect of that of awarding honours.

It might be thought that the Queen still has some discretion in exercising the royal prerogative of mercy. In practice, however, she tends to act only on the advice of the Home Secretary, who assumes responsibility for her actions.

The political neutrality of the monarchy is the governing principle which dictates every action of the sovereign, whose supreme, overriding obligation is to act in accordance with the will of the people. This means that she must invariably act on the advice of the Prime Minister and the Cabinet, who are the representatives of the people and bear the responsibility for the government of the country. Under other forms of parliamentary government it is sometimes possible for the head of state to dismiss a Cabinet with whom he disagrees, form a new government, and then dissolve Parliament to let the people decide whom they want to govern the country. But such personal rule could not be reconciled with present-day ideas of parliamentary government. The British prefer their sovereign to remain strictly above party, as the prestige of the monarchy would inevitably decline if it ever became involved in political controversies.

Yet although they do not allow the sovereign to exercise much real power, the royal prerogatives are not regarded as wholly without significance. For a decision to be taken in the Queen's name marks it out as of special importance and helps to recall that the policy, rule of law or appointment in question is a national and not merely a party issue. It also discourages ministers from thinking that their decisions have no significance outside their own departments.

It is difficult to say definitely whether these ancient prerogatives have really disappeared or not. British political practices are flexible and always liable to be changed in the process of time. At present, when there are two principal well-organised and disciplined parties, it would generally be true to say that nothing that the Queen can do could have any real effect upon the political situation. But there is always the possibility that a larger number of irreconcilable strands of public opinion might once again emerge. In that case, provided she did not compromise the political neutrality of the monarchy in any way, the sovereign might once again be able to exert some influence as an arbiter between conflicting parties. Moreover, although today the sovereign is in many respects no more than a figurehead, this does not mean that a King or Queen cannot still be a real power in the state.

III. THE INFLUENCE OF THE SOVEREIGN

The strength of the monarchy as an institution depends primarily on the personal influence of the sovereign.

It is due, in the first place, to the very fact that the sovereign is the symbol of national unity and the bonds which unite the different members of the Commonwealth. It is further enhanced by the respect, affection, loyalty and devotion which the King or Queen has been able to command among all sections of the population. Since the end of the reign of Queen Victoria the royal family have assumed a leading rôle in the religious, moral and social life of the nation, and in these spheres their influence is probably greater now than ever before. The depth of the people's feelings for the monarchy was unmistakably revealed on the occasion of King George V's Jubilee, in the concern at the abdication of Edward VIII and at the death of George VI, and by the manifestations of popular enthusiasm for the monarchy at the time of the coronation of the present Queen. Finally, the influence of the sovereign depends upon the rôle the people wish her to occupy. The British, imbued with their standards of fair play, have no desire for their sovereign to bear any political responsibility for the government of the country or have power to impose her wishes upon her subjects. Nor do they want to undermine the traditional political neutrality of the monarchy. In so far as the sovereign is able to exert any personal influence, this is, to quote Dicey, 'not because acts of State are done formally in the Crown's name, but because neither the legal sovereign power, namely Parliament, nor the political sovereign, namely the nation, wishes that the reigning monarch should be without personal weight in the government of the country'.

Bagehot summarised the ways in which the sovereign could make her influence felt as her three principal rights—the right to be consulted, the right to encourage and the right to warn. These can really be reduced to two complementary rights—the right to be informed and the right to be consulted.

The right to be informed is guaranteed by the fact that the Privy Council meets in her presence, large numbers of official papers come to her for signature and many important acts of state are performed in her name. Moreover, although she does not attend Cabinet meetings, it has always been one of the most important duties incumbent on the Prime Minister that he should personally keep the sovereign informed of what goes on in the Cabinet.

In the past, there has been some controversy as to exactly how fully and at what stage the Queen was entitled to be informed. There was no definite ruling on the subject, so what happened depended very much on the personalities of the Prime Minister and the sovereign in each individual case, and on the nature of the relationship between them. The Prime Minister used to write a personal letter informing the sovereign of what had been decided at each Cabinet meeting. Queen Victoria was by no means satisfied by this long-established custom and went much further in trying to insist that her ministers should not take any major decision without first letting her know what was in their mind.

Nowadays, this is no longer a serious problem. Papers circulated to the Cabinet by the Cabinet Office or by the departments all go to the Queen, and before any Cabinet meeting she is sent a copy of the agenda. Foreign Office despatches, reports from the Defence Committee, and communications from the Commonwealth Relations Office, are all submitted to the Queen, and if she wants any further information her private secretary asks for it on her behalf. She also has some direct personal contacts with the Governors-General of other Commonwealth countries and with colonial governors and the British ambassadors to the main foreign powers.

The sovereign also has other sources of information at her disposal. Private secretaries and trusted confidants have sometimes been able to exert a great deal of influence over their royal masters, as was the case with Sir Henry Taylor under George III and William IV, Sir William Knighton under George IV, Lord Melbourne, Baron Stockmar and General Grey under Queen Victoria, Lord Knollys under Edward VII, Sir Clive (later Lord) Wigram under George V, and Lord Hardinge under George VI. In addition, the sovereign may be greatly influenced by other personal advisers, and Edward VII often sought advice from experts in different fields.

Finally, the sovereign will be better acquainted with the general background of public affairs than the average minister, and on certain matters, such as foreign policy or Commonwealth affairs, may even be better informed than the Prime Minister. Free from the burden of administrative work and party political affairs that weigh upon ministers, the sovereign may, if so inclined, devote a considerable amount of time to objective study of the various issues with which the government is faced. A King or Queen who does this regularly over a sufficiently long period may become so well acquainted with political affairs that a government which respects the sovereign's right to be consulted is likely to receive some valuable advice.

Here again there are no rigid rules to determine what must happen in any particular case. This depends upon the personality and strength of character of individual monarchs, whether they are well informed on political questions, and how far they have taken any interest in public affairs. The influence of the sovereign also varies considerably according to the personality of the Prime Minister and the other members of his government.

Domestic affairs are now dominated by party politics, and the parties are too firmly committed on all the major issues to be likely to take much notice of opinions expressed by the sovereign. Nevertheless, they may attach some weight to the views of a King or Queen who has had many years' experience of the business of government and yet has been able to move with the times and give advice that is strictly objective and without bias in favour of any party.

It is generally impossible to form a reliable estimate of the influence of any particular sovereign until a considerable time after the end of his or her reign. Queen Victoria apparently helped to secure a compromise over the disestablishment of the Irish Church in 1869 and over the Reform Act of 1884, and some weight may have been attached to her opposition to Home Rule. Generally speaking, from 1841 onwards she tended to put difficulties in the way of Liberal governments, and after 1868 to give every encouragement to Conservative ministries. Edward VII's attitude to the conflicts between Lords and Commons at the beginning of the twentieth century does not seem to have had any significant effect upon the situation. George V's efforts in 1910 and 1911 were not a major factor in helping to settle the political issue, although he may have done something to persuade both parties to bring their policies more into line with what was acceptable to the country as a whole. George V took the initiative in calling a conference of party leaders to discuss the Irish question in 1913-14.

It is in regard to foreign policy, however, that the influence of the sovereign has always been most strongly felt. Queen Victoria's intervention helped to avert the risk of war with Prussia in 1856 and with France in 1859; her support for German unification, her anti-Russian sympathies in 1876-78, and her readiness to agree to the Russian occupation of Port Arthur are well known; and it seems probable that she was able to exert some influence when the government was deliberating whether to intervene in favour of Denmark in 1863-64 and in the Eastern Question in 1876-78. She carried on a regular correspondence with most of the other crowned heads of Europe, with whom she used to discuss current topics of international affairs. Though her successors have not had the same influence in foreign policy, the decline has been a gradual process. Edward VII certainly played a significant rôle in the forging of the Anglo-French Entente and the rapprochement between Britain and Russia, although his actions were always in line with the policy of his ministers. After the accession of George V there was a marked decline in the influence of the Crown in diplomacy, and this has continued under later sovereigns. In matters of national defence the sovereign now has practically no influence, apart from what she may be able to exert in the selection of persons for appointment to major offices.

As she does not have to bear the responsibility for the government of the country, the Queen would naturally have to be somewhat guarded in giving expression to her personal opinions. In any case, it would always be left to the Cabinet to take the final decision. Nor could a sovereign exert any appreciable influence without first putting in much hard work during a long period of apprenticeship in public affairs. Even with this preparation, a monarch could do little without the right personality, a certain political flair, and a real understanding of the rôle of the monarchy. Queen Victoria's position was somewhat exceptional, but she reigned too long ago for her behaviour to provide sound precedents for our own times, and it was only in exceptional cases and only at certain periods in her long and glorious reign that her personal opinions made any significant impression on British policy. Besides, she often acted in ways which seem quite clearly contrary to the spirit of the constitution, and it is unlikely that any sovereign would now be tempted to copy her in this respect.

Nevertheless, the sovereign remains an essential part of both the anatomy and the physiology of the British constitution. Sovereigns who, through their contacts with a series of Prime Ministers, have succeeded in making themselves familiar with public affairs and gained a grasp of political realities find nothing to stop their becoming a personage to whose advice the government will attach considerable weight. This does not call for exceptional ability on the part of whoever occupies the throne. As one Englishman put it, the Hanoverians were not chosen for their intellectual abilities, and it would be quite exceptional for any family to produce a genius in every generation in the direct line of succession. After all, ministers are themselves for the most part comparatively ordinary men, especially in a country like Britain where anyone endowed with exceptional intelligence and imagination tends to be somewhat suspect in the eyes of the general public. Monarchs who are conscientious and perceptive, who are not bereft of tact or common sense, and who are always careful never to depart from a course of strict political neutrality, should be able to exert a definite and enduring influence in the country even though they may never become a real power in the state.

The obligations of kingship make infinite demands upon the sovereign. The Queen has to fulfil both the ceremonial and the representative functions of the monarchy, to make numerous visits to foreign states and other Commonwealth countries, to provide moral leadership and help to instil a social conscience in her peoples, and to undertake a heavy programme of social engagements. This heavy burden is to some extent lightened by the great prestige of the monarchy and by its political neutrality, which it would now be inconceivable for any sovereign to infringe.

In conclusion, therefore, the monarchy is important as an institution which, in a singular combination of dignity and familiarity, personifies the entire history of a nation proud of their glorious past. Another reason for its survival is its success in transforming itself into a democratic institution and its readiness to accept this changed status. The monarchy seems certain to remain a permanent feature of the British system of democratic government. The Cabinet governs in the name of the people who have put it in power, but its position is always in some degree strengthened by the loyalty and devotion to monarchy displayed by the people of Great Britain and the other countries of the Commonwealth.

Chapter Four

THE JUDICIARY

NO general study of the British political system would be complete without a brief account of the judicial system. There are two main reasons why this is important.

In the first place, as already mentioned, the development of the constitution has, from the earliest times, been greatly influenced by the law and the interpretation of the laws, and by the judges and lawyers who at certain periods did so much to shape the course of constitutional history. The lawyers made a stand against Stuart despotism, and it was through their support that Parliament managed to strengthen its position *vis-à-vis* the Crown in the eighteenth century, thus saving the country from a violent upheaval like the French Revolution. The victory of Parliament also marked the triumph of the Common Law. In asserting their independence of the Crown, the judges did not make the mistake of trying to go too far and too fast. After the Act of Settlement, however, they came to look to Parliament to protect their rights, and arraigned themselves solidly in favour of restricting the royal prerogatives.

The other reason for the importance of the judiciary is the exceptionally great power wielded by the courts and judges. This has enabled them to reconcile the public interest with respect for the rights and liberties of individual citizens, and to preserve this equilibrium in a way which makes them the envy of other countries. The power of the judiciary has also been a vital factor in establishing the supremacy of the law, the basic principle underlying the whole of the British constitution of which Bracton wrote in his *De Legibus et consuetudinibus Angliae*: 'The King is subject unto no man. Nevertheless, he is subject unto God and unto the law, because it is the law that has made him King.'

English law, it must be remembered, is primarily case law. There is now a considerable body of Statute Law made up of Acts of Parliament and statutory regulations, but despite the volume of these enactments they are not the basic element in English law.

The Common Law is very much older. Its origins can be traced back to the thirteenth century, when a uniform system of case law began to be built up out of the decisions of itinerant justices who applied the same rules of law throughout the country, thus replacing divergent local customs by a rudimentary system of law and jurisprudence. The Inns of Court became the centres where the Common Law was taught and played an important part in its development. The system became more rigid as time passed and precedents became recognised as binding rules. As the same rules were being applied throughout the country, it was never thought necessary to make any systematic codification of the law.

Nevertheless, cases sometimes arose in which an equitable verdict or adequate redress of grievances could not be obtained from the courts of Common Law. When this happened, it became customary to appeal for equity to the King, who, as the source of all judicial power, was able to give a decision more satisfactory to the parties involved. These petitions used to be referred to the Chancellor and later to the Court of Chancery, whose decisions developed into a system of Equity, quite distinct from the Common Law and strongly influenced by the Canon Law and by Roman Law, from which the Canon Law was originally derived. Anyone going to law could choose, according to the nature of his grievance and the redress which he hoped to obtain, whether to have his case tried by Equity or by the Common Law.

In neither of these systems, however, could a satisfactory decision be given in every case simply by the application of established precedents. Entirely new rules of law were sometimes required, and this gave rise to the growth of Statute Law. This originally took the form of occasional pronouncements by the King. In time these gave way to royal ordinances made by the King in response to petitions from Parliament, and these in turn were replaced by Acts of Parliament. All Statute Law, however, has been built up on the basis of the pre-existing system of jurisprudence. A statute may alter an established rule of law, but it is always necessary to refer to the Common Law to decide how to interpret a statute in any particular case. The basic principles of English civil and criminal law are still found in Common Law and Equity. The latter are constantly being altered and adapted to changing circumstances by new Acts of Parliament, but any point on which the Statute Law is silent will always be decided by reference to previous decisions of the courts.

It follows that exceptionally broad powers are vested in the judges, who must consequently be regarded as an important element in the machinery of government in Great Britain. Their importance will become even more apparent after a brief survey of the organisation of the courts, the jurisdiction of the courts, and the position of the judges. As Scotland has a separate legal system of its own, what follows applies only to England and Wales.

I. THE MACHINERY OF JUSTICE

The main traditional features of the English judicial system have remained unaltered since the reforms of 1873. It is still a fairly complicated system, but a number of underlying general principles can be distinguished.

First, the practice of trial by a single judge is carried further in England than in any other country. This has prevented the growth of a large and badly paid corps of magistrates, and the strong and independent position of the judges means that the fact that they sit alone does not appear to have any serious drawbacks. Most cases are tried in the first instance before a single magistrate, although appeals are generally heard by three, or sometimes two judges sitting together.

Another outstanding characteristic of the English judicial system is its extensive use of juries. Reforms introduced in 1933 have made recourse to a grand jury practically obsolete, but juries are still employed to decide on matters of fact in criminal cases. They may also be used in civil cases, although not if they are decided by Equity. The judge has a fairly broad degree of discretion to order trial with or without a jury, but there is always a jury whenever a man's personal honour is implicated, as in cases of libel or arbitrary imprisonment.

Another characteristic of the judicial system is that the judges normally move about the country on circuit. This helps to avoid the disadvantages likely to be encountered in a system of justice that has always been and still is highly centralised. It also means that relatively few judges are required, so that their prestige is higher than it would be if they were more numerous. The county courts, with wide powers of jurisdiction in civil cases where the sum involved does not exceed a specified figure (£200 or £500),[1] are grouped into 59 circuits. This means that although there have been over 400 county courts since the reforms of 1846, a very small number of judges is still sufficient to enable a court to sit in each district at least once a month. Criminal courts are likewise able to manage with comparatively few judges because the lower courts are not in permanent session. Persons charged with non-indictable offences are mostly tried by Justices of the Peace in Petty Sessions, while other cases are heard at Quarter Sessions or at the Assizes, which are held three or four times a year in various provincial towns.

It is not possible here to give more than a brief outline of the various courts of law which make up the English judiciary. Altogether they form an elaborate system which is somewhat confusing on account of the overlapping jurisdiction of different courts and the fact that similar cases may be tried at several different levels.

For civil cases, county courts form the bottom rung of the judicial hierarchy. They have wide jurisdiction as courts of first instance and in fact decide a large number of civil actions. But civil proceedings may also be instituted in the High Court of Justice, the higher court of Common Law, which can decide whether to try the case itself or remit it to a county court. The High Court is made up of three Divisions, comprising thirty judges in all: Queen's Bench, the Common Law Division, includes the Lord Chief Justice and 19 puisne judges: the Chancery Division, with five puisne judges, is the court of Equity and has concurrent jurisdiction with Queen's Bench; lastly the Division of Probate, Admiralty and Divorce consisting of a President and four puisne judges, deals with a varied range of cases formerly within the jurisdiction of the ecclesiastical courts, including the probate of wills, matrimonial causes, and Admiralty affairs such as shipping and prize cases.

In civil cases there is a right of appeal from the county courts and the High Court of Justice, at least on points of law. Appeals are decided by the Court of Appeal, a central tribunal sitting

[1] The limit on the competence of county courts in actions of contract, tort, etc., was increased from £200 to £400 in 1955.

in London. Besides a number of *ex officio* members who do not normally take part in its work, the active members of the Court of Appeal are the Master of the Rolls and eight Lords Justices of Appeal. Any three of these may confirm or annul the decision of a lower court or remit the case to the court of first instance for retrial if they find that the jury were not properly instructed at the first trial.

The supreme court of appeal is the House of Lords or, to be more precise, the small body of Law Lords who sit specially to hear appeals brought before them by petition. This is an expensive process and very rarely used. The appellate functions of the Judicial Committee of the Privy Council are in practice almost exclusively confined to appeals from the decisions of courts in the colonies or those Commonwealth countries which have not yet abolished this right of appeal.

For criminal cases, the lowest courts are those of the Justices of the Peace, whose office dates back to the Middle Ages when the King charged certain leading men in each district with the duty of maintaining the peace in their counties. Their modern counterparts are unpaid magistrates, without legal training, who now number about 19,000, including nearly 4,000 women. Only London and a few other large towns have replaced these lay justices by professional stipendiary magistrates. Elsewhere, individual justices have jurisdiction over minor offences for which the penalty does not exceed a fine of £5 or 14 days' imprisonment. Persons charged with non-indictable offences are usually tried by two or more justices of the peace in Petty Sessions. Groups of justices also sit in Quarter Sessions, held four times a year in each county, where they sit with a jury to try persons charged with indictable offences, and without a jury to hear appeals from lower courts. The most serious criminal offences are tried at the Assizes, held throughout the country at regular intervals by judges of the Queen's Bench Division on circuit, sitting with a jury of twelve members. In addition, there are coroner's courts which frequently sit with a jury and perform functions comparable to those of a *juge d'instruction* in France by conducting investigations before a case is brought to trial. In criminal cases only those convicted by a lower court have the right to appeal. Appeals are heard by the Court of Criminal Appeal, constituted from judges of Queen's Bench Division, who have power in certain cases to quash the verdict of the court of first instance. A final appeal to the House of Lords is occasionally possible, but only if the Attorney-General certifies that the case raises a point of law of exceptional public importance.

II. THE COMPETENCE OF THE COURTS

An exceptionally wide range of cases comes within the jurisdiction of the ordinary lawcourts whose competence is far from being confined to actions involving only private persons.

A substantial body of administrative law has developed since the end of the nineteenth century, when Dicey still found it possible to maintain that the term would be unintelligible to an Englishman without further explanation. According to Dicey, the principle of the supremacy of the law meant that there could only be one system of law, applied and interpreted by a single system of courts, to govern the actions of every citizen whether acting in a private capacity or in the execution of some public function. This is certainly no longer true today. Even in Great Britain there is now a large volume of administrative law which, as Professor Robson has pointed out, includes not only the law—Statutes, Common Law and Equity—controlling public administration but also the law emanating from administrative authorities and the usages and conventions of the executive.

There are obviously a large number of special rules governing the activities of executive organs in Great Britain and their relations with private citizens. Although not regarded as a separate code of law, they may nevertheless be likened to the administrative law of countries that have a separate system of administrative courts, since they recognise that public authorities must be given a certain amount of legal immunity and cannot be treated as exactly equal to private persons in the eyes of the law. This is clearly true of many rules relating to public administration, local government, taxation and the organisation of public services, that are laid down in Acts of Parliament and, at greater length, in delegated legislation.

The great increase in government activities, partly as the result of the two World Wars, has meant that new government departments have been established, public administration has extended into many new fields, administrative regulations have grown more and more complex, and entirely new juridical relationships have been created. This has given rise to new kinds of cases that could not be decided by established legal precedents. It was not thought appropriate to place these matters under the jurisdiction of the ordinary lawcourts, so there has been a series of piecemeal innovations which have gradually destroyed the traditional monopoly of the courts over every kind of litigation.

Judicial or quasi-judicial powers have been vested in a number of government departments, such as the Ministry of Health, the Ministry of Housing and Local Government, the Ministry of Transport, the Ministry of Pensions and National Insurance and the Ministry of Education. Special executive organs or even genuine administrative tribunals have been set up to exercise judicial functions in respect of such matters as railway and canal traffic, national insurance, pensions, town and country planning and social security. In 1948 there were no less than 207 of these tribunals, of which 41 were attached to the Ministry of Transport, 40 to the Ministry of Agriculture and Fisheries, 20 to the Ministry of Health, 18 to the Home Office, 14 to the Ministry of Labour and 10 to the Ministry of Fuel and Power. Such tribunals should be able to decide many cases relating to technical or administrative matters far more quickly and cheaply than would be possible in the ordinary lawcourts, provided that they employ specialist judges and follow a procedure which gives adequate safeguards for individual rights. The last twenty or thirty years have seen considerable improvements in the procedure and effectiveness of these forms of 'administrative justice'.

Those who adhere to the traditional liberal principle that to remove any matter from the jurisdiction of the courts is a violation of the Rule of Law have expressed great concern at the way that the executive appears to be taking upon itself powers which properly belong to the courts. Under modern conditions, however, it is no longer realistic to try to give the Rule of Law the strict interpretation placed upon it in the nineteenth century. On the other hand, as the British usually proceed by way of gradual change and adaptation, it seems unlikely that they will ever acquire a separate and unified system of administrative courts such as exists in France. The traditional supremacy of the courts has not been seriously challenged, and it is usually—though not always—possible to seek redress in the ordinary lawcourts against the decision of an administrative tribunal.

Moreover, the decision of an administrative authority is always open to review by the courts unless there is some express statutory provision to the contrary. The courts still retain their traditional power to determine whether the executive has acted in accordance with the law. It rests with them to decide how the prerogatives of the Crown are to be interpreted and whether delegated legislation is consistent with the terms of the Act under which it is made. They also have power to review the legality of any acts of any executive organ, including its judicial or quasi-judicial decisions.

Judicial review of executive acts may be instituted by means of various special orders which have now replaced the old prerogative writs. The latter were originally issued by virtue of the King's power to require judges and magistrates faithfully to carry out the duties committed to their charge, but subsequently came to be sought as a means of obtaining redress against public authorities. *Mandamus* is issued to compel the performance of a public duty. Its application to the Crown and government departments is somewhat limited, but it may be used to annul the decisions of local authorities and administrative tribunals and to compel them to fulfil their legal obligations. An order of prohibition restrains an authority from exceeding its jurisdiction. *Certiorari*, an order of wider application, can be used to secure annulment or alteration of an administrative decision.

It is also possible to obtain a declaratory judgment from the courts, stating how the law would apply in a particular case, and public authorities have not usually questioned any private rights declared by the courts. In addition, the doctrine of *ultra vires*, comparable to the French concept of *excès de pouvoir*, has been deployed with considerable skill as a means of restraining arbitrary action by the executive, although it does not apply only to public authorities.

Finally, another powerful deterrent to arbitrary acts is that public officials have always been to a large extent personally liable for any damages to private persons occurring in the course of their official duties. This was because the old rule that the King can do no wrong meant that there were many cases in which it was impossible to bring a claim against a public authority. Here, however, there has recently been an important reform, as the Crown Proceedings Act, 1948, makes it possible to sue the Crown in civil proceedings without recourse to a petition of right. This opens up a wide range of cases in which damages are now recoverable from the Crown itself instead of from its agents in their personal capacity.

The English legal system is still based on the principle of a single system of law equally applicable to public and private personages and enforceable by the ordinary courts of law which retain general powers to review executive acts. The supremacy of the courts became firmly established through their long struggle to secure recognition of the rights of individual citizens against arbitrary government. The Rule of Law continues to be respected today because the courts have acquired great authority which is unlikely to be undermined because of the strong position of the judges.

III. THE JUDGES

The special position of the judges in Great Britain is due principally to the way in which they are recruited and to their absolute independence, which are the main reasons for their unparalleled prestige.

The judiciary is not a distinct profession to which a man devotes the whole of his working life, since judges are always men who have previously had a distinguished career at the bar. Judges, barristers and solicitors form the three distinct branches of the legal profession, each of which regulates the training of its members and administers its own affairs.

Solicitors, who have their autonomous organisation in the Law Society, now combine the functions of solicitor and attorney which were formerly quite distinct. They advise lay clients, make arrangements for the conduct of their cases, and may themselves appear on their behalf in the lower courts.

A barrister's functions are similar to those of an advocate in France. At the present time there are about 2,000 barristers, all of whom belong to one of the four Inns of Court—Grey's Inn, the Middle and Inner Temples on the site once occupied by the order of the Templars, and Lincoln's Inn which specialises in Equity. Each is a closely knit corporate body of barristers, former barristers who have become judges, and students. The benchers supervise the training of the students, who are subsequently called to the bar by a system of co-option which helps to preserve the traditions of the profession. One section of the barristers are known as Queen's Counsel, a title conferred by the Lord Chancellor on the more senior and distinguished members of the bar. The Lord Chancellor's is the highest office in the judiciary, but there is of course no equivalent of a Minister of Justice. The two Law Officers—the Attorney-General and the Solicitor-General—are members of the government and appear on behalf of the state in important lawsuits and act as government spokesmen in Parliament. These are both temporary political appointments carrying a fixed salary. In most cases, however, ordinary barristers appear on behalf of public authorities in both civil and criminal proceedings.

Judges are appointed by the Crown from among barristers who are Queen's Counsel. Puisne judges and county court judges are appointed on the recommendation of the Lord Chancellor, and other judges on the recommendation of the Prime Minister. In either case, however, the Lord Chancellor and the Prime Minister usually consult with each other before recommending any name to the sovereign. County court judges must be barristers of at least seven years' standing, and High Court judges barristers of at least ten years' standing, while a Lord Justice of Appeal must have had fifteen years at the bar or else have already been a High Court judge for at least a year. In practice, however, a barrister is hardly ever appointed to the bench before the age of 40 or 50, and the average age of judges is consequently high.

This is possibly a disadvantage in so far as a relatively elderly bench of judges who have spent many years defending powerful and well-established interests at the bar may tend to be somewhat conservative in its outlook. On the other hand, English judges are appointed, not—or at least not primarily—for political reasons, but under a system which ensures that they are distinguished lawyers thoroughly well versed in their profession. These arrangements also help to maintain the high standard of judicial integrity since, as A. B. Keith pointed out, 'judges are conscious that they are under the continuous scrutiny of men with like experience' who were formerly their colleagues at the bar. Moreover, judgeships have always been too much sought after to become simply a refuge for those who have been a failure at the bar. A distinguished barrister often welcomes the prospect of spending the last years of his career as a judge, and is quite prepared to give up the high fees he could command as a leading counsel in exchange for the independence and prestige of the bench.

A number of different factors combine to guarantee the independence of the judiciary. In the first place, judges have security of tenure. By the Act of Settlement of 1701, they are appointed for life and hold office during good behaviour. They cannot be dismissed except by the sovereign in response to an address from both Houses of Parliament, a procedure which has not been employed for over two hundred years. The sovereign could in theory dismiss judges in the lower courts, but in fact they too enjoy complete security of tenure.

Judges are sufficiently well paid to prevent their being tempted to compromise their independence from financial motives. Their salaries may not compare very favourably with the fees of a leading barrister but are substantially higher than those of any other public employees. The Lord Chancellor receives a total salary of £12,000, being £4,000 as Speaker of the House of Lords and £8,000 in respect of his judicial functions as President of the Court of Appeal and of the House of Lords when it sits as the supreme court of appeal. The Lord Chief Justice, who presides over Queen's Bench, the Court of Criminal Appeal and the High Court of Justice, has a salary of £11,000 a year. A Lord Justice of Appeal and a puisne judge both receive £8,000 a year, and judges in the lower courts from £2,000 to £2,800. Judges' salaries, it will be remembered, are charges on the Consolidated Fund and do not come up for discussion in Parliament as part of the annual budget. A judge may resign voluntarily, in which case he receives a pension— £3,500 a year for a puisne judge and £5,000 for the Lord Chancellor. There is no compulsory retiring age, this being thought undesirable in view of the fact that judges are appointed late in life and no one wishes to deprive the bench of its most experienced members. There is, however, a considerable body of opinion in favour of making all judges retire at the age of 72 or thereabouts, and county court judges do in fact retire on reaching this age.

Another factor which strengthens the independence of the judges is that they are not normally looking for further promotion. Once appointed, the vast majority of English judges occupy the same position until they retire from the bench. Promotions are rare, and in any case the prospect of advancement is not sufficiently lucrative to be sought after for financial reasons.

The judiciary has also succeeded in maintaining its independence in its relations with the general public, and no third party may bring an action against a judge in respect of anything done by him in the course of his official duties. Finally, the judiciary is well protected against any attempt to frustrate the course of justice or any attack on a judge personally or on his conduct of a case. Such activities are regarded as contempt of court, punishable on summary conviction by a fine or imprisonment. Contempt of court is not limited to offences committed in court while the case is being heard, but also covers any other act or publication designed to discredit the judiciary. The protection thus afforded to the bench is often held to be excessive because it deters what might be salutary criticism and violates the rule that no one should be judge in his own cause. Nevertheless, English judges still enjoy this protection, which serves to enhance their independence and is also a mark of their high prestige.

Their small numbers and high social standing have undoubtedly helped to preserve this prestige. Another contributing factor is the extremely serious tone of all legal proceedings, which are governed by a strict code of etiquette that rules out any kind of theatrical declamations. Moreover, judges have no thought of securing further promotion for themselves, and carry out their duties with unfailing and universally recognised impartiality. Finally, judges are thoroughly imbued with the traditions of the judiciary and of the legal profession, so that they endeavour to administer justice in such a way as to uphold the supremacy of the law.

The English legal system is, inevitably, not without its weaknesses. Administrative tribunals could with advantage be made more independent of the executive, and a considerable body of opinion favours the creation of a new division of the High Court or some other special tribunal with power to review all judicial decisions of administrative authorities. Another point often criticised is the way that a large proportion of criminal cases are still tried by laymen serving as justices of the peace for the district. This has been condemned as an anachronism, though some anomalies of the system were removed by the Justices of the Peace Act, 1949. Moreover, despite its many good features, the judiciary does perhaps tend to suffer from some of the weaknesses found in most exclusive professional groups, such as uniformity of outlook and a generally conservative disposition. The greatest defect of English justice, however, is its expense. Legal procedure is extremely complex, and although cases are settled with remarkably little delay, the cost of litigation is further increased by the traditional highly centralised character of the system. The Labour government tried to tackle this problem by the Act of 1948, which extended the scope of legal aid instituted under previous legislation. Much more still needs to be done, however, before the judicial system will be truly democratic and no citizen ever debarred from going to law simply on grounds of expense.

The present English judicial system is nevertheless an outstanding example of a powerful element in the constitution which is completely independent of both the Cabinet and Parliament, does not come under the control of any government department, and is thoroughly insulated against all kinds of political pressure. The political authorities are thus constrained to act in accordance with the law and to recognise the authority of the judiciary. The judges themselves constitute a highly distinguished profession that commands universal respect. They have managed to preserve their autonomy and to remain the loyal servants of the Crown while at the same time defending the rights and liberties of the people. Their position is further strengthened because they share in the authority attached to the law itself, in a country where the people have always shown profound respect for the law and the constitution. The constitution itself has been built up partly on the basis of judicial decisions, the influence of the courts having been particularly marked in the development of parliamentary procedure, the powers of the Speaker, respect for constitutional precedents, and the British tradition of fair play in politics. The outstanding feature of the judicial system, however, is that the courts retain full jurisdiction over all acts of the government. That this should still be so under present-day conditions is a striking triumph for the cause of individual liberty.

The judiciary can thus in certain respects be likened to the British administrative system, which forms another powerful, non-political element in the constitution.

Chapter Five

THE ADMINISTRATIVE SYSTEM

THE executive can make its influence felt through the administrative system more directly, more easily and more powerfully than in any other branch of government. This is as true in Britain as elsewhere.

The structure of the administrative system and the general principles on which it operates are prescribed by law, but administration is essentially a function of the executive. The administrative machine is in effect the sum total of the organs upon which the government relies to carry the laws into effect and to manage the public services. This machinery could never operate effectively without some degree of independence.

At first glance British administrative institutions appear remarkably heterogeneous, but the Cabinet nevertheless retains supreme authority over every aspect of their work.

There are about thirty government departments which between them discharge the principal administrative functions, including both those traditionally undertaken by the government and others which it has assumed more recently. These departments appear very different in many respects. They vary greatly in age, and each has its own departmental traditions and has been established and reorganised without regard to any abstract general principles.

The Treasury has developed out of the very old office of Lord High Treasurer. This was put into commission in 1612. The Prime Minister, as First Lord of the Treasury, is thus chairman of a committee which in fact never meets. In this capacity, however, the Prime Minister has powers of control over the Civil Service and the appointment of senior officials. The Treasury itself is today the equivalent of a Ministry of Finance, with the Chancellor of the Exchequer as its effective ministerial head.

A considerable number of departments were until recently formally controlled by a board, although for all practical purposes the chairman of the board was in just the same position as any other departmental minister. The Board of Agriculture was converted into a ministry in 1919, and the Board of Education in 1944. The minister responsible for commercial affairs still has the title of President of the Board of Trade, although the board itself never meets. The Board of Admiralty retains some collegiate functions and meets regularly, but the First Lord of the Admiralty is really in charge of the department responsible for naval affairs.

Eight ministers have the title of Secretary of State, derived from the very old office of Secretary of State that was in existence in the reign of Henry III. The duties of the office came to be shared between two Secretaries and were later distributed between a number of different departments. Thus the Foreign Office and the Home Office came into being in 1782; the War Office in 1794; and the Colonial Office, previously part of the War Office, in 1854. The Air Ministry was separated from the War Office in 1919, and a Dominions Office distinct from the Colonial Office was created in 1926 and has now become the Commonwealth Relations Office. A Secretary of State for Scotland was appointed in 1926 and a Secretary of State for the Co-ordination of Transport, Fuel and Power in 1951.[1] All the Secretaries of State in theory occupy the same office, but in fact each acts as the head of his own department and their functions are quite distinct.

Besides these older departments which have not formally discarded their historic structure, there are other ministries of more recent origin which present no particularly unusual organisational features. There are also a number of subordinate departments, attached in some way or other to one of the principal government departments.

Semi-autonomous public boards and authorities commonly known as public corporations have been widely employed in Great Britain. Their development has been particularly marked in recent years, and has naturally attracted much attention from French students of the working of public corporations. Some examples of semi-autonomous public boards could be found as far back as the nineteenth century, mainly in the sphere of local government. They became more widespread as the result of increased state intervention in economic affairs in

---

[1] The office of Secretary of State for the Co-ordination of Transport, Fuel and Power was allowed to lapse in 1953.

the inter-war years, and the subsequent policy of the Labour Party has led to their being even more extensively employed. The public corporation is a device whereby a public enterprise can be to some extent freed from political control, thus making it possible for those with special knowledge of the industry to participate in its management and allowing it to be run on lines best suited to the needs of industrial and commercial undertakings.

Public corporations are invariably set up either by Royal Charter or by Act of Parliament, but they may adopt widely differing patterns of organisation. They usually have a governing board, partially if not entirely appointed by the minister to whom the corporation is accountable. Some are to all intents and purposes managed by the minister. Others, deriving the greater part of their income from their own rates and charges or from grants-in-aid, enjoy a very broad degree of independence although subject to general ministerial oversight.

Among the earlier examples of the public corporation were the National Assistance Board and the British Broadcasting Corporation. The nationalisation programme of the Attlee government resulted in the creation of many more, including the Bank of England, the National Coal Board, the British Transport Commission, the Iron and Steel Corporation of Great Britain, the British Electricity Authority and area electricity boards, and the Gas Council and area gas boards.[1] The Colonial Development Corporation and the Overseas Food Corporation were set up to administer important programmes of economic development.[2] Other public corporations such as the Atomic Energy Authority have since been created to administer enterprises which call for a combination of managerial autonomy and public control.

Despite their great variety, the government retains firm control over all these administrative agencies. Government departments are so organised that the Cabinet has full control over all their acts, for which it is in turn accountable to Parliament. Other administrative agencies are attached to some department, the head of which will have charge of a number of subordinate departments in addition to his own ministry. Every

[1] The Iron and Steel Corporation was abolished in 1953. The British Electricity Authority became the Central Electricity Authority in 1953.

[2] The Overseas Food Corporation was put in liquidation in 1954.

departmental minister must to some extent work in consultation with the Prime Minister, who can intervene personally in the affairs of any department. The Treasury exercises overall control over finance by scrutinising the estimates when the budget is in course of preparation and keeping a check on expenditure through the Accounting Officers in each department so as to ensure that there is no departure from the budget estimates.

Public control of autonomous or semi-autonomous public corporations in Britain has met with difficulties similar to those experienced in other countries. On 4th December 1951 the House of Commons appointed a Select Committee on Nationalised Industries which presented two reports on these problems, but considerable difficulties have been encountered in subsequent attempts to set up a select committee to control the accounts and operations of the nationalised industries. Nevertheless, the government has always had some powers of control over these undertakings. The governing boards are appointed by the minister, and they must seek government approval for their programmes of capital development and research and cannot borrow money without government consent. The parent minister usually has some powers over a corporation in regard to its relations with the public.

In principle, therefore, every branch of public administration in some way or other comes under the control of a minister and of the Cabinet.

Ministers are normally assisted by one or two parliamentary secretaries and sometimes by an under-secretary or minister of state. These junior ministers are regarded as in training for higher office, and are expected to exercise general oversight over the affairs of the department or over some particular branch of its work on behalf of the minister and to advise on matters of policy. Inter-departmental committees, on the importance of which we have already remarked, are used to co-ordinate the activities of different departments. A more recent experiment, in the Attlee and Churchill Cabinets, has been to give certain Cabinet ministers special responsibility for co-ordinating the activities of a particular group of departments. In the last resort, supreme authority always rests with the Cabinet and the various Cabinet committees, and with the Prime Minister. The Cabinet also has extensive power to alter the structure of the administrative system and transfer functions from one department to another under the Ministers of the Crown (Transfer of Functions) Act, 1946. Acts relating to the establishment or organisation of government departments are generally brief and leave much to the discretion of the Cabinet.

The British administrative machine has undergone considerable expansion in recent years in consequence of the extension of government activities, intensified by six years of Labour rule. Many new agencies and public corporations have had to be established to undertake additional functions, and all these are public authorities and as such come under the control of the Cabinet. The growth of delegated legislation and the increase in the powers of the executive have been accompanied by a corresponding broadening of administrative discretion, which is one aspect of the 'New Despotism' that has aroused so much misgiving among liberal-minded persons in Great Britain.

Nevertheless, the administrative system contains two strong bulwarks against any threat of dictatorship. The first is the Civil Service. This certainly provides the government with able and loyal administrators, but Great Britain has surpassed all other democracies in keeping her Civil Service out of politics and maintaining complete political neutrality even among the highest officials. The second safeguard is the system of local government, which has always been to a large extent autonomous. In recent years local authorities have been subjected to closer control from the centre, but they still have sufficient power and independence to be a considerable check on the central government.

I. THE CIVIL SERVICE

The Civil Service came into being as a result of the movement to do away with the old system under which public offices were treated as political spoils.

The origins of the modern Civil Service can be traced back to 1855. Until then, administrative posts were regarded as the property of the Crown and filled by a system of patronage under which appointments were largely determined by birth and connections and—after the emergence of parties—by political affiliations. Little attention was paid to the personal merits of the candidates. There were many sinecures, remuneration was more or less arbitrary, there were no definite prospects of promotion and absolutely no security of tenure. Any change of government was followed by a redistribution of offices quite as extensive, if not so systematic, as occurs in the United States today. The patronage system reached its zenith in the eighteenth century. By then, however, it had begun to be attacked, and in the later eighteenth and early nineteenth centuries there was hardly a break in the demands for thorough-going reform, voiced by Fox, Burke and Bentham. Only a few abuses were removed until the movement for administrative reform gained momentum after the Reform Act of 1832 and the ascendancy of the middle classes. Between 1830 and 1840 many new administrative organs and public services were created, the framework of the British administrative system was established and there was a greater awareness of the need to root out irregularities and abuses in the public services.

In November 1848 the Prime Minister, Lord John Russell, and the Treasury took the initiative in appointing Sir Charles Trevelyan, then Permanent Secretary to the Treasury, and Sir Stafford Northcote to undertake a thorough inquiry into the Civil Service. Shortly before this, examinations had been re-introduced and made the general practice at the universities. Haileybury had been founded in 1813 as a special college for training officials to go to India, and competitive entry to the Indian administrative service was introduced by the Act which renewed the East India Company's Charter in 1833. These provisions were not wholeheartedly enforced in practice, but the opposition to patronage gathered momentum until the Charter Act of 1853, influenced on this point by Macaulay, made competitive examinations obligatory for recruitment to the Indian Civil Service. The principles underlying these reforms were accepted by Trevelyan, and the report which he and Northcote submitted to Parliament in 1854 recommended recruitment by competitive examination, separate competitions for different grades of posts, and selection on the basis of a liberal education.

The Northcote-Trevelyan report was greeted with derision, coolness or scepticism in many quarters, including the Court. But Gladstone supported its recommendations. The Civil Service Commission was consequently established, by the Order in Council of 21st May 1855. It consisted of three members who were to examine candidates for admission to the Civil Service, who would then be appointed by ministers on the basis of certificates granted by the Commissioners. The Superannuation Act of 1859 consolidated this system by making the Commissioners' certificate a necessary qualification for a retirement pension. The reform was completed by the Order in Council of 4th June 1870. This made recruitment by open competition compulsory for all posts except where the Commission had granted a special dispensation, or in a limited number of cases where appointments can be made by the Crown without reservations. The Treasury was empowered to approve rules drawn up by the Commission and the departments concerning recruitment. Promotion remained under the control of heads of departments.

The development of the Civil Service has continued since 1870. A number of reforms have been made in the light of investigations by various Royal Commissions and Committees: the Playfair Commission of 1875, the Ridley Commission of 1886-90, the Macdonnell Commission of 1912-14, the Gladstone Committee of 1918, the Tomlin Commission of 1929 and the Assheton Committee of 1944.[1] There have in fact been great changes in the Civil Service over the past century. Its numbers have grown enormously, and with broader opportunities for university education it has become a much less exclusively aristocratic corps of administrators. In January 1950 the top grades of civil servants actually took the unprecedented step of protesting to the Labour Prime Minister against the freezing of their salaries. The high calibre, efficiency and impartiality of the Civil Service make its services of immense value to any government, and with its traditional independence and political neutrality it provides a singularly effective guarantee against dictatorship.

The organisation of the Civil Service follows certain basic general principles. In the first place, the 700,000 civil servants outside the industrial grades are divided into a hierarchy of classes. These class divisions are to some extent a reflection of the social structure of England, and correspond to a classification of duties much more elaborate than that between

[1] Another Royal Commission under the chairmanship of Sir Raymond Priestley was appointed in 1953 and reported in 1955.

'intellectual work' and 'routine work' originally proposed by Trevelyan.

The Administrative Class comprises about 2,631 civil servants, including 206 women, ranging from Assistant Principals, the lowest grade (£360-£720 a year),[1] to the permanent heads of departments at the top of the hierarchy (Deputy Secretaries and Permanent Secretaries earning £2,500-£3,500 a year).[2] Their official duties cover the key functions of government—'the determination of policy, the co-ordination and improvement of the machinery of government, the general administration and control of the departments'. Formerly the Administrative Class was almost a distinct social caste, recruited from well-to-do families and nearly all educated at Oxford or Cambridge. It is still an élite, who constitute the most influential class of civil servants, united in loyalty to their traditions and to the service of the state. The Executive Class forms a lower hierarchy of about 68,000 civil servants, including nearly 11,000 women, ranging from Executive Officers to Chief Executive Officers (£230-£1,200).[3] They have important functions, both executive and supervisory, especially in such branches as supplies, revenues, payments and accounts, where an official's duties can be fairly narrowly defined. Membership is not confined to any particular social class.

Below this comes the very large Clerical Class with about 120,000 members for general clerical duties whose salaries range from £150 to £625 a year.[4] Then there is the Clerical Assistant Class of women engaged on subordinate office duties, and a Typing Class of women typists and shorthand-typists.

Finally, there is the Scientific Civil Service, which was established on an inter-departmental basis in 1945. There are about 114,000 professional and technical civil servants—scientists, actuaries, statisticians, architects, doctors, lawyers and engineers—who form a separate hierarchy on their own.

The outstanding features of this system are, first, the very marked dominance of the Administrative Class, and second, the segregation between classes which has by no means disappeared, particularly at the highest levels. It is comparatively easy to obtain promotion from one class to another as far as the Executive Class, but fewer manage to enter the Administrative

---

[1] £605-£1,055 in 1956.
[2] £3,250-£4,500 in 1956.
[3] £365-£1,845 in 1956.
[4] £240-£1,000 in 1956.

Class from below, even though there has recently been some attempt to make this more democratic. Yet, in spite of these rigid distinctions between classes, the Civil Service is essentially a unified service. This is particularly true of the highest class, who form an integrated staff of administrators freely inter-changeable between departments. Nevertheless, the work of the Treasury and the Civil Service Commission ensures that a high degree of integration is maintained throughout the Service.

The Treasury has special responsibilities for the control of the Civil Service, in addition to its general control over finance which gives it a considerable authority over the activities of other departments. The Order in Council of 22nd July 1921, consolidating a long series of earlier orders in council, gives the Treasury control over grading, remuneration and all matters of organisation and office management. There is an Establishments Branch, under an Establishments Officer, in each department to handle staff questions and promote im-provements in organisation and methods. The Establishments Branch is formally accountable only to the head of the depart-ment, but it also comes under the direct control of the Treasury, which is advised and assisted by a standing committee of estab-lishments officers under the chairmanship of an Under-Secretary to the Treasury. The Establishments Department of the Treasury deals with all questions of principle in regard to the numbers and grading of staff in the various departments, promotion, pensions, remuneration and the organisation of the Service. Since 1919, the Permanent Secretary to the Treasury has had the title of Head of the Civil Service and as such receives a salary of £5,000 a year.[1] There is some doubt as to whether the Treasury, with its economic and financial pre-occupations, is the department best fitted to control the Civil Service. It has been suggested that this function be transferred to the Cabinet Secretariat under the Prime Minister, but while that might be a more logical arrangement, there does not appear to be any pressing reason for interfering with the tradi-tional supremacy of the Treasury in these matters.

The other unifying factor is the Civil Service Commission,

[1] Since 1956 there have been two Permanent Secretaries to the Treasury —one solely concerned with its economic and financial business and the other, who is also Secretary to the Cabinet, concerned with the Civil Service and machinery of government; the latter is 'Head of the Home Civil Service'.

which deals with recruitment to the Civil Service subject to the overriding authority of the Treasury. Its intervention ensures that selection is carried out impartially on the basis of individual merit. The Commission was originally established in 1855, when it had three members; three extra commissioners have recently been added. They are all civil servants of long standing who are appointed by order in council, so that their tenure is virtually as secure as that of a judge. They have a staff of about 700 to assist them in their important duties covering all matters relating to recruitment.

Subject to the approval of the Treasury, the Civil Service Commission prescribe methods of recruitment. They conduct the various competitions, issue the certificates which are a prerequisite for appointment to any position in the Civil Service, and draw up the lists from which the departments and offices select their personnel. The method of entry to each class is geared to the British educational system: the age limits and examinations for the Administrative Class are designed for university graduates, those for the Executive Class for entrants from the top classes of secondary schools, and those for the Clerical Class for candidates who have had several years' secondary education. The examinations and competitions are designed primarily as a test of general education or a means of assessing intelligence, personality and powers of reasoning. Far from being in any way specially related to the functions of a particular department, they tend to eliminate candidates with too specialised qualifications. The Selection Boards include a high proportion of university teachers and some private individuals. The century-old concept of the civil servant as a general administrator and not a technical expert is still generally accepted, even in regard to the lower classes. In the Scientific Civil Service, however, it has not been applied so strictly, and recruitment is often based upon professional qualifications.

The Administrative Class provides the most striking illustration of this concept of non-specialisation. There are two methods of entry, both open to British subjects of either sex between 20½ and 24 years of age. Under the traditional method the competition falls into three parts. First, there is a general examination: an essay on a subject chosen from among several alternatives, an English paper and a paper on current cultural, social, political and scientific affairs. This is followed by papers in two or three subjects selected from a list of 77 which cover practically every field of human knowledge. Even at this stage the aim is to discover not merely what the candidate knows but also his powers of reasoning and self-expression. Finally, there are two interviews, the first being a preliminary to the second, when the competitors appear before a Final Selection Board, under the chairmanship of the First Civil Service Commissioner. This is intended as a test of both intelligence and personality. Over half the total vacancies are filled by this method, appointments being offered to the candidates in the order of their final marks.

An alternative method of entry was instituted in 1947 for a trial period of ten years. This is modelled on the system used by the War Office for the selection of officers in the second World War. Candidates must have a degree of a recognised university with at least second class honours. The competition consists of a general written examination, a general intelligence test, personality tests and interviews. Up to half the vacancies may be filled by this method.

In 1954 there were 51 successful candidates for the Administrative Class, 36 by the first method and 15 by the second. These may be classified in accordance with their educational background as follows: 13 came from public schools and 38 from other schools; 22 had been at Oxford University, 18 at Cambridge, 5 at London, 2 at Glasgow, 1 each at Manchester, Edinburgh and St Andrews, and 1 at University College, Hull. This high proportion of Oxford and Cambridge graduates does not have the same social significance as formerly, since there are now many scholarships available at these universities.

It should be added that there is a probationary period of one or two years before entrants become established civil servants. Much importance is also attached to in-service training under the system instituted in 1945 whereby various forms of training are organised by the different departments under the supervision of a Director of Training and Education at the Treasury. This helps to compensate for the lack of pre-entry training for the Civil Service.

Civil servants are regarded as 'servants of the Crown', and their status as such has been determined largely by custom. In theory they hold office during the pleasure of the Crown, but in fact their appointments are permanent and their tenure secure. Their pay, though 'the gracious gift of the Crown', is just as securely guaranteed as that of officials in other lands. As in other countries, salaries in the Civil Service are somewhat if not substantially lower than in comparable private employment. Nevertheless, the Administrative Class is relatively well paid and there is a fairly wide range of salaries generally, with annual increments for all provided that their work is satisfactory. Women have continued to receive much lower salaries than men, the difference having been about 20% to 25%, but this inequality will disappear in the fairly near future.

Promotion within each class is by selection, with guarantees against arbitrary decisions by the head of a department. Promotions are made on the recommendations of a board of senior civil servants, who receive annual reports on every civil servant and may consult staff representatives. Decisions are subject to appeal to the Head of the Civil Service, who may refer the case to the promotion board or to some other body, and a staff association may support such appeals. Promotion between classes is not so simple a matter. Since the second World War, however, more liberal arrangements have been introduced whereby a definite percentage of vacancies are filled by promotion from the class below on the results of the limited competitions organised from time to time by the Civil Service Commission.

In theory, Civil Service discipline is strict, and officials are liable to dismissal at the pleasure of the Crown. Yet in practice it is quite exceptional for anyone to be dismissed, and tenure is quite as secure as that of civil servants in France. No civil servant may be dismissed or subjected to any other severe penalty except in compliance with a procedure designed to safeguard his rights.

Superannuation comes as a royal favour, but it is granted as regularly as though it were a legal right of all civil servants when they reach the retirement age. This is between 60 and 65, or may be over 65 if specially authorised by the Treasury. Each year of service entitles a civil servant to a pension equivalent to 1/80th of his average salary in his last three years, with a maximum of 40/80ths; in addition, he receives a lump sum equal to three years' pension. Pensions at proportionate rates are paid to those who resign on grounds of ill-health.

Civil servants are under special obligations such as are

usually imposed on public servants in regard to disinterestedness, official secrecy and restrictions on business activities. For many years all active participation in politics was forbidden, and this is still the case in the two highest classes. A civil servant must resign before he can stand for Parliament, and if a member of Parliament accepts a post in the Civil Service he automatically vacates his seat. On the other hand, a civil servant will usually be able to obtain permission from the head of his department to take part in local government. The main point is that he must never let his own political convictions in any way compromise his official impartiality.

Civil servants are allowed to form staff associations, to which nearly four-fifths of them now belong. After the great General Strike of 1926, Civil Service staff associations were prohibited by the Trades Union Act, 1927, from joining any outside trade union organisations. This ban was lifted in 1947, and the government now looks upon the associations as valuable organs for the representation of staff interests.

There is also a system of joint consultative committees, known as Whitley Councils, whereby civil servants have the same opportunities as persons in private employment to take part in discussions of matters in which they are interested. This machinery was set up as a result of the recommendations of the Whitley Committee of 1917-18 on the improvement of relations between employers and employees. It includes a National Whitley Council for the Civil Service and Whitley Councils for each department, composed of official and staff representatives in equal numbers. These provide a medium for joint consultation, discussion and study on all questions affecting staff interests, such as improvements in organisation and methods, administrative reforms, grievances or conditions of service. The National Council has a leading rôle, but is mainly concerned with broad general principles, while the departmental councils give more detailed attention to staff questions arising in their own particular departments. Nevertheless, it does not seem that in practice this system has fully lived up to the hopes of its creators.

These methods of recruitment and organisation have produced a Civil Service which provides the Cabinet with a corps of administrators of high quality, unquestionable integrity and outstanding efficiency. Senior officials are undoubtedly ready to serve loyally under any government, and would never contemplate any underhand dealings with the opposition, which would be quite unworthy of their office.

On the other hand, the Civil Service is a politically neutral instrument through which every government has to work. The select band of officials at the top of the hierarchy wields great influence. It has been said, without much exaggeration, that Britain is governed by the Civil Service, and it would be no exaggeration at all to say that senior officials do play a major part in determining British policy. As government business has grown more complex and ministers generally lack specialist knowledge, the influence of higher civil servants has tended to increase until most legislation and many important political decisions now originate with officials. Unless he has a pre-conceived policy and a strong personality, a minister will always find some difficulty in going against the advice of the chief officials in his department, who form the permanent administrative apparatus of the state. The Administrative Class is now becoming more democratic, so it no longer presents the same problem of power concentrated in a single social group. The issue is rather one of the possible political influence of civil servants, a problem not peculiar to Great Britain. Nevertheless, should any British Cabinet try to abuse the power which it has obtained by popular vote, the Civil Service is sufficiently strong and impartial to be a very effective safeguard against any attempt at arbitrary government.

II. LOCAL GOVERNMENT

Another restraint on the power of the executive lies in the substantially autonomous system of local government. Local authorities undertake many important administrative functions which, despite the recent multiplication of national public services and the fairly pronounced tendency towards centralisation, still remain outside the jurisdiction of the central government. Great Britain has a very long tradition of local government by autonomous authorities with very wide powers. This contrasts with the present system of local government in France, which is little more than the Napoleonic administrative system in which the more authoritarian features have been slowly and discreetly eliminated in response to the spread of democratic ideas. As the term 'decentralisation' implies, local authorities have only such powers as have been explicitly conceded to them by the state. The system of administrative tutelage gives officials of the central government extensive powers of control or at least of indirect influence over the activities of local authorities. Local initiative is also restrained by lack of financial resources. Liberal measures of decentralisation were checked at a relatively early stage by the rise of *étatisme*. In Britain, on the other hand, it was not until very recently that there were any serious inroads into the freedom and initiative of local authorities. Now, owing to social change, because many problems formerly capable of varying local solutions have become national issues, and because local authorities are in need of financial assistance, the central government has assumed additional functions. There has also been an increase in central control over local services, leading to closer co-ordination and possibly greater uniformity. Yet this inevitable increase in the powers of the central government has not produced any undesirable effects or altered the long and firmly established liberal concept of local autonomy which remains a fundamental principle. A strong and viable system of local government is generally considered one of the vital elements in democratic government, and its principal characteristics have been unimpaired by the tendency to greater centralisation.

Most of the present organs of local government have a very long history. Boroughs existed in Saxon times and have been administrative areas since the reign of Alfred the Great. Parishes were ecclesiastical units in the Middle Ages, and became the earliest districts to be administered by an elected local council with power to raise taxes to provide for the needs of the community. Counties were created before the Norman Conquest by grouping several hundreds together under the jurisdiction of a count, and they still keep their historic boundaries substantially unchanged, although these now bear very little relation to present-day administrative requirements. The Sheriff, the Justice of the Peace and the Coroner are all very old administrative offices. These local authorities had a variety of functions relating to the administration of justice and the conduct of elections and carried out a wide range of duties entrusted to them by the King or by Parliament. The time-honoured system continued, with all its anomalies, until the middle of the nineteenth century. History alone provides any explanation for the persistence of such extremely diverse forms of organisation and fiscal systems, and the lack of co-ordination and duplication of functions.

The movement towards a simpler and more rational structure began with the establishment of the Local Government Board in 1871. Some changes in borough government were introduced in 1882, and more important and extensive reforms inaugurated by the Local Government Act of 1888 were brought to completion in 1919. The law relating to local government has now been consolidated in the Local Government Act of 1933. It is still a complex system. Its structure is the outcome of history rather than logic, and the old forms of elected authorities have been retained. Local autonomy still survives despite the recent increase in centralisation. The powers of local authorities may have been curtailed, but they are still extensive. Central control over the exercise of local powers is greater than formerly but by no means unlimited, and local authorities still enjoy a large amount of freedom.

The system of local government laid down in 1933 embraces no fewer than six types of elected local authority: administrative counties, county boroughs, non-county boroughs, urban districts, rural districts and parishes. These vary greatly in importance.

The counties, of which there are 62 in England and Wales, have kept their traditional boundaries almost unaltered, although this results in enormous disparities in population, ranging from 18,000 in Rutland to over 2 million in Middlesex. Each county is divided into districts, either urban districts, rural districts or non-county boroughs. These are in turn subdivided into parishes, of which there are 1,000 altogether, but these do not have administrative functions except in rural districts. To create a new county, a private Act of Parliament is normally required.

County boroughs, of which there are at present 83, are towns large enough to have been given the most autonomous form of local government. County borough status is conferred by private Act of Parliament. It was laid down in 1888 that it should not be accorded to towns with less than 50,000 inhabitants, and the qualifying level of population has now been raised to 100,000.

The local autonomy which is characteristic of the whole

system is enjoyed in some degree by every local authority. It is particularly marked, however, at the two highest levels—the counties and county boroughs. Another outstanding traditional feature of English local government is that the supreme power is always vested in an elected body and never in a single person. The chief executive, who occupies so important a position in local government in France and in the United States, has no equivalent in Britain. The mayor and the leader of the county council have only ceremonial functions. The local executive is always an elected council, except in parishes with a population of less than 300, where a meeting of the inhabitants constitutes the executive. Councillors are normally elected by universal suffrage for a term of three years, one-third being re-elected each year. The mayor or chairman of the council is elected by the councillors, and their choice is not limited to members of the council. In addition, up to one-third of the council may consist of aldermen co-opted by the council for a term of six years, one-half being reappointed every three years. They are generally chosen from outside the council, being distinguished and able persons who would not be inclined to stand for popular election. The size of the council varies greatly: from 5 to 15 members in a parish; 30 to 40 in a borough or an urban or rural district; 50 to 60 in a county; and 100 to 150 in a large county borough. Most of the work of the council is done through statutory, standing or special committees, whose decisions come before the council for approval. There is a permanent administrative staff headed by the Town Clerk and various other local officials. The vital point, however, is that the council always has complete freedom of meeting and discussion and no official of the central government has any authority over it. The British tradition of local government respects this independence, which is fundamentally different from the autonomy granted to organs of decentralised administration in France. But to appreciate the position of the various types of local authority it is necessary now to consider their functions.

The most remarkable thing about these is their diversity, itself a consequence of local autonomy. A local council can only exercise such powers as have been conferred upon it by the central government. These powers vary enormously, not only between the different classes of local authority but between one county or one borough and another. Generally speaking, the functions of a county borough are more extensive than those of a county, since in the counties administrative functions are divided between the county, the county districts and the parishes. The more populous districts also tend to have more powers than smaller boroughs or urban districts.

The chief reason for this diversity of functions, however, is that within the general statutory framework individual local authorities may be granted special powers. This can be done in the instrument creating the authority—a royal charter in the case of a borough or an Act of Parliament for any other authority—or else by subsequent legislation. Any local authority except a parish council has the right to ask Parliament to pass a private or local Act to give it special powers or to authorise it to undertake some new activity regardless of any general legislation on the subject. Many such Acts have been passed by Parliament, by a special procedure rather different from that on public bills. The more important local authorities have secured large numbers of private Acts: the London County Council, for instance, has over a hundred in which its own particular powers and duties are defined. Special powers may also be granted by a provisional order made by the appropriate department after holding an inquiry and confirmed by Act of Parliament. This procedure involves less delay and means that the local authority does not have to contend with opposition in Parliament.

These provisions clearly give considerable scope for local initiative, which also finds other openings through permissive legislation. The latter leaves local councils free to decide whether to adopt Acts in which Parliament lays down the conditions under which they may provide such services as public libraries, street lighting and public health. The powers of a local authority in these spheres depend on whether it has asked for the Acts to be applied in the area under its jurisdiction. Although Parliament remains the supreme legislative authority, its enactments have done quite as much to increase as to detract from local autonomy, and local authorities are frequently under no compulsion to exercise the powers they have been granted. 'Local government' may not be a strictly logical term, but it does at least help to emphasise the difference between the independence of local councils in Britain and the limited competence of the organs of decentralised local administration like the French, with uniform powers laid down in laws of general application.

There is also a great difference in the scope of activities of local authorities in the two countries. In Britain local authorities still have a wide range of important functions in spite of the increase in centralisation which has been especially marked since the second World War. At the county and county borough level at least, local councils are still responsible for a number of services which could quite conceivably have been taken over by the central government. Public health, housing, town and country planning, public works and public assistance are all local services. Even education, at the primary and secondary stages, has remained a local responsibility, and so has the police. It is indeed a point of great significance, both politically and administratively, that there is no national police force but only a series of county and borough police forces. It should be added that county councils often have statutory powers to delegate certain of their functions to other local authorities. They also have power to make by-laws consistent with national legislation, and to enforce these in the area under their jurisdiction, thus exercising a legislative function which makes them the intermediary between Parliament and the private citizen.

Although they have not entirely escaped the financial problems which beset local government in other lands, local authorities in Britain have comparatively extensive financial resources and a fairly broad amount of discretion as to their use. The system of rates or local taxes on real property may be open to criticism on grounds of equity, but it does provide the source of about half of all local expenditure. Responsibility for valuing property for rating has now been transferred from local councils to the Board of Inland Revenue, but this has not seriously undermined the financial autonomy of local authorities. The growth of government grants has undoubtedly given the central government much more influence over local affairs. Nevertheless, these are often very substantial subsidies and constitute an extremely important source of local revenue. They cover 50% of local expenditure on police, 30%-65% on education and 20%-75% on public works. There are also some unit cost grants which do not involve such detailed control of local expenditure, and a general Exchequer Equalisation Grant which varies according to the expenditure incurred under certain heads and the rateable value of the district.

A certain amount of central control is only to be expected when local authorities have very extensive functions that involve a high level of expenditure and are often of far more than merely local significance. Yet although the powers of the central government have increased substantially in recent years, this process has not gone nearly so far in Britain as in other countries. Proceedings on private bills provide an obvious means of parliamentary control, and this is clearly justifiable when new or special powers are being granted. Nevertheless, Parliament has no means of exercising detailed supervision over local authorities. The courts have evolved various forms of judicial control. All public authorities are liable to be sued in the same way as a private individual. Actions may be brought against them for *ultra vires* acts, negligence or damages. The Attorney-General may, in the public interest, institute various forms of proceedings against a local authority to compel it to fulfil its legal obligations or to desist from exceeding its powers. Such proceedings do not in any way interfere with the rights of aggrieved persons to take legal action. The cases come before the ordinary lawcourts and are not excessively costly. There are also a few respects in which county councils may exert some slight powers of control over lower tiers of local authorities.

Lastly, local authorities are subject to control by the executive. This is exercised by government departments and takes many different forms: inspection of grant-aided services when the grant is being allocated; approval of borrowing; audit of accounts by the district auditor; inspection of public health, transport, police and education services by the appropriate departments; and the issue of regulations in regard to certain activities. The Ministry of Housing and Local Government in particular, and to a lesser extent the Ministries of Transport, Health and Education, have fairly broad powers of control over local authorities. Since the second World War, government departments have also on occasions been authorised to make schemes which become binding on local authorities, as provided for by the Education Act, 1944, and the Town and Country Planning Act, 1947. In recent years, local authorities have been deprived of some of their former powers, as has occurred under the Trunk Roads Acts, 1936 and 1946, the Electricity Act, 1947, the Gas Act, 1948, the National Health Service Act, 1946, and the National Assistance Act, 1948. Other functions have been transferred from lower-tier authorities to counties and county boroughs, as was done by the Police Act, 1946, the Town and Country Planning Act, 1947, and the Fire Services Act, 1947.

An increase in the powers of the central government is a widespread modern phenomenon, and there is a general need for larger financial resources and closer co-ordination in the public services. In Britain, however, there has only been a limited amount of centralisation, and local authorities have been allowed to retain, wherever possible, their traditional functions. The local government service still employs 40% of all public officials in Britain. Local authorities still administer an important range of public services, including many which in other countries have always been state services or have by now been taken over by the central government. Central control of local services operates in such a way as to arouse no misgivings, since it is definitely not regarded as a means of obtaining political power. It is essentially a form of expert supervision by a number of different departments. No one department is responsible for controlling every aspect of local government, although the Ministry of Health and the Ministry of Housing and Local Government both have extensive powers in this connection. The Home Office is only concerned with elections and the police and fire services, and it is in no way comparable to the Ministry of the Interior in France. There is no equivalent of the French system of tutelage in Great Britain and no officials corresponding to the French prefects. Local activities are influenced by the government's financial policies, but the local budget is adopted by the council and does not have to be approved by any higher authority.

Some aspects of the British local government are undoubtedly in need of reform. Some revision of boundaries and rationalisation and redistribution of functions will be necessary if the system is to meet modern administrative requirements. But basically it is sound and viable. The Committee set up in 1949 to consider possible reforms based its investigations on the assumption 'that local authorities are responsible bodies competent to discharge their own functions, and that they exercise their responsibilities in their own right'. A considerable range of public services is thus almost completely outside the jurisdiction of the central government, although not always outside the sphere of party politics. The British system of democratic government is based upon the will of the people and owes much to the long tradition of local government, in which many citizens have received a large part of their political education. The growing influence of Whitehall runs counter to these traditions and institutions, but some fundamental principles remain unshaken: the idea that public functions should be divided between the central government and other public authorities; the conviction that free democratic government cannot exist without a strong system of local government; and the belief that preserving the traditional independence of local authorities is also the way to safeguard some vital aspects of individual liberty.

Chapter Six

THE LIBERTIES OF THE SUBJECT

CIVIL liberties provide another guarantee against arbitrary government. In Great Britain the political and judicial safeguards of the liberties of the subject, like the other restraints on the power of the executive, are very different from those which exist either in the United States or on the Continent.

This is another sphere in which firmly established and respected customs and conventions, together with a deep-rooted aversion to any kind of arbitrary rule and the general concern to abide by democratic principles of fair play, have been far more important than any actual laws in ensuring respect for individual freedom. Between them, these provide a formidable series of safeguards that make it virtually impossible for the executive, however powerful it may be, to do anything that would undermine the rights of any individual or group of citizens.

The British have never thought it necessary to protect their liberties by defining them in precise terms in a fundamental constitutional Act or declaration of rights. Magna Charta, the Habeas Corpus Act, the Petition of Right and the Bill of Rights were major landmarks in English constitutional history, but they contain few provisions that are still of any real importance for the protection of individual liberties at the present time. There is hardly any respect in which such acts as these are at all comparable to the declaration of rights that are found in other constitutions. Nor have the English lawcourts any power to decide whether a law or Act of Parliament is compatible with the constitution. The most recent legislation invariably supersedes all pre-existing laws, however important they may have been in their time. The sovereignty of Parliament means that, if the British had a declaration of the rights of the subject, while it might be of fundamental importance politically, from the legal point of view it would be no different from any other Act of Parliament and could be amended at any time without recourse to any special procedure. The British have never inclined to the view that the best way to protect the liberties of the subject is to define them in as minute detail as possible, so as to form a code of individual rights that the executive will then be obliged to respect. In some other countries, and notably in France, great importance is attached to the precise definition of individual rights. In Britain, however, such elaborate codification would appear to be superfluous. Individual liberty is not conceived as a series of specific rights, but rather as a general state of individual freedom that springs from the fundamental principle of the supremacy of the law which is enshrined in the Common Law and manifests itself in every sphere of human activity.

This respect for individual freedom, like all the specific liberties of the subject, is founded upon the Rule of Law. This is the fundamental principle of the whole constitution. It has never been laid down in any written text, but the monarchy, Parliament and the courts have all come to acknowledge its paramount importance. It has traditionally been held to have three distinct meanings.

First, it means the supremacy of the law of the land, regardless of its origin, and excludes the existence of prerogative, of arbitrariness or even of wide discretionary authority on the part of the government. In recent years it has become recognised as a logical corollary of the Rule of Law that Parliament should retain control over delegated legislation, and that if any discretionary powers are delegated to the executive, the manner in which they are to be exercised shall as far as possible be laid down by Act of Parliament. The supremacy of the law, in this sense, imposes unwritten restrictions upon the power of Parliament itself, and is therefore one of the fundamental bases of British democracy.

Secondly, the Rule of Law implies that all, whether individuals or corporate bodies, private persons or public officials, are equal before the law of the land administered by the ordinary courts. Attachment to the Rule of Law, in this classic sense, and aversion to anything savouring of privilege, is what has always made the British reject the idea of a separate hierarchy of administrative courts and a distinctive system of administrative law. Some special administrative tribunals have been created in recent years, but they are still regarded with suspicion in some quarters. They are generally considered undesirable except where their competence is confined to matters formerly decided by government departments, and they accept precedents as binding and give reasoned decisions which are, as far as possible, subject to a right of appeal to the ordinary courts.

Finally, the Rule of Law means that the courts have been primarily concerned with defining and enforcing the rights of individuals in accordance with the basic principles of English law which, by the action of Parliament and the courts themselves, have gradually been so extended as to determine the position of the Crown and of its servants. The courts consider themselves bound by the established rules of law unless these are specifically superseded by Act of Parliament, and it is never easy to obtain legislation to set aside such fundamental principles. This is why English law does not include any detailed codes of civil rights such as figure so prominently in French jurisprudence. Except at times of special national emergency, respect for individual liberty is assumed as the basic premise of the British constitution. It is the prerogatives of the executive that require express statutory authority.

That really sums up the whole concept of the relationship between the individual and the state in Great Britain. This basic political philosophy is what has always made other democratic countries look upon Great Britain as the pre-eminent example of a state which respects the liberties of the subject. Every freedom-loving state in the world today owes some debt to the British for the passionate struggles they have waged over the course of the centuries in the cause of individual liberty. Practically every other attempt to take a stand against arbitrary rule has drawn its inspiration from Great Britain, even though few have had much success in their efforts to rekindle the spirit of British institutions on alien soil. It also follows from this concept of the liberties of the subject that, even though protected by such strong guarantees, individual freedom in Great Britain is still, to a greater extent than in other countries, something readily perceived but not nearly so easy to analyse. This will become clear after a brief survey of the principal liberties of the subject in Britain today.

I. PERSONAL FREEDOM

The right to individual freedom is firmly assured. It was laid down in Magna Charta and had been implicitly recognised at an even earlier date. It was one of the principles which Parliament strove to defend against arbitrary encroachments by the Stuarts under guise of the royal prerogative. The first major clash between Parliament and the King was over the case of Darnel in 1626. There is no need at this juncture to recall all the details of this famous case, which arose from the refusal of Sir Thomas Darnel and four other knights to comply with the King's letters patent ordering certain of his subjects to subscribe to a forced loan. The offenders were arrested by order of the Privy Council, but, as there was no other warrant for their imprisonment, Darnel obtained a writ from the court of King's Bench against the keeper of the prison, ordering his release. Once he had been set free, however, a fresh warrant was issued for his imprisonment, this time on the ground that this was the express order of the King, who could 'do no wrong'. The Parliament elected in 1628 therefore drew up a Petition of Right, largely inspired by the ideas of Sir Edward Coke, under the terms of which it would be impossible for anyone else in future to be arrested simply by virtue of the royal prerogative. This was accepted by the King but very narrowly interpreted by the courts.

In 1679, however, a firmer guarantee against arbitrary arrest was obtained by the passage of the Habeas Corpus Act. It has thus become the rule that, except in cases of felony, breach of the peace or a number of other offences specified by Act of Parliament, no one may be arrested or deprived of his liberty except by order of a court and after conviction on a definite charge for failure to comply with a statute or for an offence against the Common Law.

The procedure of habeas corpus is designed to prevent both arbitrary arrest—which is practically unknown—and preventative detention, which is only employed on a very modest scale. The Habeas Corpus Acts of 1679 and 1816 merely gave statutory authority to rules of Common Law which had long been generally accepted until the Stuarts attempted to set them aside.

Anyone believed to be unlawfully arrested or imprisoned can seek to recover his liberty by means of a writ of habeas corpus.

This used to be obtained from the King and is now issued by a court. Anyone deprived of his liberty or any other person interested in his case or acting on his behalf is entitled to ask the court to examine whether there is any legal justification for his detention. The application, supported by affidavits establishing the facts of the case, must be made by a barrister to a judge of Queen's Bench or, in exceptional cases, to some other High Court judge. The person detained always has a right of appeal to a higher court.

The court will then issue a writ of *habeas corpus ad subjiciendum* whereby, in the name of the sovereign and on the authority of the Lord Chief Justice, whoever has the custody of the prisoner is solemnly ordered to bring him before the court on the day and at the time appointed, and to show lawful grounds why he should be deprived of his liberty. The court examines the reasons given and decides whether it is necessary to detain the prisoner in order that a case may be brought to trial. If not, the court will order that he be either restored to his full liberty or else released on bail. If a court refuses to order the release of anyone charged with treason, felony or a grave misdemeanour, the case must be brought up for trial at the next session of the appropriate court unless the prisoner has meanwhile obtained some other remedy.

At every stage in the procedure of habeas corpus there are strong sanctions to ensure that the decision of the court is respected. There can be no appeal against an order to release a prisoner. Anyone who contrives, whether in a private or an official capacity, to secure the imprisonment of any person without lawful justification, may be sued for damages by the party concerned. This pecuniary sanction acts as a powerful deterrent against arbitrary arrests and ensures that no one will be deprived of his liberty except where this is strictly necessary and provided for by law. A writ of habeas corpus may be sought in an extremely wide range of cases. It may be granted in civil actions relating to such matters as the custody of children or the internment of aliens, and in criminal cases it will secure the release of anyone except those detained on charges of treason, felony or contempt of court.

In war-time, the scope of habeas corpus has had to be somewhat restricted, but even then British governments have always been extremely reluctant to deprive anyone of this guarantee against arbitrary imprisonment. Habeas corpus was retained except for certain particularly suspect categories of persons by both the Defence of the Realm Act in the first World War and the Emergency Powers Act, 1939, and the Special Powers Act, 1940. The executive has never been granted more than extremely circumscribed powers to detain anyone under arrest without a proper trial.

Public opinion is always very easily aroused against any interference with the personal freedom of any citizen, except as provided for by law. The heavy sentences imposed for such offences serve as a solemn warning against arbitrary arrests or imprisonment. In one case, when a local authority had erroneously detained a person later found to be of sound mind, it hastened to offer him an apology and £500 in compensation rather than run the risk of being taken to court, while the Home Secretary also expressed his regret at the mistake. In the Savidge Case of 1926 the prolonged interrogation of Miss Savidge by the police led to the appointment of a royal commission, and the traditional liberties of the subject in this respect were subsequently reaffirmed. The whole system of criminal procedure, the laws of evidence and the jury system have all been inspired by respect for individual freedom and make it possible to ensure that this is not interfered with and yet that justice is none the less sure and effective.

The courts have taken a firm stand against any infraction of individual liberty by the executive. One important instance of this is the law forbidding house-to-house searches unless specially authorised by law. If the object is to recover stolen property, obscene or blasphemous literature, forged currency, explosives or documents specified under the Official Secrets Acts or the Incitement to Disaffection Act, 1934, a court will allow the houses of persons in custody to be searched and the goods in question removed. In these and a few similar cases, a search may be authorised by warrant of the court. Otherwise, the home is inviolable, and to enter it without the consent of the occupier is an offence punishable by law.

II. FREEDOM OF RELIGION

Freedom of religion is now as highly valued as any other aspect of individual liberty, but it was a long time before this became the recognised right of every citizen. Even today its status remains somewhat anomalous, as the Church of England is a state church 'established by law', and its position is regulated by legislation, in particular by Acts dating from the reigns of Henry VIII, Edward VI and Elizabeth I.

The Thirty Nine Articles of Religion and the Book of Common Prayer derive their authority from Acts of Parliament, and the Prayer Book cannot be revised without the consent of Parliament. The organisation of the Church is governed by the Church of England Assembly (Powers) Act, 1919, and other statutes. Bishops and Archbishops are nominated by the Queen on the advice of the Prime Minister. Parliament has a joint Ecclesiastical Committee which reports to both Houses on all public bills relating to Church affairs, and each House begins its sittings with prayers. The competence of the ecclesiastical courts has been gradually narrowed down until their jurisdiction is now confined to strictly ecclesiastical affairs, but there is a right of appeal against their decisions to the Judicial Committee of the Privy Council. Every reigning monarch has the title of 'Defender of the Faith' and takes a solemn oath to defend the established Church.

With these close links between the state and the Anglican Church, it is hardly surprising that the right to freedom of religion was not recognised until comparatively recently. The Episcopal Church of Scotland was always quite distinct from the Church of England and has never been a state church. The Irish Church, on the other hand, was established until 1869, and the Act to disestablish the Church of England in Wales was not passed by Parliament until 1914 and was not put into effect until 1920.

Individual Catholics, Nonconformists and Jews were long deprived of many important civil rights, and it is well known how those fleeing from religious persecution in England played a leading part in founding the American colonies in the seventeenth century.

Catholics were long excluded from the leading professions and it was impossible for them to sit in Parliament because they could not subscribe to the oath that all members were required to take. Their disabilities did not begin to be removed until the end of the eighteenth century. In 1813 they were admitted to the armed forces and in 1817 to the Civil Service. Finally, in

1829, Peel and Wellington succeeded in passing the Catholic Emancipation Act whereby Catholics became eligible to sit in Parliament and to hold any public office other than that of Regent, Lord Chancellor, a judge in the ecclesiastical courts, or—until the office was abolished in 1920—Lord Lieutenant of Ireland. The last restrictions on the wearing of ecclesiastical vestments by Roman Catholics were not removed until 1920, and it would still apparently be impossible for a Catholic to become Lord Chancellor. Nevertheless, partly as a result of the first World War, Britain has entered into diplomatic relations with the Vatican and established an harmonious relationship with the Catholic Church. Individual Catholics now enjoy complete religious toleration and in fact appear to wield considerable influence in politics, particularly in the Labour Party.

Members of the various Nonconformist churches, though for many years subject to much the same disabilities as Roman Catholics, did not have to wait so long for religious toleration. By the beginning of the eighteenth century some of their disabilities had already been wholly or partially removed, although they still could not be married or buried or have their children baptised except in accordance with the rites of the Church of England. They were also debarred by the Test and Corporations Acts from all public and political offices. The chief remaining obstacles to full toleration for Nonconformists were removed by the institution of civil marriage in 1836 and the repeal of the Test and Corporations Acts in 1828. This made it possible for dissenters to hold any of the offices from which they had hitherto been excluded provided that they took the oath 'on the true faith of a Christian'.

Jews had been in much the same position as Nonconformists since the middle of the eighteenth century, but they could not of course subscribe to the oath provided for in 1828. They had to wait until 1839 before being allowed to take an oath on the Old Testament. In 1845 they became eligible for membership of municipal corporations. Finally, between 1858 and 1866, a new form of oath for members of Parliament was evolved which made it possible for Jews to sit in either of the two Houses.

The last stronghold of religious intolerance was in the ancient universities. Oxford and Cambridge did not open their doors to students who were not members of the Church of England until 1871, although such persons had been admitted to the University of London ever since 1836.

There can be no doubt that the right to freedom of religion is now genuinely respected and firmly guaranteed in Great Britain. Nevertheless, the Church of England still occupies a decidedly privileged position. In the past, it could exert considerable influence simply because it was the church of the aristocracy, the great landowners, the ancient universities and the wealthiest sections of the community. Today, partly because religious issues do not excite such strong passions, the Church is no longer such a powerful force in the life of the nation but it is still an important national institution. It meets with no active opposition, it appears in an active rôle on numerous public occasions, and it is still able to make its influence felt among the youth of the country. Many of the principles of social ethics generally accepted today have been inspired by Christian precepts, and the Church endeavours to see that they do not fall into disrespect. In its political outlook the Church tends, broadly speaking, towards conservatism, despite the contrary opinions of some members of the episcopal bench. Parliament and the executive still not infrequently find themselves up against forces whose inspiration is basically religious. This was why, during the reign of Queen Victoria in particular, governments attached so much importance to their function of nominating bishops and archbishops. In the twentieth century, however, it has become impossible to decide these appointments on political grounds. Men appointed to high positions in the Church today have been nominated by the Crown primarily as being persons acceptable to the Church itself and appearing the best qualified to discharge the duties of their office. Church appointments are thus decided in a way which still further broadens the scope of religious freedom in Great Britain today.

III. THE RIGHT OF PUBLIC MEETING

The right of public meeting is, of all the liberties of the subject, perhaps the one that is most typically associated with Great Britain, where it is universally acknowledged and can be freely exercised, with protection from the police should the need arise. Nevertheless, it has no foundation in any special law. It has simply become recognised that the right to personal freedom implies that men are entitled to meet together to hear and deliver speeches and to discuss any matter whatever, provided only that they do not break the law, interfere with the rights or property of any person, cause an obstruction, or commit a breach of the peace. Peaceable public meetings are regarded as a valuable safety valve for a system of democratic government. People are free to congregate together wherever they please, even on the public highway. The famous Speakers' Corner in Hyde Park, though probably the most celebrated, is by no means the only place where public speakers can be seen vigorously attacking the government under the watchful eye of a policeman. From time to time, processions are organised to march with a petition to Parliament or to present some special demands to members of Parliament. The right to hold such meetings is guaranteed by the Park Regulation Act, 1872. Local authorities are empowered to make further regulations as to the conduct of public meetings. No meeting may be forbidden or broken up by force except in cases expressly provided for by law, such as those specified in the Riot Acts which contain statutory definitions of a riot and an illegal assembly, and in the Public Meeting Act, 1908.

The important point, however, is that these legal restrictions have always been interpreted in an extremely liberal sense. A meeting is never held to be illegal simply because it is held on the public highway. The police can break up a meeting if it is causing a disturbance, but they can only do this if there is no other way of preventing a breach of the peace, and in this case they must first of all try to apprehend the ringleaders. In 1936 the danger of subversive activities by fascist organisations and the increase in the number of public meetings led Parliament to pass the Public Order Act in order to simplify the work of the police in seeing that the right of public meeting was not abused. It was made illegal to wear uniforms or carry arms at a public meeting, and local authorities were empowered to ban all public meetings for a specified period if the chief officer of police considered this necessary in order to prevent disturbances. These restrictions were entirely justified by the need to ensure that the public peace would not be disturbed by political agitators. By present-day standards they are remarkably liberal. Even in the twentieth century the British have never had to contend with mass demonstrations and outbreaks of violence in the streets, and their traditional right of public meeting remains substantially unimpaired.

IV. FREEDOM OF ASSOCIATION

Freedom of association is simply one aspect of the Common Law right to enter into contracts and form trusts and companies. This has been expanded until it covers the formation of non-profit-making organisations of all kinds, ranging from clubs to political parties and from trade unions to charitable foundations. The right to carry on such activities has never been seriously challenged except in the case of the trade unions, whose position has since 1871 been regulated by a series of Trade Unions and Trade Disputes Acts, the details of which need not be considered at this juncture.

Apart from the special position of the trade unions, it would be true to say that English law does not impose any restrictions on the right to enter into associations. Any association may be lawfully constituted without first having to seek special authorisation from the government. Associations are free to pursue their objectives by any means they think fit provided they do nothing expressly forbidden by law. They have power to acquire and dispose of property and to sue and be sued, and are not subject to any special control by any public authority. Freedom of association has facilitated the growth of organisations representing different economic, social, cultural and religious— not to mention political—interests, and every one of these is free at all times to voice its opinions.

These interest groups are not really comparable to the political pressure groups that exist in other countries such as the United States or France. The technique of 'lobbying' has not developed to nearly the same extent in Great Britain. There are two main reasons for this. In the first place, if any interest group has no special constitutional channel through which it can make its influence felt, it will usually have a spokesman in one or other of the political parties who will endeavour to impress its views upon the Cabinet or the leaders of the opposition. Secondly, party discipline under the British two-party system is both stronger than in the United States and less easily defied than in France or other countries where there is a large number of parties. Consequently the parties in Parliament normally vote solidly for or against the government in every division and sectional interests can best be advanced by securing the support of one of the political parties. This is most easily done by obtaining the backing of individual members of Parliament or by trying to work on public opinion through the press or other media of mass information.

V. FREEDOM OF SPEECH AND SELF-EXPRESSION

The freedom of the press is generally considered to be closely connected with freedom of speech, and both are protected by the same legal sanctions. Freedom of speech, however, has always been regarded as a natural right, while the freedom of the press has, in Great Britain as in other countries, only been attained after a hard struggle against the efforts of the government to suppress or control this powerful means of influencing public opinion.

As soon as the Crown became at all apprehensive as to the possible consequences of the dissemination of the printed word, the sovereign sought to establish some form of control over the press. A system of censorship was set up under an ordinance of 1586, in which it was reaffirmed that all printing was a monopoly of the Crown. The government endeavoured to control the press, and contrived to do so extremely rigorously through the court of Star Chamber. The struggle between government censorship and the people's desire for information on public affairs continued until the end of the seventeenth century. The Licensing Act of 1662 imposed rigorous censorship in advance of publication for every kind of printed matter. This continued for a considerable time until finally, in 1695, the House of Lords followed the lead of the Commons and decided not to renew the Licensing Act. The press thus became free from state control. As the eighteenth century advanced, the press grew more independent and influential and began to attract more attention from the political parties. Governments meanwhile strove to keep it under restraint by the usual expedients of high taxation—gradually increased until, for newspapers, it reached a maximum of 4d. a copy in 1851—and by reducing the powers of the jury in cases relating to the press. Nevertheless, the freedom of the press survived intact. Trial by jury was not eliminated, censorship was never reimposed and, as its influence increased, the press became more independent of outside pressures, especially those emanating from the government. The origins of the modern press can be traced back to the end of the eighteenth century, when *The Times* was launched by John Walter (1785-88), James Perry inaugurated the Whig *Morning Chronicle*, and Daniel Stuart built up the *Morning Post* as the principal organ of the Tory Party. The development of the press continued throughout the nineteenth century, and the twentieth century saw the advent of the 'popular press'. Large 'chains' of cheap papers with vast circulations were built up through the efforts of men like the Harmsworth brothers, Lord Northcliffe and Lord Rothermere, who made the *Daily Mail* and the *Daily Mirror* into what they are today.

Anyone in Britain is now perfectly at liberty to found a newspaper and to say, write, print or publish anything he wishes. The only limitation is that he is always liable to be sued for contempt of court, libel or slander, or the use of blasphemous or obscene language or any expression with a seditious intention. 'Sedition' can cover a great deal, including anything spoken or written with intent to bring into hatred or disrespect the Queen, the government, Parliament or the constitution, to encourage any attempt otherwise than by lawful means to alter any matter in church or state by law established, or to promote feelings of hostility and ill-will among the people at large. In fact, however, there are quite adequate safeguards against arbitrary interference with the freedom of the press. Its implications have been fairly narrowly defined by law, and there is always the right to trial by jury before an independent judiciary which has itself played a leading part in establishing the freedom of the press. In practice, no one is ever charged with showing a seditious intention unless he has published something that constitutes a serious threat to law and order or has made allegations against some public official too serious to be overlooked.

The main threat to the freedom of the press today is that a great many papers with enormous circulations are controlled by a small number of extremely powerful and wealthy proprietors. The papers with the largest circulations in the country, between them accounting for 45% of the circulation of all newspapers, are all controlled by one or other of the five great proprietors or 'chains'. The Rothermere Group controls the *Daily Mail* (circulation 2,200,000), the *Evening News* (1,800,000), the *Sunday Dispatch* (2,200,000) and a number of provincial newspapers. The Kemsley Group controls the *Daily Graphic* (800,000), the *Sunday Empire News* (2,200,000), the *Sunday Graphic* (1,200,000) and the *Sunday Times* (500,000), besides more than fifteen provincial papers, for example the *Manchester Daily Dispatch*, and a great many periodicals. London Express Newspapers, Ltd., controlled by Lord Beaverbrook, owns the *Daily Express* (4,000,000), the *Evening Standard* (850,000), the *Sunday Express* (2,700,000) and the *Glasgow Evening Citizen*. Lord Camrose,[1] a brother of Lord Kemsley, controls the *Daily Telegraph* (1,000,000) and the Amalgamated Press, which produces a large number of other newspapers and periodicals. Lastly there is the Cadbury Group, which owns the *News Chronicle* (1,600,000) and the *Star* (1,200,000).

Many independent journals still remain outside these big chains. Altogether nearly 4,000 newspapers and periodicals are published in Great Britain, and about 110 of these are dailies. Pre-eminent among the independent newspapers is *The Times*, whose importance is out of all proportion to its relatively small circulation of 250,000, owing to the high quality of its editorship and reporting and the influential circles in which it is read. A daily of great repute is the Liberal *Manchester Guardian*, while the *Observer* (386,000) is a high-class independent Sunday paper. All the same, there are only nine national daily newspapers, all printed in London, and seven of these are controlled by one or other of the big chains. The *News Chronicle* and the *Star* are both Liberal or at least inclined towards Liberal views, but all the other papers controlled by the big chains are predominantly Conservative in outlook. The Communist Party publishes the *Daily Worker*, but this has an extremely small circulation and very little financial backing. Only two big dailies support the Labour Party—the *Daily Herald* (2,000,000) and the theoretically independent *Daily Mirror* (4,000,000). The Labour Party also obtains further backing from its two Sunday papers, the *People* (over 4 million) and *Reynolds News* (700,000). Among the weeklies, the *New Statesman and Nation* reflects the views of the left wing of the Labour Party and to some extent acts as a counterweight to the *Economist*, a high-class journal with a great reputation despite its comparatively small circulation, which now tends to express a relatively right-wing point of view.

[1] Lord Camrose died in 1955.

On the whole, it seems fair to conclude that the average level of the British press is extremely high. It is certainly not independent *vis-à-vis* some major financial interests, even though many readers of Conservative papers must vote for the Labour Party, a substantial number of socialist journalists have worked for the Beaverbrook press, and Lord Kemsley told the Royal Commission on the Press that he had never tried to exert any influence over the opinions expressed by his editors. Nevertheless, it would probably not be very easy for a paper controlled by one of the big chains to publish any unorthodox views, although there are always other papers to give vent to different points of view. All the same, the power of the Press Lords and the consequent tendency towards monopolist control of the press has come under heavy attack from the Labour Party. The Royal Commission on the Press, after spending two years examining the whole question and producing a massive report, reached the guarded conclusion that there was no monopoly but merely a tendency towards concentration of ownership, and that even this was less marked in 1948 than it had been in 1921. The Royal Commission did not deny that the Press Lords could exert considerable political influence, but maintained that they did not in fact use their powers to try to suppress other points of view.

Public opinion would soon react strongly against any government that tried to interfere with the freedom of the press or to forbid the publication of any information that it might not wish to be disclosed. Consequently the press remains a formidable restraint on the power of the executive in Great Britain. That is particularly true when there is a Labour government, even more than when the Conservatives are in office. No country in the world can hope to have a completely independent press, for it would never be able to survive for lack of financial backing. The British at least have the assurance that their press will be too much concerned with maintaining its vast circulations either to embark on anti-democratic political propaganda or to become dangerously rigid in its outlook.

In the field of broadcasting, the government has extensive powers of control over the B.B.C. This is a corporation created by Royal Charter and virtually a public authority with a statutory monopoly. It is subject to control by the Postmaster-General, although it enjoys a broad degree of autonomy in the day-to-day conduct of its affairs. It has a duty to broadcast any announcements that the government may require, and the Postmaster-General is empowered to forbid the broadcasting of any matter or programme. Nevertheless, the British broadcasting system manages to avoid the worst evils of a state monopoly. The Cabinet has always used its powers with admirable restraint, except in a very few instances when government intervention has invariably met with strong public criticism. The B.B.C. has always had the right to announce on the air when it is broadcasting a statement at the request of a government department. Moreover, all broadcasts are closely scrutinised by both the Labour and Conservative parties, so the B.B.C. has consequently been obliged to remain strictly impartial in all its reporting of political affairs.

This brief survey of the liberties of the subject shows how the existence of individual liberty in Great Britain is not dependent upon specific rights defined and guaranteed in a constitution or any other special law. A more thorough examination of English judicial decisions would only add weight to this conclusion.

Individual freedom in its broadest sense is securely established in Great Britain. Its importance is manifest in every sphere of human activity, where the implications of this abstract idea have been worked out in application to all kinds of concrete situations. The liberty of the subject in Great Britain means that the individual is free to do anything not expressly forbidden by the law as applied by the ordinary courts. The authority and prestige of the judiciary ensures that its decisions are respected by the people, and at the same time prevents the government from riding roughshod over the rights of private citizens.

One point of particular interest is the attitude which British governments have adopted towards extreme right-wing or left-wing political movements and propaganda. Sir Oswald Mosley was left free to carry on his political campaigns, subject only to the general prohibitions imposed by the Public Order Act, 1936, against the wearing of uniforms and the formation of associations of a military character. The Communist Party is allowed not merely to exist but actually to propagate its doctrines, to hold meetings, to put up candidates in elections and to attack the government, provided only that it does not try to overthrow it by force. Communists managed to gain considerable influence in the trade unions, especially in the Transport and General Workers' Union, but their power probably reached its height in 1944 or 1945, and has declined substantially since 1948. Communists from abroad are not allowed to enter British territory for the express purpose of carrying on political activities, but they usually have no difficulty in obtaining visas for short visits, and a limited number are even allowed to attend the annual conference of the British Communist Party and the Communist Youth Organisation. Members of the British Communist Party are not legally debarred from any of the professions. They have not even been excluded from the Civil Service, although the latest regulations introduced by the Attlee government forbade their employment in any position where they would be concerned with security questions or matters relating to national defence. Even so, there has still been no systematic security check. Inquiries were instituted in respect of 17,000 civil servants considered to be in sensitive positions, but only 148 were provisionally suspended. By 1954, 21 of these had been rehabilitated after further investigations, 69 had been transferred, 19 had resigned, and in 9 other cases a decision had still to be reached. Only 23 had actually been dismissed, and these were officials whose qualifications were such that they could not be transferred to alternative positions in the Civil Service. That such a remarkably small number of civil servants have been suspended or dismissed is a striking illustration of how little the British are troubled about 'the defence of the constitution'. Practically the entire nation supports the existing regime, and the political maturity of the people prevents their becoming obsessed with the fear of subversive movements. These, they believe, can best be combated by free discussion rather than by any form of repressive legislation.

CONCLUSION

MANY reasons might be given to explain the remarkable development and survival of liberty in Great Britain. The most obvious is probably the independence of the judiciary.

Parliament has been another important bulwark of individual liberty. This could never have been achieved had not Parliament taken a stand against the executive in the first place, and Acts of Parliament have often served as a defence against arbitrary rule. In recent years it has sometimes been necessary to curtail the rights of the individual in the national interest, but these restrictions have generally been kept to an absolute minimum, and the intention has always been to remove them as soon as circumstances should allow. The opposition, although relatively co-operative, remains fully alive to the importance of its functions and is always on the alert to challenge any illegal action on the part of the government. By means of parliamentary questions, the executive is exposed to continuous and effective criticism, in which no error or failing of a minister or his department is allowed to pass unnoticed. The government is thus virtually constrained to keep within the bounds of the law and the rules of fair play in politics.

The liberties of the subject are respected by the executive, not merely because the whole constitutional system tends to secure this or makes it impossible for those in power to behave in any other way, but also because British governments have never set out uncompromisingly to enforce the will of the majority with the least possible delay. The task of the Cabinet is rather to ensure the execution of policies acceptable to the people, to safeguard the national interests and to see that the Rule of Law is respected, while at the same time interfering as little as possible with the liberties of the subject. As regards the maintenance of order, it is significant that the police is organised on a local basis, the Home Secretary having only general powers of supervision which help to ensure that order is preserved without any encroachment on individual liberties and the rights of the individual are fully respected. In this connection it is important to note that proceedings against the police in respect of acts committed in their official capacity can be brought before the ordinary lawcourts. Moreover, in so far as there is any central control of local legislation, its purpose is to ensure that this is compatible with the law and does not violate the liberties of the subject.

Yet individual liberty obviously depends far more upon the people themselves than upon any institutions. The British people have been ready to face any danger, no matter how severe, and to make the greatest possible sacrifices in defence of their liberties. Over the course of the centuries they have jealously guarded their civil rights, and this has led to the emergence of a public opinion as genuine and spontaneous as it would be possible to find in any democracy. This vigorous public opinion is both the source of the power of the Cabinet and at the same time a guarantee that neither the Cabinet nor Parliament nor the courts shall be able to ride roughshod over the liberties of the individual. Public opinion can also be brought to bear on national policy through many different channels, both direct and indirect, including elections, political parties, public meetings and the press.

This, then, is the most important conclusion which emerges from a study of British government. Constitutional rules have clearly played a vital part in the process of adaptation, still going on today, whereby institutions steeped in tradition have been gradually modified to create a democratic political system. Today, as in the past, the British have shown themselves singularly successful in managing to meet the political exigencies of the moment while still respecting the established laws of the land. Yet political institutions by themselves reveal very little of the true secret of the British constitution. This is something which can better be described as a state of mind.

Although the Cabinet derives its strength from its majority in Parliament and its policies are those of the majority party, this majority allows the government a very large measure of independence in carrying out its policy. The opposition are content to do no more than criticise the government, with the hope that they will in time be called upon to take its place. The executive is dominant, and its power is not restrained by any finely adjusted checks and balances designed to create an equilibrium. The bicameral system is no more than a façade.

The Crown, though still important in other respects, is politically a mere figurehead with no effective power. The judiciary sees that the Rule of Law is maintained, there is a vast sphere in which individual freedom is regarded as sacrosanct, and in no other country are the liberties of the subject more securely established. Nevertheless, no special institutions or procedures exist to protect the individual against the exceptionally powerful executive. The political system is based upon popular elections and the party system, which are potentially extremely powerful instruments of democracy. In practice, however, their function is to assist the machinery of government to operate efficiently and yet with such restraint as not merely to ensure respect for the rights of every individual citizen but actually to leave the opposition completely at liberty to do all in their power to bring down the government and set themselves up in its place.

The essence of liberal democracy in Great Britain is not to be found in any single institution. It is not wholly personified in the leader of 'Her Majesty's Opposition', the judges in their traditional garb, the Speaker of the House of Commons, or the strong Civil Service. It is not to be identified with the autonomy of local authorities, the speakers in Hyde Park, or habeas corpus; nor with the power of dissolution and the complete freedom of elections; nor yet with the Prime Minister, the 'ancient and undoubted privileges of the House of Commons', or even the King and Queen who in the struggle against Nazi aggression shared the lot of their faithful subjects throughout the London Blitz. The true essence of British democracy does not lie in any one of these institutions but rather, as we have tried to show, in the whole complex taken together.

The people favour a strong executive because they know that it will also be democratic. At the same time, they have a passionate desire for liberty. Their strongest safeguard against oppression is not any constitutional mechanism, but the extraordinary solidarity with which the whole fifty million are prepared to defend their freedom. The entire nation would, it seems, wholeheartedly endorse the sentiments expressed by John Stuart Mill: 'We can never be sure that the opinion we are endeavouring to stifle is a false opinion; and if we were sure, stifling it would be an evil still. If all mankind minus one were of one opinion, and only one person were of the contrary opinion, mankind would be no more justified in silencing that one person, than he, if he had the power, would be justified in silencing mankind.'

In some circles in Britain today one hears constant talk of 'the despotism of the executive', 'an omnipotent bureaucracy' and 'moving towards totalitarianism'. Such language hardly seems applicable to the British political system. Its use, however, is clear evidence that public opinion is far too much on the alert against totalitarianism for any attempt at anything savouring of dictatorship to have the slightest chance of success.

The British political system is thus an enviable model of democratic government. One can only regret that it could not possibly be transplanted to any other country.

SELECT BIBLIOGRAPHY

Works which appeared after the French edition of this book are marked with an asterisk.

GENERAL WORKS

Adams, G. B., *Constitutional History of England*, 1941.

Amery, L. S., *Thoughts on the Constitution*, 1947.

Amos, Sir Maurice, *The English Constitution*, 1935.

Anson, Sir William, *The Law and Custom of the Constitution*, 2 vols., 1922-36.

Bagehot, W., *The English Constitution*, 1872.

Bailey, S., *Parliamentary Government in Britain*, 1949.

Burdeau, G., *Traité de sciences politiques*, 5 vols., 1943-53.

Campion, Lord (ed.), *British Government since 1918*, 1950.

Dicey, A. V., *The Law of the Constitution* (ed. Wade), 1945.

Esmein, A., *Éléments de droit constitutionnel français et comparé*, 2 vols., 1927.

Finer, H., *The Theory and Practice of Modern Government*, 2 vols., 1932.

Halévy, E., *History of the English People in the Nineteenth Century*, 1924-34.

Jenks, E., *Parliamentary England*, 1903.

Jennings, Sir Ivor, *The Law and the Constitution*, 1948.

Keir, Sir David, and Lawson, F. N., *Cases in Constitutional Law*, 1949.

Keith, A. B., *The Constitution of England from Queen Victoria to George VI*, 2 vols., 1940.

Laski, H. J., *Parliamentary Government in England*, 1938.

Lewis, R., and Maude, A., *The English Middle Classes*, 1949.

Lhomme, J., *La Politique sociale de l'Angleterre contemporaine*, 1953.

Lowell, A. L., *The Government of England*, 1908.

Morrison, H., *Government and Parliament*, 1954.

Muir, R., *How Britain is Governed*, 1932.

Ogg, F. A., *English Government and Politics*, 1936.

Ridges, E. W., and Keith, A. B., *Constitutional Law*, 1939.

Robson, W. A., *The British System of Government*, 1952.

Rowntree, B. Seebohm, and Lavers, G. R., *English Life and Leisure*, 1951.

Siriex, P. H., *Le Régime parlementaire anglais contemporain*, 1935.
Stout, H. M., *British Government*, 1953.
Trevelyan, G. M., *English Social History*, 1944.
Visscher, P. de, *Les Nouvelles Tendances de la démocratie anglaise*, 1947.
Wade, E. C. S., and Phillips, G., *Constitutional Law*, 1951.
Zweig, E., *The British Worker*, 1952.
*Alexander, W. P., *Education in England*, 1954.
*Keeton, G. W., *The United Kingdom: the Development of its Law and Constitution*, 2 vols., 1955.
*Smellie, K. B., *The British Way of Life*, 1955.
*Wheare, K. C., *Government by Committee*, 1955.

THE ELECTORAL SYSTEM

Baker, J., *The Law and Practice of Parliamentary Elections*, 1940.
Butler, D. E., *The Electoral System in Britain, 1918-1951*, 1952.
—— *The British General Election of 1951*, 1952.
Butler, J. R. M., *The Passing of the Great Reform Bill*, 1914.
Cadart, J., *Régime électoral et régime parlementaire en Grande-Bretagne*, 1948.
Hogan, J., *Election and Representation*, 1945.
McCallum, R. B., and Readman, A., *The British General Election of 1945*, 1947.
Nicholas, H. G., *The British General Election of 1950*, 1951.
*Benny, M., Gray, A. P., and Pear, R. H., *How People Vote*, 1956.
*Butler, D. E., *The British General Election of 1955*, 1955.
*Schofield, A. N., *Parliamentary Elections*, 1955.

POLITICAL PARTIES

Attlee, C. R. (Earl Attlee), *The Labour Party in Perspective*, 1937.
—— *As it Happened*, 1954.
Belloc, H., and Chesterton, G. K., *The Party System*, 1911.
Bulmer Thomas, I., *The Party System in Great Britain*, 1953.
Cole, G. D. H., *A History of the Labour Party from 1914*, 1948.
Cruikshank, R. J., *The Liberal Party*, 1948.
Duverger, M., *Political Parties*, 1951.
Hogg, Q. (Lord Hailsham), *The Case for Conservatism*, 1947.
Lavau, G. E., *Partis politiques et réalités sociales*, 1953.

Mabileau, A., *Le Parti Liberal dans le système constitutionnel britannique*, 1953.

Ostrogorski, M., *Democracy and the Organisation of Political Parties*, 2 vols., 1912.

Pollock, J. K., *Money and Politics Abroad*, 1932.

Renaudeau, F., *Le Parti travailliste de Grande-Bretagne*, 1947.

Trevelyan, G. M., *The Two-Party System in English Political History*, 1926.

Viereck, P., *Conservatism Revisited; the Revolt against Revolt*, 1950.

Wilkinson, W. J., *Tory Democracy*, 1925.

The British Party System (Hansard Society), 1952.

*McKenzie, R. T., *British Political Parties*, 1955.

*Pelling, H., *The Origins of the Labour Party, 1880-1900*, 1954.

THE EXECUTIVE

Allen, Sir Carleton, *Law and Orders*, 1945.

Anderson, Sir John (Lord Waverley), *The Machinery of Government*, 1946.

Carr, Sir Cecil, *Delegated Legislation*, 1921.

Delthil, L., *Le Conseil privé* (Law thesis, Paris), 1937.

Fitzroy, M., *The History of the Privy Council*, 1928.

Giraud, E., *La Crise de la démocratie et le renforcement de l'exécutif*, 1938.

—— *Le Pouvoir exécutif dans les démocraties d'Europe et d'Amérique*, 1938.

Hankey, Lord, *Government Control in War*, 1945.

Heath, T. L., *The Treasury*, 1928.

Hewart of Bury, Lord, *The New Despotism*, 1929.

Jennings, Sir Ivor, *Cabinet Government* (revised edition), 1951.

Keith, A. B., *The British Cabinet System* (revised edition, ed. N. H. Gibbs), 1952.

Mersey, Lord, *The Prime Ministers of Britain, 1721-1921*, 1922.

Sibert, M., *Étude sur le Premier Ministre en Angleterre* (Law thesis, Paris), 1909.

Tilley, Sir John, and Gaselee, S., *The Foreign Office*, 1933.

Troup, E., *The Home Office*, 1925.

*Jeffries, Sir Clive, *The Colonial Office*, 1956.

*Newsam, Sir Frank, *The Home Office*, 1954.

*Strang, Lord, *The Foreign Office*, 1955.

PARLIAMENT

Chastenet, J., *Le Parlement d'Angleterre*, 1946.
Gordon, S., *Our Parliament*, 1946.
Jennings, Sir Ivor, *Parliament*, 1939.
Lucy, H., *Lords and Commoners*, 1921.
May, Sir Thomas Erskine, *Parliamentary Practice* (revised edition), 1946.
Pollard, A. F., *The Evolution of Parliament*, 1928.
*Campion, Lord, and Lidderdale, D. W. S., *Parliamentary Procedure in Europe*, 1955.

THE HOUSE OF COMMONS

Campion, Lord, *An Introduction to the Procedure of the House of Commons* (revised edition), 1950.
Chubb, B., *The Control of Public Expenditure*, 1952.
Dasent, A. I., *The Speakers of the House of Commons from the Earliest Times*, 1922.
Pasquet, *Essai sur les origines de la Chambre des Communes* (thesis), 1914.
Porritt, E., *The Unreformed House of Commons*, 2 vols., 1909.
Ross, J. F. S., *Parliamentary Representation*, 1948.
Taylor, E., *The House of Commons at Work*, 1951.

THE HOUSE OF LORDS

Allyn, E., *Lords versus Commons*, 1930.
Lees-Smith, H. B., *Second Chambers in Theory and Practice*, 1923.
Lindsay, M., *Shall we Reform the Lords?*, 1948.
Marriott, Sir John, *Second Chambers*, 1927.
Roberts, G. B., *The Function of an English Second Chamber*, 1926.
Rowse, A. L., *The Question of the House of Lords*, 1934.
*Bailey, S. D. (ed.), *The Future of the House of Lords*, 1954.

THE MONARCHY

Barker, Sir Ernest, *British Constitutional Monarchy*, 1943.
Erskine of Marr, *The Crown of England*, 1937.
Fletcher, I. K., *The British Court, its Traditions and Ceremonial*, 1953.

Hardie, F. M., *The Political Influence of Queen Victoria*, 1935.
Keith, A. B., *The King and the Imperial Crown*, 1931.
—— *The Privileges and Rights of the Crown*, 1936.
Lee, S., *King Edward VII*, 1927.
MacDonach, M., *The English King*, 1929.
Martin, K., *The Magic of Monarchy*, 1937.
Nicolson, Sir Harold, *King George V*, 1952.

LAW AND THE JUDICIARY

Amos, Sir Maurice, *British Justice*, 1940.
David, R., *Introduction à l'étude du droit privé de l'Angleterre*, 1949.
Denning, Sir Alfred, *The Changing Law*, 1953.
Geldart, W. M., *Elements of English Law*, 1912.
Hanbury, H. G., *English Courts of Law*, 1944.
Howard, P., *Criminal Justice in England*, 1931.
Jackson, R. M., *The Machinery of Justice in England*, 1940.
James, P. S., *Introduction to English Law*, 1953.
Jenks, E., *The Book of English Law*, 1932.
Potter, H., *A Historical Introduction to English Law and its Institutions*, 1949.
Robson, W. A., *Justice and Administrative Law* (3rd edition), 1951.

THE CIVIL SERVICE

Bridges, Sir Edward, *Portrait of a Profession*, 1950.
Cohen, E. W., *The Growth of the British Civil Service*, 1941.
Eaton, D. B., *The Civil Service in Great Britain*, 1880.
Finer, H., *The British Civil Service*, 1927.
Gaudemet, P. M., *Le Civil Service britannique*, 1952.
Gladden, E. N., *The Civil Service: its Problems and Future*, 1948.
—— *Civil Service Staff Relationships*, 1943.
—— *An Introduction to Public Administration*, 1949.
Léger, B., *Les Syndicats de fonctionnaires en Angleterre* (Law thesis, Paris), 1929.
Walker, H., *Training Public Employees in Great Britain*, 1935.
*Craig, Sir John, *A History of Red Tape*, 1955.
*Robson, W. A. (ed.), *The Civil Service in Britain and France*, 1956.
*Wheare, K. C., *The Civil Service in the Constitution*, 1954.

LOCAL GOVERNMENT

Chester, D. N., *Central and Local Government*, 1951.
Cole, G. D. H., *Local and Regional Government*, 1947.
Finer, H., *English Local Government*, 1934.
Hasluck, E. L., *Local Government*, 1948.
Jackson, W. E., *Local Government in England and Wales*, 1945.
Robson, W. A., *The Development of Local Government* (3rd edition), 1954.
Warren, J. H., *The English Local Government System*, 1946.
Webb, S. and B., *English Local Government*, 1922.
*Clarke, J. J., *A History of Local Government*, 1955.

THE LIBERTIES OF THE SUBJECT

Coase, R. H., *British Broadcasting: a Study in Monopoly*, 1950.
Hart, J. M., *The British Police*, 1951.
Herd, H., *The March of Journalism*, 1952.
*General Council of the Press, *The Press and the People*, 1955.
*Giles, F. T., *The Criminal Law*, 1954.

INDEX